Shared Governance in Higher Education

Shared Governance in Higher Education

Vitality and Continuity in Times of Change

VOLUME 3

Edited by

Sharon F. Cramer and Peter L. K. Knuepfer

Preface by
Nina Tamrowski

Introduction by
Gwen Kay

Published by State University of New York Press, Albany

© 2020 State University of New York

All rights reserved

No part of this book may be used or reproduced in any manner whatsoever without written permission. No part of this book may be stored in a retrieval system or transmitted in any form or by any means including electronic, electrostatic, magnetic tape, mechanical, photocopying, recording, or otherwise without the prior permission in writing of the publisher.

For information, contact State University of New York Press, Albany, NY
www.sunypress.edu

Library of Congress Cataloging-in-Publication Data

Names: Cramer, Sharon F., editor | Knuepfer, Peter L. K., editor.
Title: Shared governance in higher education : vitality and continuity in times of change / edited by Sharon F. Cramer and Peter L. K. Knuepfer; preface by Nina Tamrowski; introduction by Gwen Kay.
Description: Albany : State University of New York Press, [2020] | Includes bibliographical references and index.
Identifiers: LCCN 2016031462 (print) | LCCN 2016047976 (ebook) | ISBN 9781438478708 (ebook) | ISBN 9781438478692 (hardcover) ISBN 9781438478685 (pbk.)
Subjects: LCSH: Education, Higher—United States—Administration. | Teacher participation in administration—United States. | Student participation in administration—United States.
Classification: LCC LB2341 (ebook) | LCC LB2341 .S44779 2017 (print) | DDC 378.1/01—dc23
LC record available at https://lccn.loc.gov/2016031462

10 9 8 7 6 5 4 3 2 1

Contents

Preface: Enduring Shared Governance at SUNY — vii
Nina Tamrowski

Introduction — xiii
Gwen Kay

Editor's Note: Governance Undimmed — xvii
Sharon F. Cramer

Part I.
Perspectives on the Key Elements of Shared Governance

1 Characteristics of Shared Governance — 3
   Diane Bliss, Renee Lathrop, and Jeffrey Steele

2 Framing the Role of Faculty Governance Toward Institutional Diversity and Inclusion — 15
   Gordon Bigelow and Noelle Chaddock

3 Shared Governance: Valuing Each Other and Achieving More Together — 25
   Belinda S. Miles, Cliff L. Wood, and Kristine Young

Part II.
Shared Governance in Times of Change: Necessary Components

4 Developing Rapport and Relationships with New Administrators — 41
   Margaret Ann Hoose and Barry Spriggs

5 The Rights, Wrongs, and Challenges of Governance Communications — 63
   Joe Marren

Part III.
Avoiding Governance Quicksand: Pragmatic Considerations

6 The Campus Concept Committee: A Case Study in
   Shared Governance   75
   Lisa M. Glidden and Deborah F. Stanley

7 Reflections on the Process for Developing a Rubric for
   Assessing Shared Governance   91
   Deborah L. Moeckel

8 Back to the Past: Imagining the Future of Academic
   Governance   147
   Michael DeCesare

Part IV.
Lessons Learned

9 Chancellor Nancy Zimpher and SUNY's Shared Governance   165
   Kenneth P. O'Brien

10 Lessons in Process: "It's Not Just About #Transparency,
   It's About #SharedGovernance"   183
   Philip L. Glick and Domenic J. Licata

11 Nassau Community College at a Turning Point   197
   Valerie H. Collins

12 Accreditation Academy! An Organic Approach to Preparing
   for an MSCHE Site Visit   217
   Olin Stratton and Wendy Tarby

13 A Comparative Analysis of Regional Accreditors: Role of
   Shared Governance in Accreditation   235
   Peter L. K. Knuepfer

Contributors   267

Index   281

Preface

Enduring Shared Governance at SUNY

Nina Tamrowski

"The State University of New York system, established in 1948, is the largest and most recently founded system of public higher education in the country. By the first decade of the twenty-first century, it encompassed sixty-four campuses, including the state's thirty community colleges. Unlike in other public university systems, the research universities, comprehensive colleges, health science centers and medical schools, specialized colleges, contract colleges, and community colleges are all integral parts of the SUNY system. The different institutions have individual presidents or other presiding officers, but the system is governed by one chancellor and one board of trustees (the community colleges also have local boards of trustees as a part of their governance structure)" (Tamrowski et al., 2017).

The 64 campuses of this complex system are fortunate to have had leadership from the top that has modeled respect for the concept of shared governance, which works to realize best practices. Influence over system decision-making can be affected by administrators, faculty, staff, students, and trustees through a truly iterative policy review process.

The chancellor of SUNY from 2009 to 2017, Nancy L. Zimpher, helped institutionalize shared governance by building the very concept into her first strategic plan. The faculty governance leaders of the University Faculty Senate and the Faculty Council of Community Colleges worked to build a determinate shared governance plan that would show growth and measurable goals that could be accomplished over time. Among their outcomes were conferences on shared governance; trainings for campus governance leaders; support for hiring interns; support for faculty and student exchanges at each other's meetings, and (so far) three edited volumes on shared governance, such as this one, that contain conference presentations.

This initiative and the resources for these events, publications, travel, and support was branded SUNY Voices. With a vision, a strategic plan, a business plan, and a budget, SUNY Voices has become institutionalized at SUNY as a demonstration of system support for shared governance.

The SUNY system has successfully transitioned from Chancellor Zimpher, who retired in fall 2017, to a new chancellor, Dr. Kristina Johnson. She was selected in 2017 after a nationwide search, bringing an eclectic background in government, the private sector, and academia to the position. Dr. Johnson has likewise embraced SUNY's commitment to shared governance.

Upon Dr. Zimpher's retirement, SUNY's student and faculty governance bodies, the Student Assembly, the Faculty Council of Community Colleges, and the University Faculty Senate decided to create a Joint Statement on Shared Governance (see Appendix A to this preface). This declaration provided a record of the shared governance practices that had been established over the past decade at SUNY.

The introductory paragraph of the Joint Statement states "Shared governance has been instrumental in *moving SUNY forward*, especially in recent years when public higher education has endured many challenges." The statement goes on to enumerate the ways shared governance is accomplished at SUNY.

The features of shared governance that are delineated include the presence of the student and faculty governance elected leaders as members of the SUNY Board of Trustees; their inclusion in the chancellor's cabinet; the inclusion of faculty governance in any policy with academic implications and inclusion of students in policies affecting student affairs; regular meetings among the governance leaders with the chancellor; and the attendance of the chancellor and provost at plenaries of the three governance bodies.

The last characteristic, one of the most important items, states: "These principles and practices of SUNY system shared governance should serve as a model for effective shared governance at the campus level." This is the hook that allows our faculty, staff, and student governance leaders on every campus to establish inclusive structures and transparent processes with the goal of improving shared governance on their campuses.

"Moving SUNY forward": This is why shared governance is essential to producing better outcomes. Not only are the constituent parts better engaged in institutional success if they have accepted roles in shared governance, but decisions reflect those inputs. This is true at the system or campus level. The State University of New York has institutionalized the concept and, more important, the practices that represent the best in shared governance.

The chapters in this volume illustrate the many varied ways shared governance is exemplified at the campus and system levels, often with our faculty, staff, and student governance bodies in the lead.

References

Tamrowski, N., Good, T., Knuepfer, P., & O'Brien, K. (2017, May–June). SUNY Voices: A successful joint effort to institutionalize faculty governance. *Academe*. https://www.aaup.org/article/suny-voices#.XbhIm-dKjUI.

Appendix A
Joint Statement on Shared Governance for the State University of New York

Introductory Statement

The following short summary on Shared Governance in the system has been prepared by the Faculty Council of Community Colleges (FCCC), the Student Assembly (SA) and the University Faculty Senate (UFS) to express the state of shared governance at the system level of the State University of New York. Shared governance has been instrumental in moving SUNY forward, especially in recent years when public higher education has endured many challenges.

Summary Statement on the Principles and Practice of Shared Governance in SUNY

SUNY Shared Governance refers to the structures and processes through which constituent groups, including the above governance organizations and the SUNY Board of Trustees, participate in the development of policies and decision-making that affect the institution. Collaboration, communication and collegiality are the hallmarks of shared governance within the SUNY System, the facilitation of which includes, but is not limited to, the following:

1. The president of the SA is a voting member of the SUNY Board of Trustees. The presidents of the FCCC and the UFS are currently non-voting members of the Board.
2. SUNY System Administration and the campuses contribute to the financial and organizational stability of the FCCC, SA, and UFS.
3. SUNY Voices sponsors events and publications intended to strengthen shared governance across the system;
4. Regular meetings between the presidents of the FCCC, the SA, and the UFS, are held with the Chancellor, the Provost, and other senior administrators as appropriate, to discuss issues of concern and develop a common agenda;
5. Chancellor's Cabinet membership includes the presidents of the FCCC, the SA, and the UFS.
6. Elected governance organization leaders and/or their representatives are included in strategic planning as well as development, implementation, and evaluation of system-wide initiatives;
7. Presidents of the FCCC, the SA, and the UFS (or their designees) are included in all search committees for senior system-wide university officers;
8. Consultation and approval processes on all major SUNY policies are articulated and followed prior to their submission to the Board of Trustees, recognizing that faculty have primary responsibility for academic policy, curriculum, and standards, and that such consultation with students is also essential for student affairs policies.
9. Senior system administrators, especially the Chancellor and the Provost, attend each of the scheduled plenary or conference events held by the FCCC, the SA, and the UFS around the state.
10. These principles and practices of SUNY system shared governance should serve as a model for effective shared governance at the campus level.

The FCCC, the SA, and the UFS look forward to working with the Board of Trustees, the Chancellor, and the Provost to continue to evolve the principles and practices of shared governance enumerated above, to serve as a model of shared governance at universities across the country, and to be a resource for all colleges and universities within the SUNY System.

Approved by Faculty Council of Community Colleges (FCCC),
Student Assembly (SA) and University Faculty Senate (UFS)
April 2017

Introduction

Gwen Kay

"Everybody talks about shared governance, but nobody does anything about it." With all respect to a paraphrased Mark Twain, this statement is incorrect. With appreciation to former SUNY Chancellor Nancy Zimpher for allocating funding for discussions about shared governance, SUNY Voices has made it possible: We talk about shared governance in shared spaces, and we try our best to get it right. As the essays in this volume illustrate, there are many different ways, strategies, and approaches to "getting it right." From campus-specific examples to system-wide rubrics, SUNY campuses are committed to shared governance.

The contributions in this volume are from two SUNY Voices conferences with a resonant theme: empowering and including as many people as possible to make the life and work of our campuses a shared process. At its essence, each essay works to grapple with how and what shared governance is, using examples of success and occasional failure to learn from mistakes and highlight best practices.

In the beginning, there was shared governance, and it was good. But "good" might be in the eyes of the beholder. In "Characteristics of Shared Governance," Diane Bliss, Renee Lathrop, and Jeffrey Steele ferret out key elements of shared governance. Comparing systems across three different institutions allows for a high-level view of common practices and evolving issues. Because shared governance should be both dynamic and responsive, some policy areas, such as how to be more inclusive of part-time staff within a governance structure, are currently unresolved. As Noelle Chaddock and Gordon Bigelow remind us in "Framing the Role of Faculty Governance Toward Institutional Diversity and Inclusion," governance can be a place and space for new issues. Are there ways shared governance can be more inclusive and more responsive to larger campus issues of diversity and inclusion? Can shared governance spaces model best practices and infuse this vision across campus? Finally, three neighboring community college presidents, Belinda S. Miles, Cliff L. Wood, and Kristine Young, present their views on shared governance particularly in regard to Middle States Commission of Higher Education standards. The perspective of campus leaders is a good contrast to the faculty, the other side of shared governance. Their advice and insight about working under tight deadlines, transitions, and a continual influx of new students offers an illuminating look at the challenges (and frustrations) shared by our partners in governance.

With a common language and understanding, what does it take to make governance work smoothly? The three keys are communication, communication, and communication. Joe Marren highlights specific and generic strategies that can be used on a campus level in "The Rights, Wrongs, and Challenges of Governance Communication." The use of social media may or may not work on a specific campus, but the common tools of basic communication, properly deployed, will ensure that everyone on campus has the ability to be well informed. The ability to communicate well, honestly, and openly is at the heart of "Developing Rapport and Relationships with New Administrators" by campus governance leader Margaret Ann Hoose and Provost Barry Spriggs. A new governance system and a new leader could be a difficult transition, but with open conversation and adherence to bylaws, an institution can move forward in a productive and inclusive manner, with buy-in from faculty and staff, students, and administration.

Communication does not always mean that honest and open conversations are occurring, however. To that end, we offer some best practices across SUNY and the American Association of University Professors (AAUP). Deborah F. Stanley, president, and Lisa M. Glidden, campus governance leader, offer a case study from SUNY Oswego. A committee set up through shared governance allowed this campus to think creatively and long term about the needs and desires of the campus to grow and expand its physical facilities. Working collaboratively enabled the committee to think big and position itself well: when resources were available, the campus was ready with a process, a plan and a goal in mind. Another example of best practices is "Development of a Rubric for Assessing Shared Governance," which came out of the SUNY Committee on Assessment. Deborah L. Moeckel shares the rubric and the process for creating something applicable across a varied 64 campuses. Finally, Michael DeCesare uses the AAUP's 1966 "Statement on Government of Colleges and Universities" to bring us "Back to the Past: Imagining the

Future of Academic Governance." He balances breakdowns on some campuses with suggestions for strengthening shared governance.

All of these tools and best practices can be seen in the shared lessons learned. Kenneth P. O'Brien reflects on "Chancellor Nancy Zimpher and SUNY's Shared Governance" from his position as president of the SUNY University Faculty Senate in Zimpher's first four years. A champion of shared governance, he assesses two particular cases in which working with governance leaders was fruitful to Zimpher's larger agenda. Taking Zimpher's words about shared governance to heart, campus governance leaders Philip L. Glick and Dominic J. Licata argue that transparency is perhaps the best tool deployed in shared governance. They argue that transparency fosters shared governance, just as true shared governance fosters transparency.

Are transparency and communication enough? When Middle States Commission on Higher Education (MSCHE), an accrediting body, comes to visit, the answer can be varied. As Valerie H. Collins illustrates in "Nassau Community College at a Turning Point," sometimes it takes hard work through shared governance. A new university president and a new vice president of academic affairs arrived on campus in fall 2016, following MSCHE putting the campus on probation. Building trust and using tools from AAUP and Middle States, the campus regained its footing and was fully accredited. Olin Stratton and Wendy Tarby, in "Accreditation Academy: An Organic Approach to Preparing for the MSCHE Site Visit" offer a proactive response to MSCHE. In advance of accreditation, they held campus-wide workshops to inform everyone about the process, timeline, and responsibilities. This helped ensure that everyone was familiar with accreditation and ready for the visit, having fully been involved in preparing the report. Finally, in "A Comparative Analysis of Regional Accreditation Guidelines: Role of Shared Governance in Accreditation," Peter L. K. Knuepfer compares accreditation bodies across the United States to find similarities and differences. The commonalities are reassuring, the disparities somewhat surprising.

From basic definitions and a common understanding to accreditation, from failure to success, shared governance offers campuses a path to collaborative and productive wins for faculty, staff, students, and administrators. These essays offer a unique perspective on shared governance, with applicability beyond the specifics.

Editor's Note

Governance Undimmed

Sharon F. Cramer

Since 2015, the SUNY Press Shared Governance series has been a part of my life. I have had the privilege of working with 55 academic authors from 23 institutions of higher education. They chose to investigate topics about which they were curious, and often passionate, and to channel their thoughts into scholarly contributions. My own research on the topic of shared governance over the decades in scholarly journals yielded publications that were largely theoretical. I was confident that our series, with authors who had many sleepless nights before arriving at true shared governance, would make a unique contribution to the field.

The centennial of World War I and a visit to the National World War I Museum and Memorial in Kansas City, Missouri, sharpened my sense of what shared governance leaders have on the line when they fight for the flags of collaboration and transparency. This analogy is apt, as the generals (like those erudite governance scholars) often viewed their battles from afar. Governance officers and members, like the soldiers, rarely take time to look up from their trenches. Unexpected things happen—on the battlefield, in campus governance. Only the lucky and the strong manage to not only dodge the perils but evolve because of the challenges. Just as many soldiers left the battlefields experiencing shell shock (now known as post-traumatic stress disorder, or PTSD), most people wander away from governance service without recording what they learned. Relieved to have their email inboxes empty of governance-related matters, they rarely take time to reflect on (much less write about) their governance experiences.

These volumes changed the landscape of what is available to governance members and leaders who want to avoid reinventing the wheel. For the first time, battle drums are used to keep time and as part of surprising (and sometimes funny) musical compositions: the music of governance is no longer exclusively used to keep the regiment in line. Within these volumes, music inspires. Governance members who contributed to this volume tell complicated, layered stories of their experiences to help others avoid becoming casualties of war. The journey readers can take through the three volumes, and especially this one, shows how SUNY governance leaders have offered a field not of memorial poppies but of vegetation that flourishes and nourishes.

I am grateful to many for enabling me to serve the SUNY University Faculty Senate as editor of these volumes. To each author, I express thanks for partnering with me to make chapters better. To our SUNY Press colleagues, Donna Dixon, Ryan Morris, and others, you filled in the potholes on the bumpy road to publication. To our indexer, Dave Prout, who took so much care with our authors' work, helping their intentions emerge. To Former SUNY Chancellor Nancy Zimpher, for creating and funding SUNY Voices, beginning in 2014. To current SUNY Chancellor Christina Johnson, for endorsing continued commitment to shared governance. To the Faculty Council of Community Colleges (FCCC) presidents Tina Good, Nina Tamrowski, and Christy Fogel, I appreciate all you have done and will do to keep SUNY Voices and this series vibrant and strong. To the SUNY University Faculty Senate (UFS) presidents Ken O'Brien, Gwen Kay, and Pete Knuepfer, thank you for your confidence and support: It has been my privilege to serve you.

With this volume, I take my leave, after 27 years as a governance member and leader in SUNY. These years have taught me that governance only works when it is shared. Governance matters because our process enables us to influence and better our campuses and ourselves. We are inspired by problems, invigorated by aspirations. We can take pride as we read the words of our colleagues, who took the time to grasp the wisps of their experiences and mold them into chapters. This series has been, and ideally will continue to be, a gift from me and our contributors to governance colleagues within and beyond SUNY. We fervently hope that because of our governance work, and sharing it through publications, the lives of students, faculty, staff, and administrators have been and will continue to be improved.

Part I

Perspectives on the Key Elements of Shared Governance

1

Characteristics of Shared Governance

Diane Bliss, Renee Lathrop, and Jeffrey Steele

The popular term "shared governance" is often misused. This chapter contrasts definitions of shared governance with elements of a shared governance system. Although institutions of higher education may have idiosyncratic governance structures, key factors are present in all shared governance systems, and these are discussed. The process of achieving shared governance is constantly evolving to meet specific needs. The chapter concludes with a paradigmatic challenge—the question of the inclusion of part-time or contingent staff in shared governance structures.

Although not a new concept, as the decision-making processes at institutions of higher education evolve, the term "shared governance" is increasingly used more broadly, often equated with various models of decision-making. To more fully understand current decision-making trends in the environment of higher education, a starting point must be to define shared governance and the essentials of a shared governance system. In this context, it is possible to explore the impact of (and needs for) the evolution of shared governance.

What Does "Shared Governance" Mean?

In its 1966 *Statement on Government of Colleges and Universities*, the American Association of University Professors (AAUP) recognized that "A college or university in which all the components [governing board, president, faculty, and to some extent students] are aware of the usefulness of communication among themselves and of the force of joint action will enjoy increased capacity to solve educational problems" (AAUP, 1966, introduction). In other words, shared governance is a joint responsibility among faculty, administrators, and trustees. AAUP further "emphasizes the importance of faculty involvement in personnel decisions, selection of administrators, preparation of the budget, and determination of educational policies. Faculty should have primary responsibility for such fundamental areas as curriculum, subject matter and methods of instruction, research, faculty status, and those aspects of student life which relate to the educational process" (AAUP, 1966, section 5, para. 1). Although the AAUP focuses on the role of faculty in shared governance, it does recognize that there is a role and responsibility for each group of decision-makers.

A similar body overseeing another group of stakeholders, the Association of Governing Boards (AGB), stated in 2015 that "Shared Governance is a set of guidelines about the various roles and authority of the board, faculty, and administration in such things as academic decisions, budget decisions, selection of the President and other operational decisions" (excerpted from Bahls, 2015). Here, the focus is on shared governance as a set process—decisions are made through the efforts of faculty, administrators, and boards, thereby reinforcing the AAUP statement in terms of the legitimacy, importance and authority of the roles taken by these three groups in certain decisions.

The Middle States Commission on Higher Education (2011) stated in "Characteristics of Excellence in Higher Education: Requirements for Affiliation and Standards of Accreditation" that

> Institutions should seek to create a governance environment in which issues concerning mission, vision, program planning, resource allocation and others, as appropriate, can be discussed openly by those who are responsible for each activity. Within any system of shared governance, each major constituency must carry out its separate but complementary roles and responsibilities. Each must contribute to an appropriate degree so that decision-makers and goal-setters consider information from all relevant constituencies. (Middle States Commission on Higher Education, 2011, p. 12)

Despite this standard's best-practice approach to collegial and transparent shared decision-making, the commission's 2014 revision is less specific about shared governance in higher education, indicating in Standard VII: Governance, Leadership, and Administration simply the need for "a clearly articulated and transparent governance structure that outlines roles, responsibilities, and accountability for decision making by each constituency, including governing body, administration, faculty, staff and students" (MSCHE, 2014, p. 13). This shift points to the need for professional organizations such as the AAUP and AGB to continue championing the principles of shared governance in higher education as the hallmark of college and university decision-making processes. Nevertheless, these higher education professional organizations recognize the strength of a collegial system of shared decision-making with clearly defined constituency roles and established processes in advancing the mission, goals, and quality of higher education.

The State University of New York's (SUNY) statement on shared governance is similar to the foregoing statements but introduces students into this decision-making process:

> In a shared governance system, faculty, professional staff, administration, governing boards, and students participate in the development of policies and in decision making that affects the institution. SUNY has three main bodies that interact with each other and the Board of Trustees: The University Faculty Senate, Student Assembly, and Faculty Council of Community Colleges. By coming together with different constituent groups who have different opinions on how an institution should be governed, the shared governance process can become the desired way to help institutions implement changes. (SUNY, 2017)

Including students in the SUNY model speaks to the recognition that this group is in fact greatly affected by decisions and brings a perspective that might otherwise escape the consideration of boards, administration, or faculty. Although the emphasis in SUNY is on different constituencies (among them the students) coming together to develop policies that affect an institution, "participation" is not identical for groups interacting with the board of trustees. Although the faculty representatives on the SUNY Board of Trustees are trustees, they are nonvoting. Their participation is limited to gathering and voicing perspectives of faculty and professional staff members, as well as providing expertise about policies. However, there is a recognition here that many decisions may put faculty in positions raising conflicts of interest were they voting members of the board. On the other hand, the student trustee represents student interests and shares the unique student perspective on decisions that directly affect their educational experience and thus has a vote. An important point here is that within the SUNY shared governance process, not all individuals have equal votes on all issues. Some constituencies are included but with limited roles (e.g., can provide input but are excluded from having a vote in the decision-making process) by virtue of their positions at the institution, a topic discussed later.

The Faculty Council of Community Colleges (FCCC) 2008 statement on faculty's role in shared governance is consistent with the AGB statement, emphasizing the set process or procedure for decision-making. There is primacy in the decision-making process of certain constituencies. For instance, faculty have primacy in curricular decisions, whereas administrators have primacy in budget decisions. Nonetheless, there should be collegial and cooperative communication among the groups (FCCC, 2008). Both the AAUP statement and the Faculty Council statement accord faculty well-established roles in decision-making in higher education, especially in educational and curricular matters but also in areas such as planning and mission creation. With those roles are concomitant responsibilities.

Emerging from these examples is clear evidence that shared governance includes a set process through which better decisions can be made. Although no details constrain the process, and no particular model is preferred, these professional bodies clearly recognize (1) that multiple groups offer a variety of voices and ideas, and (2) that diverse areas of expertise should be represented in all decision-making processes. Most important, (3) the decision-making process used at an institution should be a consistent and well-established one, not an ad hoc system or structure. There should be clearly written charges or statements that define various constituent roles in the process, determine how constituents communicate with each other, and delineate how to advance recommendations if decisions involve various campus offices and positions. The expected norm of shared governance should be collegiality in decision-making, with an appropriate level of respect and authority for those in clearly defined roles or with specific expertise or accountability. The resulting recommendations arising from such an established and codified process should likewise be given consistently respectful and authentic consideration.

Elements of Shared Governance

Although there is no single accepted model of shared governance, the following key elements should be present in every shared governance organization.

- **A governance structure has bylaws and/or a constitution.** The establishment of bylaws and a constitution is a first step in making a formal decision-making structure, whether at institutions of higher education or in governance bodies. Bylaws define everything, including such details as who is a member, how meetings are conducted, how formal recommendations are made, and to whom those recommendations are sent. Such clarity strengthens and makes permanent a process that is not altered at the whim of any one individual or small group. Organizational boards of trustees and faculty governance groups, such as senates or assemblies, each have bylaws. These groups conduct formal business that requires majority or consensus approval to advance actions and decisions. Presidential cabinets do not necessarily have bylaws. As a group of senior administrators, they may advise a college president but may not necessarily vote in a formal way to take an action or make decisions.

- **Governance bodies have a formal process by which they conduct their meetings, generally parliamentary procedure.** Boards of trustees/colleges use parliamentary procedure to conduct their business, and most faculty groups use either *Robert's Rules of Order* or the Sturgis Standard Code of Parliamentary Procedure. A formal, recognizable process is used to conduct meetings and provide order to the decision-making process. Groups that do not use a formal process are probably informal groups, not formal governance bodies.

- **Shared governance requires clearly defined lines of communication.** How are recommendations communicated to the college's boards or president? If the president does not approve of the recommendation, how does the faculty governance or assembly know about the difference in opinion or the decision the president makes? If a student organization makes a recommendation, does it go to the president or the faculty governance body? How are different groups convened, and how do they communicate on issues of shared importance? These are important questions that must be codified in advance; if they are not, any governance body is likely to fail. Failure to work out these lines of communication can lead to time-consuming and disjointed decision-making and implementation, as well as an inefficient and ineffective use of time and resources.

- A governing body should have groups of people who have been given responsibility to make decisions/recommendations. For example, a curriculum committee should be composed of faculty or people who teach; their primary roles at the institution would determine their expertise in evaluation of curriculum. Individuals in nonteaching positions might be invited to provide input into decisions (e.g., tutors, students, or administrators might be affected by curriculum decisions), but faculty are the caretakers of curriculum; by their professional role, they have primacy in making curricular decisions. In contrast, there are aspects of the institution wherein faculty voices are not central. Issues of grounds or building maintenance are primarily roles of nonfaculty groups; faculty might be invited to participate in discussions as they use the grounds and facilities for learning activities, but they should not drive decisions. Each group has a level of expertise to bring to the discussions. It would be important to have a predetermined process for decision-making on which decision-makers can rely. For example, open, well-publicized meetings should be held on topics of broad interest. Campus members can be invited to attend and provide their input, directly or indirectly through their representatives, as the case might be. However, only those given the authority to make the decision, by virtue of their role as defined in the bylaws or their administrative position, are given a vote in the decision-making process. Ideally, decision-makers in a shared governance structure are selected by a vote of their peers. Whether for a representative body, such as a faculty senate, or a more inclusive body of the whole, such as an assembly, when it comes to committee work, a committee should be composed of those who have been selected by their peers to serve on the committee. This democratic process is valuable in ensuring that each constituency supports the work of the shared governance committees while discouraging the sense that members must agree with or meet the approval of administrators to be a part of the decision-making process. Thus, the decisions or recommendations being put forth are more authentically the product of shared governance and thus more likely to be effective.

- Shared governance must specify the means by which representatives communicate with and hear the ideas of those they represent. It is important in a governance structure that there be complete and accessible records so that those not able to attend a meeting can be informed and can provide input and feedback to those who represent them. Sometimes there is a tendency for college leaders to assemble "task forces" or ad hoc committees outside the governance structure. Although this may be well intentioned, these people often may be hand-chosen by administrators, rather than elected by their peers, and the resulting decisions may be made without the broader input and perspectives that would be available through shared governance. In such cases, the ability to make a truly effective and "best" decision is hampered in the name of expediency, and thus commitment to its success is limited.

These key elements form the bedrock of effective governance organizations, in that they create a forum for predictability. When governance is most effective, it capitalizes on precedent and promotes respect among its members. Transparency of process and effective, established lines of communication reduce suspicion and increase confidence in decisions. In a time of change—administration turnovers, political climate, financial stresses, or shifts in societal priorities—a well-established system and process of shared decision-making can make all the difference in terms of the institution's effectiveness and success, promoting collegial problem-solving and mutual respect and advancing its educational mission. Those who seek to engage in shared governance must also be aware that this approach to shared decision-making also brings its share of challenges.

What Is Often Problematic About Governance Committees or Structures?

One of the criticisms of shared governance is that it is a slow process. This is true: the members of the governance body must figure out the problem, identify all components, determine what needs to be fixed, discuss their ideas and perspectives, research possible solutions and best practices, and build agreement or consensus—and all these steps take time. In addition, in a representative structure, representatives must take time to hear from constituencies, educate those who did not attend meetings, propose acceptable solutions or recommendations, and listen to and consider reactions or feedback, so even more time is required. The speed of the process depends greatly on how well the processes are defined and followed, as well as how well groups work together. Ideally, a culture of deliberative and collegial shared governance is present and engaged on the campus, but if not, the process may be problematic. To address the speed of the process, shared governance bodies may need to (1) consider reviewing processes for redundancies or unnecessary steps, and (2) review communications mechanisms, such as online form submissions or communication tools, to expedite information transmittal. Equally important is establishing ground rules and formal procedures to promote an atmosphere of collegiality and respect for the process.

Respect and collegiality may help avoid another criticism of governance structures that arises when there are conflicting points of view or results that leave some constituents unhappy. Governance is not a guarantee for, nor should it be about, making everyone happy. Faculty may express unhappiness at not being included in a decision-making process, and at the same time, administrators become disillusioned when they engage in shared governance only to hear that faculty are unhappy with the result. Conflict is natural in any decision-making process. A governance structure, or the use of a governance process, is not a simple fix to all conflicts on a campus; instead, it is a means for arriving at the best and most realistic recommendations and solutions through a deliberative process that approaches the issue from several perspectives. There still will be conflict; some may be unhappy with a decision, but if the decision went through the governance process, it should have considerable support from many of the constituencies involved. Having the unrealistic expectation that a governance process will make everyone happy with every outcome sets a system up for failure. A well-functioning system of shared governance should leave those who may have desired a different outcome still satisfied with the process itself and their role in that process. What shared governance should do is foster stronger understanding, a stronger sense of shared decision-making, and greater respect among the various constituencies on a campus. It relies on and should also promote an expectation of collegiality. In such an environment, adaptively responsive decisions can be more quickly and efficiently implemented.

Sometimes, those who are in decision-making positions try to protect their "right" to make those decisions unilaterally; people not in such positions but with expertise or interest in the decision-making area may be left out of the process. As mentioned earlier, in some cases, administrators may think they are engaging in shared governance when they seek input from specific people or form administrative task forces or ad hoc committees outside the formal governance structure. In such cases, the administrator actually bypasses the governance structure, and this can result in mistrust of the decision-making process or the administrator. Alongside problems with shared decision-making that is not formally shared governance are those constituents who are not part of the formal system, and this can also work to an institution's disadvantage. Recently, the topic of diversity has been prevalent in governance discussions. Although diversity may immediately bring to mind people who look differently or have different cultures or beliefs, in terms of shared governance it includes those who bring differing perspectives to the table. What many institutions of higher education and some private companies have learned is that having a group of diverse thinkers debate and discuss ideas often brings better information, better understanding, and more respect to the decision-making process. Governance organizations at colleges would do well to look at who is involved in their process. Institutions of higher education are not limited to deans and faculty; they include support staff for students, grounds staff, part-time faculty, and part-time staff who have often not been involved in decision-making. Some systems have made concerted efforts to involve students in their decision-making process, as evident in the inclusion of the Student Assembly within SUNY's defined shared governance system. Likewise, some higher education institutions within SUNY, particularly some of its community colleges, have inclusive governance bodies consisting of not just faculty but also professional staff, support staff, and students.

Although inclusion is a good goal, some difficulties with college community members (such as contingent faculty, part-time staff, and even students) is that they have temporary positions or limited time at the institution. A person in a temporary position or at the college for a limited time realistically may not be expected to have much knowledge of the situation, useful advice, or suggestions. If a person's job is contingent, they may not be willing or open to criticizing or suggesting changes to the current administration or their supervisors. In addition, adjuncts or contingent faculty generally are paid only to teach and are not for the time to participate in committee meetings or shared governance meetings. Furthermore, faculty who have been granted tenure tend not to be as fearful of making suggestions that are not as popular with the current administration. Tenured faculty usually are at an institution for longer and can offer historical perspectives on certain decisions being considered. Finally, students at a community college might be in attendance for as little as one semester or for one or more years. The question is, how effective or even wise is it to involve people who are transient within a college community in that institution's decision-making processes? This is not to say that faculty voices are more important than others, or that a governance structure should not be designed to hear these other voices. There is a need to make sure those voices that are transient or unprotected are heard, and tenured faculty—with their history and commitment to the institution that allows them to consider and experience short-term and long-term effects of decisions—have the responsibility to help ensure those voices are heard in the process.

Conclusion

It is often exciting to be at a stage of transition. Historically, most governance structures at colleges were either boards of trustees and/or faculty governance structures. With issues of diversity and the shift to an increase of contingent faculty and part-time staff on campuses, the question is now what does this mean for these same governance structures? Should shared governance organizations change, and—if so—how should they change? The idea that there is no one model of what a "good" shared governance structure looks like has made this even more difficult for each campus to answer.

Regardless of what a campus decides in terms of including other voices in their shared governance structure, the elements of a shared governance process offered here are crucial for shared governance success—including clear bylaws that detail how decisions are made, who is included in those decisions, and to whom recommendations or decisions are sent, as well as some accountability for the ultimate decision. An archive of minutes should exist in a public or semi-public place where information from the meetings can be accessed by all constituents and perhaps those outside the decision-making structure. Parliamentary rules of order for the meetings should be routinely followed and reviewed so that people understand how to comment or call for a vote on issues, and business can proceed in an orderly fashion. Last, all parties should foster an environment where collegiality, trust, and open communication is modeled and respected.

If a campus makes the effort to ensure that their governance structure responds to the changing needs of the institution and the suggestions offered in this chapter, they should be on their way to having a truly responsive and effective governance structure. If they experience difficulties, the suggestions offered here have been designed to help them know they are not alone in their struggles. Campus dialogue regarding these bedrock principles can provide starting points in moving toward stronger, more effective shared governance. With more effective shared governance in higher education, we can better continue the principle of including those who will be affected by decisions in the actual decision-making process, and we will be more successful in accomplishing our educational mission in the midst of change.

References

American Association of University Professors. (1966). *Statement on government of colleges and universities.* Retrieved from https://www.aaup.org/report/statement-government-colleges-and-universities.

Bahls, S. (2015, Dec. 21). What is shared governance? *Association of Governing Boards.* Retrieved from https://www.agb.org/blog/2015/12/22/what-is-shared-governance.

Faculty Council of Community Colleges. (2008, Oct. 18). *The role of faculty in shared governance. Faculty Council of Community Colleges.* Retrieved from https://www.fccc.suny.edu/governance/FCCCsharedGov_10_18_08.pdf.

Middle States Commission on Higher Education. (2011). *Characteristics of excellence in higher education: Requirements for affiliation and standards of accreditation.* 12th ed. Philadelphia, PA; MSCHE.

Middle States Commission on Higher Education. (2014). *Standards for accreditation and requirements of affiliation.* 13th ed. Philadelphia, PA: MSCHE. Retrieved from https://www.msche.org/publications/RevisedStandardsFINAL.pdf.

State University of New York. (2017). Shared governance. *State University of New York.* Retrieved June 14, 2017, from https://www.suny.edu/about/shared-governance/.

2

Framing the Role of Faculty Governance Toward Institutional Diversity and Inclusion

Gordon Bigelow and Noelle Chaddock

This chapter addresses the question of shared governance, particularly the role of faculty governance, in the academic institution's work to promote a diverse and equitable community. The authors offer reflections and recommendations regarding recruitment and hiring, perceptions of and responses to bias, and faculty committee organization. The essay considers the process by which colleges and universities can advance the work of diversifying campuses and creating inclusive cultures. The authors suggest that effective work toward institutional diversity and inclusion must take place across the whole institution, and that a strong and widely understood practice of shared governance is therefore a crucial element of this work. The authors invite colleagues to a conversation about a changing professoriate, a shifting student demographic, a troubled pipeline, and the evolving roles of faculty governance and leadership around diversity, equity, and inclusion in academia today.

Introduction: Noelle Chaddock

As we write this chapter, I have been an upper-level administrator for more than three years. I have seen colleges welcome a diversity of "first-identity" presidents and witnessed the importance of the preparatory work of the outgoing (often white male) leadership. I have watched incoming student cohorts reach record-setting racial diversity and seen colleges working very hard through committee, commission, and outside consultation. Our institutions across the country have spent countless hours reviewing policy, procedure, and practice while generating reports and recommendations. All of this has been good and necessary work. Where institutions get stuck and campus constituents become frustrated is at the point of implementation.

In my years in higher education, I have found that the place where all of this becomes particularly difficult for campus communities is around the gap between institutions that are incredibly willing yet terribly unready. The difference between willingness and readiness has become where I focus most of my attention. I have found faculty governance leadership and faculty committees to be the nexus point, where movement from "willing" to "ready" happens in academic institutions.

As a willing community, constituents come to the table. Members of institutions are willing and intentional about reading, training, and planning around creating a diverse, equitable, inclusive, welcoming, and value-filled campus community.

Many institutions fall short around their readiness—the ability to implement and sustain diversity and inclusion efforts through the realities and experiences of the fear-filled and the implicated. I would identify the spaces of tradition, fear, and self-preservation as where good diversity and inclusion intentions go to die. The impact, and thus the lack of readiness, is felt in institutional and individual performances of these same areas— tradition, fear, and self-preservation.

The "willing" but "not ready" campus is a particularly common institutional reality. It looks like many well-intentioned people trying to do the right thing while trying to maintain space for the things they are familiar with, the things that reflect their values in campus communities and higher education.

The greatest struggle has been and will continue to be guiding a population of people who are privileged in many ways to create space for those who have not had access. It is crucial that they do not feel displaced or implicated in the exclusion of these populations.

Unlike other kinds of change in higher education, demographic changes along with shifts in institutional focus around the diversification of faculty populations truly feel like change on the ground. Feelings of threat around displacement are often articulated as a sense that those who have been doing the work of examining and teaching race and identity for the past 25 years are no longer wanted because they are white (or male, or older). In fact, the good work of race and identity scholarship and education had long been white men teaching white students. That population of our professoriate, in relation to diverse classrooms, now feel white.

As I began to really appreciate the power of this relationship, I was presented with opportunity after opportunity to learn about our community from its members. Almost immediately, members of the faculty governance bodies at the institutional and state levels started to show up to welcome me and help acclimate me to my various roles. I found these campus members far more aware and critical of diversity and inclusion issues than I anticipated. They articulated strong awareness of the gaps in our efforts as scholarly communities to bring privileged members along and to help the institutions meet their goals around diversifying the professoriate. Broadly, this has become a governance priority for faculty leadership in the past five years. Issues of institutional marginalization, the lack of demographic representation in our faculty hires, cultural climate in the classroom, and issues of bias and discrimination are now part of what faculty governance bodies take up as an ongoing part of their work. Many if not most governance bodies suffer from the reality that the demographics of leadership no longer reflect that of the faculty or the diversifying student body. By the time I started this work at an administrative level in 2010, faculty governance leaders were ready and willing to support me in a diversity leadership role.

The collaboration between faculty governance and diversity administrators is imperative for creating and maintaining the spaces this work moves through to cultivate budding cultures of diversity, equity, and inclusion. In the coming pages, Gordon Bigelow and I think together about how this work is evolving from our unique but not disconnected experiences and perspectives.

I. The Task

US colleges and universities seeking to diversify their campus communities are acting at a time when long-standing practices around college governance are under pressure, sometimes strained to the breaking point. Seeking to respond to changing economic forces and shifting political currents, many institutions have taken the view that long-standing practices of consultative decision making, based on the principle of shared expertise, are no longer viable. Recent studies of shared governance in US higher education, including a new white paper from the Association of Governing Boards, have underscored this problem.[1] In this environment, best practices for campus-wide planning and decision making around inclusion and equity across many areas have become unclear or in dispute at many institutions. Meaningful study, planning, and innovation to promote diversity and inclusion requires sustained participation from every part of the community, touching on faculty recruiting and curriculum planning, admission and financial aid, athletics, campus life, development, and so on. So how do faculty, presidents, students, and trustees collaborate on these crucial matters when earlier patterns of academic governance have fallen out of use?

Our contention is that a broadly shared understanding of campus governance and decision-making processes is necessary for diversity initiatives to take hold and create change at the level of campus culture and climate. These governance practices need to be clear and widely understood among the student population as well as faculty, administrative staff, and trustees. The role of each group involved needs to be well defined, with a clear sense of how groups will work together to gather information, identify specific challenges, and address them. This shared understanding is crucial for fostering the trust in the process that will invite potentially vulnerable members of the campus community to contribute their voices.

Without using an inclusive process to design and undertake substantive change, collaborative governance will likely fail in creating lasting change, as it will tend to highlight the views of faculty, students, and staff in positions of relative security and institutional authority and exclude those with different views. At the same time, even well-conceived initiatives around diversity and equity, if imposed by one office without broad collaboration, often produce reactivity, opposition, or half-hearted support from stakeholders if they are not involved throughout the process. In that case, even an otherwise effective campus governance system cannot facilitate meaningful and lasting change.

We propose that to be successful, college and university leaders in all campus constituencies—faculty, presidents, trustees, and students—must work together from the outset. Issues of shared governance and inclusivity need to be thought through together, and every effort to advance these aims needs to function in parallel to other efforts. Dr. Daryl Smith, senior research fellow at the Claremont Graduate University and author of *Diversity's Promise for Higher Education*, does this work in a way that locates this relationship between administration and faculty as essential to the success and sustainability of equity and inclusion efforts. Presidents who willingly make diversity and inclusion part of their platform, who act as standardbearers for broad participation in diversity and inclusion initiatives, create a space for holding colleagues accountable for their participation.

This essay focuses on institutions with a clearly stated aim of participating in the work of diversity and inclusion. We consider institutions whose governing documents articulate good principles of shared governance and at least partially clarify the roles of faculty, trustees, and the president's office in crafting major decisions. Even at such institutions, the understanding of these principles is often neither deep nor widely shared. In many places, faculty see decisions affecting the academic program to have been made without systematic and meaningful faculty input. To begin to establish or reestablish clear shared government practices, one step faculty can take would be to generate a statement articulating their understanding of the roles different campus constituents play in making major decisions. A statement of this kind can clarify existing, if neglected, procedures or bylaws and draw attention to the need for a shared process.

II. The Tools

Student and campus climate surveys can yield information regarding the understandings that students and faculty have of the environments in which they work and study. When provided the opportunity to respond in these surveys, students of color are able to point out the role biases play inside and outside their classrooms, and how they disrupt the academic experience. Faculty are able to report experiences of intimidation or exclusion, and recently hired female faculty and faculty of color have often made these reports in disproportionately high numbers. Institutional inventories of this kind—provided that they are designed through a collaborative process—are crucial for establishing baselines for diversity and equity work, allowing voices not usually heard to come to the fore.

Based on this and other survey data, colleges can move toward building lasting infrastructure for their work on diversity and equity. We have found this step to be crucial. Rather than responding reactively and ad hoc to separate campus incidents or obstacles, colleges and universities need regular structures where information can be collected, problems identified and addressed, and new ideas fostered. At this point, faculty governance bodies can begin to think about the role faculty might play in sustainable equity and inclusion work. Their work can productively intersect with that of diversity administrators, most notably the chief diversity officer. This particular place of intersection between faculty and administrative leadership can be a fertile one for collaborative thinking and implementation, potentially broadening the scope of diversity and inclusion work at the institution.

However, if shared governance procedures are not already in place and routinely practiced by a broadly representative cross-section of the community, new diversity and equity initiatives can easily be hindered. For many faculty harmed in a toxic climate, time matters. The time to implementation for shared-governance initiatives, while administration and faculty are in the stages of discussion and consensus building, often feels like stalling to those being harmed. Faculty of color, women, and LGBTQ+ faculty may feel that faculty representation and governance processes are merely tactics to delay or avoid addressing their experiences with bias, discrimination, and a marginalizing campus climate. The shared governance space can become easily perceived as a privileged space where majority faculty avoid having difficult conversations around pervasive white normativity, gender bias, homo- and transphobia, bullying, accessibility, socioeconomic disparity, and so on.

Implementing bias-related and Title IX incident reporting systems can become a pressure point in this process and may serve as a useful example of our thesis. At colleges and universities without a regularly used and commonly acknowledged structure of shared governance, a new policy aimed, for example, at addressing the prevalence of sexual violence on campus can be resisted on the grounds of bad governance. Opponents of the policy, whatever their grounds, can gain cover here, enabling them to speak out not against Title IX enforcement—a position few would be willing to take—but against what they see as a lack of systematic community involvement in the development of the procedures. The accusations of a lack of procedural transparency and faculty involvement, especially on campuses where the initiatives and responsibility have come out of offices of student life or human resources, can lead to calls for delay on the grounds that faculty concerns have not been adequately addressed early on. Once the discussion arrives at this complicated place, it becomes difficult to gauge the scale (and the rationale) of community concern on the issue, as opposing voices all end up grouped under the heading of "shared governance."

At the same time, other faculty members may continue to report being harmed by delays in implementation. Declarations from some faculty that the administration failed to follow the shared governance process are seen by others as intentional tactics to stall or derail the implementation of a system that they felt was crucial. They are concerned for themselves and for the students with whom they are most closely identified, believing these procedures are necessary prerequisites for moving campus cultures to a place of authentic inclusion and equity. For others, however, these claims were heard as another attempt to "run a new policy through" without full faculty input and consensus. Lingering tensions present an obstacle to understanding and addressing the problem that was initially identified.

An example of the power of shared governance that counters the one given above would be the work that faculty governance leadership can accomplish by prioritizing diversity in the faculty hiring processes. Usually part of the responsibility of governing faculty bodies is to evaluate requests from departments and programs for faculty positions, both new and renewed. When faculty bodies overhaul procedures for submitting requests for faculty lines, building in more sustained thinking about attracting diverse candidate pools and developing relationships with a broad range of graduate programs that might supply candidates, these procedures are more than cosmetic. Recruiting a broadly diverse faculty is partly a curricular matter. At many institutions, program representatives and faculty groups responsible for leading curricular change may not be representative of the range of experiences and backgrounds reflected in the student body. Recruiting diverse pools of applicants for faculty positions is thus not simply a matter of counting bodies but a matter of enhancing the long-term intellectual viability of the college's academic program.

There are a variety of practices that can be considered with regard to faculty hiring. Modifications can be made to how departments generate faculty line requests, outlining steps for designing positions effectively, and planning for a successful search. Some institutions have ended up developing departmental action plans that laid out the strategies for diversifying the candidate pools. Others have looked toward more universal prescriptions for action. Again, crafting these procedures can be a place for productive engagement between faculty leaders, diversity professionals, and administrative staff. Consider, for example, the common procedure that requires a trained diversity officer or administrator to serve on a search committee to help departments with each hire. Although faculty often value the inclusion of these members of their search committees, feeling that this affords them a level of protection during a difficult process, others may criticize the policy as administrative interference. Again, we contend that the process that implements procedures of this kind is crucial and may lay the ground for its success or failure.

In some circumstances, faculty as a body can lead the institution in setting priorities around diversity and equity. A faculty frustrated by the lack of clear and ongoing institutional strategy on equity and inclusion might consider creating of a standing faculty committee to work on these matters. This move leverages the sociopolitical capital faculty have with their peers. These committees can contribute to the building of lasting structures for proactive conversation, rather than simply reacting to crises. If an institution is unresponsive to broad community concerns about diversity, or if diversity administrators are siloed in particular offices, a faculty body can organize to advocate for best practices across the institution. A standing committee of faculty can consider matters related to faculty affairs, student life, athletics, and so on.

These examples, chosen from among many, suggest to us that shared governance leadership can play a crucial role in moving an institution toward a diverse and inclusive campus culture. These examples and structures are not unique. Shared governance has been a long-standing space for institutional reimagining and progress, but the way shared governance functions at some institutions works to minimize faculty leadership and full faculty involvement in general. What we want to highlight is that without intentional, systematic, full faculty involvement, diversity efforts in particular will struggle. More broadly, if any part of the institution is left out of these initiatives, problems may ensue.

We have come to understand the profound need for parallel and simultaneous work on governance and campus diversity. The relationship between faculty governance leadership and diversity administrators can play a significant role in this work. All the parties need access to space for long-term thinking, where the perspectives of campus constituencies can be shared. This can also be a supportive space that directly affects faculty and administrative retention, especially when those roles intersect with underrepresented and marginalized identities and lived experiences.

Conversations around diversity and equity can arguably proceed more effectively in institutions that already have a clear and widely understood set of processes for consultation and collaborative innovation, between (and within) academic and administrative units. Likewise, promoting shared governance—both nuts-and-bolts procedures and a larger sense of purpose—may perhaps be simpler on a campus that had already devoted long years of deliberate effort to promoting a culture of equity and justice. But in working to better understand the obstacles and difficulties we have described, we learned a lot about the general existing state of things in institutions—in terms of governance and administrative structures and in terms of culture. This enabled us to determine exactly where we would recommend institutions begin to create meaningful change. Campus constituents do not simply want new forms and web pages on college websites—not simply new procedures or even new offices. Our interest is in practices that can help institutions act when they determine change is necessary, practices that can promote a deep-rooted, long-term shift in the campus culture, allowing the community to learn, respond, and change.

Moving forward, institutions, faculty governance leaders, and diversity administrators all have work to contribute. As presidents create more clear directives about institutional diversity and inclusion as major priorities, conditions are created for faculty to reach out across the institution. The commitment of administrative leaders can position various divisions of academic affairs to partner with faculty governance bodies and with each other in this work.

We hope that as US colleges and universities continue to explore the best ways to cultivate equitable and accessible campuses, the question of governance can be part of this exploration. Shared governance in general has been a neglected element of the work of colleges and universities in the past few decades, and the often difficult conversations around racial equity, LGBTQ+ support, first-generation access, sexual violence, and other issues are not made easier when no one has a clear sense of how and where important decisions will be made. Issues of equity and inclusion and policies aimed to promote change will affect all members of a campus community, and they all have a role to play in shaping the important decisions that will affect them. One productive step we suggest is for other institutions to host conferences or symposia on the role of shared governance in institutional diversity and inclusion. We believe there is a need to share best practices across the academy for addressing problems in these overlapping fields, problems whose solutions may lie in good collaboration and transparency between faculty leadership and senior administrators.

Note

1. Association of Governing Boards of Universities and Colleges (2017). Rhodes was among the case studies compiled by the AGB as part of this initiative.

Reference

Association of Governing Boards of Universities and Colleges. (2017). Shared governance: Changing with the times." *Association of Governing Boards of Universities and Colleges.* http://www.agb.org/reports/2017/shared-governance-changing-with-the-times.

3

Shared Governance

Valuing Each Other and Achieving More Together

Belinda S. Miles, Cliff L. Wood, and Kristine Young

A hallmark of the State University of New York and its 64 colleges and universities is a strong commitment to the long-standing practice of shared governance. The Middle States Commission on Higher Education also has shared governance as an expectation for all colleges and universities it accredits in the mid-Atlantic region of the United States. Shared governance is widely hailed as both a model and overriding objective of administration, faculty, staff, and students for effective collaboration and beneficial action on behalf of the academy. The opportunity to achieve shared governance is iterative and requires intent, flexibility, communication, understanding, and resolve. In this chapter, three community college presidents from the Lower Hudson Valley of New York state share their insights and perspectives on several key areas relevant to fostering effective shared governance in the shifting landscape of higher education. This chapter addresses best practices for collectively developing and sustaining an inclusive climate of shared governance to facilitate innovative institutional change, a positive environment that values all stakeholders, and results that matter. Particular themes and highlights include shared governance during presidential and other administrative transitions, urgent timelines, and constant influx of new and increasingly diverse student cohorts.

A hallmark of the State University of New York (SUNY) and its 64 colleges and universities is a strong commitment to shared governance. During an address to the University-wide Faculty Senate, SUNY Chancellor Kristina Johnson reinforced the role of shared governance in asking for help in addressing the challenges facing higher education and the SUNY system

(Ellis, 2018). SUNY further affirms that "by coming together with different constituent groups who have different opinions on how an institution should be governed, the shared governance process can become the desired way to help institutions implement changes" (SUNY, 2017a). In addition, through its Shared Governance Award, the SUNY system acknowledges the "inclusive and participatory" nature of the process, where "administration, faculty, staff, and students engage in a cooperative effort to create timely, inclusive, well-researched and well-supported institutional policies and decisions that benefit from the differing expertise, perspectives, and areas of responsibility of those constituents" (SUNY, 2017b).

Shared governance is a long-standing value in academia. It defines and integrates various roles and sources of input for collaborative decision-making and juxtaposes the authority of trustees and executive leadership with broad input from faculty, staff, and students as key stakeholders affected by administrative policies and decisions (AAUP, 1990).

The Middle States Commission on Higher Education (2015), responsible for the accreditation of the 64 institutions in the SUNY system, emphasizes effective governance as an expectation for colleges and universities under Standard VII, Governance, Leadership, and Administration. Specifically, the commission calls for "a clearly articulated and transparent governance structure that outlines roles, responsibilities, and accountability for decision making by each constituency, including governing body, administration, faculty, staff and students" (MSCHE, 2015).

The effective practice of shared governance is the overriding objective for collaborative and action-oriented decision making in our institutions. This is a worthy ideal. Accordingly, the process of achieving shared governance is dynamic, iterative, and purpose-driven; the people involved must make use of their personal and institutional capacities for flexibility, understanding, and resolve. Yet striving to achieve these goals can become a muddled process when parameters are not clearly defined or when constituents feel their concerns are not effectively represented or addressed.

The inclusive nature of the community college access mission is a value connected to shared governance. A uniquely US institution, community colleges are committed to broader access and opportunity to higher education in America (President's Commission on Higher Education, 1947). SUNY institutions provide quality, affordable, and accessible higher education to New Yorkers, whether their families have been here for generations or they are new residents of our state. In alignment with this mission of broad access, it is fitting that our institutions operate within the inclusive framework of shared governance, maximizing input from multiple sources. In simple terms, we need a community governance system for our community colleges. Our reflections on this topic yielded six key areas of discussion, which provide a framework for this chapter and offer valuable insights to effective shared governance processes.

Unified by Mission, Attentive to Culture

A shared commitment to and embrace of the college's mission often serve as the driving force for shared governance processes. At least by association, all constituents are united by the mission of the institution. Accordingly, the efforts of every initiative should be relevant to aspects of that mission. As institutions launch new initiatives or reset existing practices, it is critical to ask whether the initiative, however well researched or data-driven, aligns with the core tenets of the mission. Grounding institutional change efforts in standard mission-based processes, like accreditation reviews and strategic planning, can increase the likelihood of broad participation and adoption. In describing the role of committees in an institutional shared governance process, Tim Jones (2018) indicates that "the most gratifying part is uncovering the things that every committee member believes" and how committees serve the process of "finding fundamentally unifying ideas that shape discussion and facilitate group decision and action with more pace and shared sense of purpose." Mission as common denominator can be such a unifying force.

However, relying solely on mission alignment as a chief strategy for shared vision and governance is not advisable without regard for institutional culture. Differentiating between culture and mission and recognizing the effect of institutional culture enhances the success of shared governance efforts. The familiar phrase, widely attributed to Peter Drucker, "culture eats strategy for breakfast" (Rick, 2014), reminds us that even the best-laid plans or the clearest objectives are subject to behavioral norms and conditions that influence how things really work. Learning and appreciating the idiosyncrasies of institutional culture takes time and effort. Making space for communication can help build understanding of organizational culture, which can be leveraged to achieve strategic, mission-focused ends. As Olson (2009) writes, "the key to genuine shared governance is broad and unending communication."

Even as efforts to incorporate institutional culture ensue, increased communication can reveal that not all constituents clearly understand what a desired state of shared governance looks or feels like. In environments where hierarchical or anarchy-based governance may have existed, stakeholder groups may be so familiar with the way things have been that they cannot readily envision or adapt to the more collaborative approaches inherent in shared governance. This "better the devil you know" phenomenon can result in resistance to change. One can easily underestimate the prevalence and strength of historical practices and their impact on the effectiveness of shared governance. Nevertheless, institutional priorities may demand that change occur despite stakeholder readiness for change (or lack thereof). In Olson's (2009) words, "true shared governance attempts to balance maximum participation in decision making with clear accountability." Leaders are wise to use prudence and sensitivity in such environments, understanding that "genuine shared governance gives voice (but not necessarily ultimate authority) to concerns common to all constituencies as well as to issues unique to specific groups" (Olson, 2009).

Who's on First?

Decision making in academia involves consideration and clarification of the key activities: "voice," "vote," and "veto." What is the difference? In the presence of formal governance structures, voice is achieved with stakeholder representation. This is useful for facilitating inclusion. However, inclusion is not the same as shared governance, which typically involves the formality of voting and appropriate administrative action at the cabinet, presidential, and board level to accept or reject recommendations. To facilitate meaningful involvement that values multiple perspectives and promotes timely and mutually derived outcomes, these distinctive roles should be clarified.

Olson (2009) states that "all legal authority in any university originates from one place and one place only: its governing board [which] formally delegates authority over the day-to-day operation of the institution . . . to the president, who, in turn, may delegate authority over certain parts of university management to other university officials." For example, staff members responsible for key operations are often best suited to bring forth policy and procedural recommendations pertaining to their work units. Primary responsibility for the educational program, most notably the curriculum, is generally delegated by the president to the faculty (Pierce, 2016). Shared governance "doesn't mean that every constituency gets to participate at every stage" (Olson, 2009) of the decision-making process. Rather, "the various stakeholders participate in well-defined parts of the process."

Cowen (2018) notes that sharing in "shared governance" is not equally distributed. "The differences in the weight of each voice is determined by the reference to the responsibility of each component for the particular matter at hand" according to AAUP (1990). Ultimately, "decision making authority is held by the president and the board, the ones who are accountable for both results and shortcomings" (Cowen, 2018).

It is generally understood that the board's primary duties are fiduciary, entrusting to its members stewardship of major institutional assets like money and mission. They hire the president as their agent who more actively engages in the relationships associated with shared governance and handles the management of the college. Although the board and those involved daily in shared governance processes should be on collegial terms and serve together in select ways, more consistent direct transactions between them are not indicated. In fact, some question the degree to which a college's board of trustees should be involved at the developmental level of policies and recommendations. This participation could be construed as managing the institution, which is the president's role. An effective president will serve both the board and other participants.

Stakeholder engagement and involvement outside the shared governance process is useful for brainstorming ideas and gaining authentic input to new proposals and developments. SUNY Westchester Community College President Belinda Miles (personal communication, 2017) asserts that "communication tools, such as open office hours, town hall meetings, department meetings, college-wide summits, and blog-type messages are effective for sharing and receiving information and collaborating on systems, ideas, and operations." These may be collaborative forums in a shared atmosphere, but they are no substitute for structured shared governance practices. Understanding and using formal structures like the faculty senate, vice presidential and deans' leadership councils, staff councils, and the president's cabinet honors traditions and provides uniform processes for collaborative decision-making. A newly formed President's Communication Council at Westchester Community College (composed of members of the Faculty Senate Executive Board and the president's cabinet), has provided another layer of input and analysis of pending matters.

Cliff Wood (personal communication, 2017), president emeritus of SUNY Rockland Community College, notes that

> differentiating between shared governance and other faculty decision making groups is critical for sustained shared governance

work. There are community colleges across the U.S. with a model of shared governance that consists of a single body or a college council with representatives from all constituencies. In the college council model, there are representatives of each constituency who meet regularly to discuss, deliberate, and debate issues referred to them by the administration or concerns raised by individual representatives. Shared governance operates differently at other institutions—there are multiple governance groups that come together to discuss and debate areas of mutual concern. These groups generally focus on issues pertinent to the roles, responsibilities, and needs of their constituencies. Traditionally, these constituencies include a faculty senate, a student government group, and an administrative/staff association.

In any comprehensive model of shared governance, there must be opportunities for each constituent group to express its unique perspective when roles and constituencies inevitably conflict. At all times, the president and the board must demonstrate that they respect and value the opinions and recommendations of various governance groups. When they do not accept the recommendation(s) of a campus governance group, they should provide comprehensive and clear statements and feedback regarding such decisions, noting that "on these matters, the power of review or final decision lodged in the governing board or delegated by it to the president should be exercised adversely only in exceptional circumstances" (AAUP, 1990).

Where collective bargaining units or unions exist, the institution must clearly differentiate between the manifestation of shared governance and the role(s) of collective bargaining units, which generally focus on wages, benefits, and conditions of employment. One complication of this distinction is any issue that could be part of a collective bargaining agreement but operationally affects all members of the college community. Wood (personal communication, 2017) cites the college calendar as an example of this because "it contains the work year for faculty, as defined within their union contract, in addition to holidays, professional development days, and other events that affect other members of the college community." A key factor for an effective model of shared governance is one where the roles and responsibilities of each bargaining unit are clearly delineated as entities distinct from the purview of shared governance.

"Tyranny of the Urgent"

The pressures of balancing multiple demands with urgent timelines can disrupt even the most well-intentioned commitments to shared governance. One of the biggest challenges that shared governance participants must jointly navigate is the ever-increasing pace of change that can limit the time needed for informed and participatory decision-making. This affects institutions most acutely when major decisions and situations are required without regard to the cyclical nature of the academic calendar. For example, this can occur when demands are made by external agencies in the summer months, when many faculty are not present. The expectation of prompt responses and resolution can be thwarted during these periods because shared governance opportunities are significantly limited in the summer.

Further complicating matters, decision-making processes differ considerably among the various bodies involved in shared governance. By its very nature, the academy is purposeful and reflective. How else could knowledge, philosophies, and hypotheses be thoughtfully generated, rigorously critiqued, and broadly disseminated? This tradition is embedded in higher education and manifests publicly in formal senates and college councils. Even if a revised or new policy or statement has been advanced through many committees over a long time, every shared governance constituency is invited and expected to give input and refine the document until it is finalized and approved.

As former faculty members, we understand and respect this practice, although things look different from the vantage point of our current role as administrators. How can we continue effective collaboration and joint action through shared governance when one of the defining aspects of the academy—extended deliberation—is sometimes incompatible with the necessities of running an institution? External parties are often unfamiliar with the standard stops or pauses in the process due to summer, winter, and spring breaks. They are often unaware that a large part of our workforce is absent over the summer. As a result, the extended ecosystem of which our institutions are a part does not "get" our seemingly indefinite timelines. According to Weisbuch (2015), four specific strategies can ensure that we restart the "stalled clock" of academic decision-making: all shared governance constituents must "see the big picture; do the necessary homework; encourage risk taking; and set and keep deadlines."

The administration typically carries out these strategies while maintaining balance among constituencies. When there is time for thoughtful deliberation, administrators must give initiatives the space to be fully discussed and critiqued, make itself available for these thorough conversations, and candidly provide additional data, information, examples, and justifications as requested. Administrators must assume that suggestions and recommendations made through shared governance are worthy of consideration and incorporation. If the timeline does not allow for this level of deliberation, administrators must inform shared governance leaders of the need for expediency and the reasons for the imposed timeline, such as funding, external policy or legislative decisions, and the like. Weisbuch (2015) recommends that all shared governance constituent groups "agree, ahead of time, on an endpoint—that is, on the absolute date when a decision will be reached and on a timeline of steps to guide the process" when appropriate.

Finally, administrators should aim to develop an intrinsic and informed sense of how shared governance leaders might feel about decisions made during the (exceptional) times when full consultation is not practical. On these occasions, earnest efforts should be made to get feedback from shared governance leaders, recognizing that this input may not reflect the full consideration of the governing council. It is incumbent on all shared governance constituents, including presidents, to understand and respect the pressures each group faces. Building sufficient trust with positive joint endeavors during less stressful times can serve as "capital" to minimize tension when executive decisions must occur. Boyer (2018) posits that "the ideal scenario—in which faculty and staff members feel heard, informed, and empowered, and administrators feel they have the flexibility, trust, and partnerships to manage and lead in times of rapid change is neither a fantasy nor even unrealistic." Surely it is an ideal worthy of the effort.

Managing Turnover

Turnover of administrative leaders involved in shared governance has become the "new normal" in academia. Managing such transitions is essential to the success of institutional change initiatives, progress, and sustainability. The pace of turnover among community college presidents and provosts is evidenced by an American Council on Education report indicating that presidential tenures are shrinking, from 8.5 years in 2006 to 6.5 in 2016 (Seltzer, 2017). Although the majority of new presidents have a background in higher education administration, it remains unclear whether formative experiences along the career path provide enough familiarity with shared governance and whether this aspect of the presidential role is sufficiently addressed in leadership development programs and New President Programs.

In her transition into her role as president, Kristine Young

> couldn't miss the signal that shared governance at SUNY Orange was alive, well, respected, and valuable. I was in the Large Courtroom at SUNY System in Albany observing the SUNY Trustees' Community College Committee meeting. As SUNY Orange's president-nominee awaiting a SUNY Board vote on my selection later that day, I was taken by the deliberations of my prospective SUNY colleagues in committee. Imagine how delighted and surprised I was to learn that SUNY Orange had won the SUNY Campus Shared Governance Award earlier that academic year. I knew immediately who needed to be top of the list during my first week of meetings on the job: SUNY Orange's President and Vice President of Shared Governance. I'm grateful that I lucked into overt encouragement to seek out shared governance leadership immediately. I would have gotten there before too long, but meeting with the President and Vice President so early in my tenure gave me the chance to see the college through faculty and staff eyes.
>
> Assuredly, I received impressions of the college and expressions of hopes for the college through various lenses—the board, the cabinet, County leadership, SUNY leadership, the business community, students and alumni—but it was the leaders of shared governance who gave authentic voice to what it was like on the ground, what was really valued day in and day out, and what was truly possible. I was fortunate to discover that not only did shared governance leadership give authentic assessments of what had been, but that they were honest dealers, wanting to put in the sweat equity of creating what could be.
>
> The President and Vice President of Shared Governance and I resolved to meet monthly to discuss freely whatever was on our minds, how we could assist one another, and alert each other to possible potholes in our joint quest for student success and professional fulfillment. These monthly meetings were added to the traditional slate of my role, serving as an ex-officio member at all shared governance Executive Committee meetings and having the monthly opportunity to address the full Assembly.

In addition, my role included being welcome to recommend to shared governance Committees problems and topics that would benefit from their contemplation and/or formal recommendations. While my interactions are almost exclusively with the leadership of Shared Governance, our conversations and agreements are propagated faithfully to shared governance committee chairs and other principals.

The shared governance President continues to occupy a seat at my monthly cabinet meetings. In addition, a report from shared governance remains as a standing item on the Board of Trustees' monthly agenda. Through these inherited and invented routines, I believe outstanding lines of communication with shared governance leadership were established early and have continued to prove their value. As a result, I believe an uncommon amount of trust developed rather rapidly between shared governance leadership and myself. I credit this relationship as a major contributor to how the college and I continue to successfully navigate the preservation of SUNY Orange values, while simultaneously challenging all of us to live those values in the reality of the current environment. (Young, personal communication, 2017)

Young's instincts and expertise no doubt contributed to her ability to understand and adapt to a strong shared governance culture at Orange County Community College as its new president.

Changing Student Cohorts

Another group involved in shared governance affected by even more regular turnover than college presidents is college students. Shared governance leaders must consider the predictable, cyclical shifts in the student body. The annual change of student populations means that initiatives begun with one cohort of students may just be getting established as a new cohort enters, seeking to make their voices heard. Shifts in the student body can reflect variations in the local economy; for instance, more adult students may seek access to higher education during a recession. Student bodies also mirror demographic trends with increasing numbers of community colleges being designated as Hispanic-serving (Excelencia in Education, 2019) or minority-serving institutions. Such changes can result in widely varying areas of focus for students involved in governance roles. Although the preference may be that differences from year to year on campus are more evolutionary than revolutionary, "effective and responsive governance . . . in the face of sweeping and transformative change can help shift the thinking of boards, faculty, and staff from protecting yesterday's parochial interests to aligning efforts to address tomorrow's realities" (AGB, 2014).

Thoughtfully recognizing this potentially volatile environment should inform how institutional leaders organize communication efforts to ensure a modicum of consistency amid constantly evolving student populations.

Shared governance leaders who take the time to acknowledge, hear, and react to various student cohorts honor students' perspectives and position themselves for mutual and respectful engagement in the collaborative decision-making process. In this atmosphere, prioritized initiatives can proceed with continuity as new initiatives are introduced. Longer-lasting guiding documents like jointly created strategic plans can be particularly useful for maintaining focus and momentum on key items for implementation as adjustments are made. All shared governance stakeholders ultimately need to be held responsible for genuinely engaging each new student cohort, understanding its unique qualities and needs, and honoring its interests and contributions despite such potential obstacles as student "inexperience, untested capacity, transitory status with actions that do not carry subsequent responsibility, and the inescapable fact that the other components of the institution are in a position of judgment over the students" (AAUP, 1990).

Mea Culpa!

"As the chief planning officer, the president has a special obligation to innovate and initiate" (AAUP, 1990), guiding development of new ideas, and implementing proposals. Of course, things do not always go as planned. The ability to apologize and adjust a plan or correct a miscommunication makes leaders and constituents strong practitioners of shared governance. As we make nuanced decisions with far-reaching impact, occasional missteps occur. Acknowledging and managing those missteps is far more important than the decisions that led to them. It takes courage to recognize when things are not working well, avoid defensiveness, and accept the need to regroup and reset.

In *The Seven Acts of Courage*, Staub (2002) highlights how "the courage to confront and be confronted" serve as processes that allow leaders to lead, grow, and act wholeheartedly. Avoiding blame during this process is important and enables movement from fault to constructive questions that drive forward actions, such as: What do we do when things go wrong? What are some strategies for improving broken or nonexistent structures? Although we may want surefire, failsafe systems, we need to be flexible and allow for safe-fail environments, as well. A *Harvard Business Review* article provides relevant insight for leaders who want to avoid unnecessary pitfalls describing a spectrum of failure activities, ranging from those that yield undesired results but expand knowledge to those based on ill intent or incompetence (Edmondson, 2011). Misunderstanding and conflict can occur when difficult decisions are being made and constituent groups lack access to all data and information being considered by the board and president—sometimes due to confidentiality or for legal reasons. Often, almost all data and information pertaining to a college is accessible under the Freedom of Information Act. As such, potential conflict may be minimized when appropriate transparency is maximized.

Conclusion

With no "one size fits all" model for shared governance, presidents should rely on flexibility, persistence, and a host of emotional intelligence skills (Goleman, 1995) to create an atmosphere of truly collaborative decision-making. At its core, shared governance embeds the attributes of respect and value for the people responsible for carrying out the institutional mission. This requires much of leaders. Dr. Martin Luther King Jr. (1967) said that "a genuine leader is not a searcher of consensus but a molder of consensus." Care and effort are undoubtedly key factors in achieving this end. Also needed is the ability and space to truly hear each other and be open to solutions that may be better than the sum of the contributing parts.

Quality shared governance allows us to confront and affirm our humanity through processes that include the exchange of divergent ideas, the quest for common ground, forgiveness when errant, and celebration of jointly achieved outcomes that advance our missions and sustain our institutions. A quote from inspirational American cartoonist Tom Wilson (n.d.) sums things up tidily: "Many of us are more capable than some of us, but none of us is as capable as all of us." We should thus feel both compelled and impelled to link our talents and intellect to achieve more for our students and institutions.

Acknowledgments

We gratefully acknowledge Nicola Blake, associate professor of English at Guttman Community College at the City University of New York and American Council of Education Fellow at Westchester Community College 2016–2017, for her invaluable contribution to this chapter.

References

American Association of University Professors. (1990). *Statement on government of colleges and universities*. Retrieved March 11, 2019, from https://www.aaup.org/report/statement-government-colleges-and-universities.

Association of Governing Boards of Universities and Colleges (AGB). (2014, April 4,). How to make shared governance work: Some best practices. *Trusteeship Magazine, 22*(2). Retrieved March 12, 2019, from https://agb.org/trusteeship-article/how-to-make-shared-governance-work-some-best-practices/.

Boyer, Richard K. (2018, July 15). Want to better engage your employees? Explain the business side. *Chronicle of Higher Education*. Special report. Retrieved March 12, 2019, from https://www.chronicle.com/article/Want-to-Better-Engage-Your/243893.

Cowen, Scott S. (2018, Aug. 13). Shared governance does not mean shared decision-making. *Chronicle of Higher Education*. Retrieved March 12, 2019, from https://www.chronicle.com/article/Shared-Governance-Does-Not/244257.

Edmondson, Amy C. (2011, April). Strategies for learning from failure. *Harvard Business Review*. Retrieved March 12, 2019, from https://hbr.org/2011/04/strategies-for-learning-from-failure.

Ellis, K. (2018, Oct. 19). SUNY Chancellor Kristina Johnson speaks to university-wide Faculty Senate. *BingUNews*. Retrieved March 11, 2019, from https://www.binghamton.edu/news/story/1385suny-chancellor-kristina-johnson-speaks-to-university-wide-faculty-senate.

Excelencia in Education. (2019). *Hispanic serving institutions (HSIs): 2017–2018*. Washington, DC: Excelencia in Education.

Goleman, D. (1995). *Emotional intelligence: Why it can matter more than IQ*. New York: Random House.

Jones, Tim. (2018, Oct. 18). Putting shared governance to work. *Inside Higher Education*. Retrieved March 11, 2019, from https://www.insidehighered.com/blogs/call-action-marketing-and-communications-higher-education/putting-shared-governance-work.

King, Martin Luther, Jr. (1967). The domestic impact of the war [Transcript of a speech delivered to the National Labor Leadership Assembly for Peace]. Retrieved from http://aavw.org/special_features/speeches_speech_king03.html.

Middle States Commission on Higher Education. (2015). *Standards for accreditation and requirements of affiliation*, 13th ed. Philadelphia, PA: MSCHEW. Retrieved March 12, 2019 from https://www.msche.org/standards/#standard_7.

Olson, G. A. (2009, July 23). Exactly what is "shared governance"? *Chronicle of Higher Education*. Retrieved October 24, 2017, from http://www.chronicle.com/article/Exactly-What-Is-Shared/47065.

Pierce, S. R. (2016, Feb. 16). Shared governance in crisis. *Inside Higher Ed*. Retrieved March 12, 2019, from https://www.insidehighered.com/views/2016/02/16/mount-st-marys-and-suffolk-shared-governance-gone-awry-essay.

President's Commission on Higher Education. (1947). *Higher education for American democracy: Volume 1: Establishing the goals* [Archived government publication from Hathi Trust Digital Library]. Retrieved March 11, 2019, from https://babel.hathitrust.org/cgi/pt?id=coo.31924013013606;view=1up;seq=7.

Rick, T. (2014, June 11). Organizational culture eats strategy for breakfast, lunch and dinner. *Ameliorate*. Retrieved March 13, 2019, from https://www.torbenrick.eu/blog/culture/organisational-culture-eats-strategy-for-breakfast-lunch-and-dinner/.

Seltzer, R. (2017, June 20). The slowly diversifying presidency. *Inside Higher Ed*. Retrieved March 12, 2019, from https://www.insidehighered.com/news/2017/06/20/college-presidents-diversifying-slowly-and-growing-older-study-finds.

State University of New York. (2017a). Shared governance. *State University of New York*. Retrieved March 12, 2019, from http://www.suny.edu/about/shared-governance/.

State University of New York (2017b). SUNY Shared Governance Award. *State University of New York*. Retrieved March 12, 2019, from https://system.suny.edu/media/suny/content-assets/documents/academic-affairs/shared-governance/2018-2020_SharedGovernanceAward-Policies-Procedures.pdf.

Staub, Robert E., II (2002). *The seven acts of courage: Bold leadership for a wholehearted life*. Stokesdale, NC: Dynamic Spiral Press.

Weisbuch, R. (2015, March 23). Shared governance or snared governance? *Chronicle of Higher Education*. Retrieved March 12, 2019, from http://www.chronicle.com/article/Shared-Governance-or-Snared/228705.

Wilson, Tom. (n.d.). Tom Wilson quotes. *Brainy Quote*. Retrieved March 12, 2019, from https://www.brainyquote.com/quotes/tom_wilson_388617.

Part II

Shared Governance in Times of Change

Necessary Components

4

Developing Rapport and Relationships with New Administrators

Margaret Ann Hoose and Barry Spriggs

Adhering to bylaws and learning to work together takes time and mutual trust. Concurrently, trusting in the process of "shared governance" during the transition period of new administrators and shared governance leaders, while building and establishing trust in each other, is critical for strong shared governance. This chapter documents the challenges faced by shared governance leaders and members while examining the effects of a variety of factors (new administrators, new shared governance leaders, and a relatively untested shared governance structure). The chapter views these challenges and emerging themes through the lenses of a campus administrator and shared governance leader. "The Seven Precepts of Shared Governance," written by Chancellor Bruce Johnstone (1991) in Academic Governance in the State University of New York, *serves as the grounding reference.*

Spring 2015: Reflections from Margaret

I am a newcomer to leadership in our shared governance body. I joined the faculty at Morrisville State College in 2006. We are a two-campus college with a separate Educational Opportunity Center (EOC) at a third "campus" in Syracuse. My academic appointment was on the Norwich campus. In spring 2014, I was unexpectedly thrown into a leadership role as the chair of the Norwich Campus Liaison Committee (which is responsible for discussing, studying, and recommending ways of improving interaction between the main campus and the Norwich campus and make the College Senate and the Student Government Organization aware of important issues at the Norwich campus). This is a standing committee of the College Senate. The colleague who had been the chair moved away, and I became chairperson. Almost a year later, late on a Friday afternoon, after a challenging meeting of the committee, I discussed my concerns regarding the relationship between the Norwich and Morrisville campuses with the president of the College Senate. He reminded me of our previous conversations regarding how to keep the Norwich campus within the decision-making loop, and he asked if I was still interested in pursuing the vice president position for the College Senate. At that moment, I felt the pressing need to have the Norwich campus voice heard, and I submitted my name to the Nomination Committee. I later learned that the call for nominations closed just five minutes after that fateful submission.

When I opened the email with my election ballot, I noticed that not only was I running unopposed as vice president but the president slot was vacant! Of course, I won the office of vice president. This was my initiation into the fine print of the College Senate bylaws; the individual serving in the role of vice president "assume[s the] President's duties in his absence." Indeed, the president was absent and the Nomination Committee was serious about the vice president fulfilling the duties of the president, and the bylaws further specify that "in the event of a vacancy in the office of President, the Vice President becomes the President" (College Senate By-Laws, Article III, Section 6B, 2016).

As I thought about the choice between resigning and accepting this new role (and thereby trying to keep the Norwich campus on the radar of faculty/staff and administration decision makers), I chose to accept the position. It was then that the real work began. I met with the outgoing College Senate president and learned the details of the position. I could sense that our College Senate (newly formed four years earlier) was his "baby," and he struggled with handing over a body he had been carefully nurturing for four years. Yet after those years in office, he was tired: he had taken on the responsibilities for creating bylaws, developing and supporting committee activities, developing the academic honesty policy, and the continuing appointment and promotion process. He had worked hard to create an open and honest relationship with the administration. I felt encouraged by his observations that our provost (who had just become our new president, Dr. David E. Rogers) had been open to shared governance.

Our college had just lived through four years of a period that included three interim presidents with one appointed through the "shared services" model and linking our college to the nearby SUNY Polytechnic Institute in Utica. Prior to our shared services years, the college conducted the second national search for the provost position. Before leaving, our outgoing president chose Rogers, who was the dean of the School of Business. As provost, Rogers served in multiple roles at the college and understood what the institution was going through in relation to share services. During the shared services years, we lost several key administrators and shared the replacement administrators with SUNY Poly. The overall feeling on our campuses was that we were the forgotten stepchildren in SUNY. When we were reassigned an interim president, the college again began to breathe and found a renewed sense of hope. However, the healing process took a long time, and the college community grew tired of the extended period of transition. As we meandered through these years, Rogers often had multiple responsibilities beyond the scope of provost to keep the college engaged and productive. As I reflected on this time, I realized that when a president is in place, the provost is confident of having their support and they can easily make decisions regarding the future directions of the college. Rogers was literally on his own for the four years that he served as provost.

As I listened to my predecessor, I could understand why he was tired and looking forward to a sabbatical. He was part of the glue holding the college together. He cautioned that the president would be a willing partner as long as I kept him well informed, especially regarding any public statements from me as the College Senate president. In my naiveté, that seemed easy enough; I just had to continue to be a person of integrity.

The end of the semester arrived, and I went on to what I hoped would be a summer of bliss. One final activity in preparation for the year ahead was attendance at the SUNY Voices Leadership Institute, at the suggestion of my predecessor and senator for the University Faculty Senate. This institute had been specifically designed to help prepare new SUNY governance leaders for their responsibilities. When I attended the institute, I remember feeling great trepidation and being calmed by what I was hearing. While listening to the presenters share their experiences, I felt less alone. There were others in the room who asked questions similar to mine, who were also new to their roles. I felt encouraged that I was learning to understand the position.

One speaker's admonitions stayed with me. I will always remember the description provided by the outgoing Faculty Council of Community Colleges president, Tina Good. Although I do not remember her exact words, I remember the gist of her talk: we are not members of administration, we are faculty members, and we are in a unique role. We have an insider's view of the college. We must treat our position with respect and consider how and when to share our knowledge.

After returning from SUNY Voices, I met with the president for my first shared governance/administration meeting. I was encouraged—things did not seem too hard yet! I also had a conversation with my predecessor regarding the conference. He concurred with my summary of Good's presentation. He agreed that I was going to learn about many pieces of the college that had been invisible to me as a faculty member. I was also going to witness firsthand many of the complex challenges to be addressed. Moreover, in words that I later realized were understatements, I would find that many decisions are not as straightforward as they seem. When leaving our conversation and starting my summer break, I was thankful that I did not have to think about these issues for a while.

My break abruptly ended on August 8, 2015, when I had my first official phone call from my predecessor, alerting me to a task I knew nothing about. I was visiting family and swimming. As I came out of the water to answer the phone, I heard him ask me if I realized that by 5 p.m. that day I needed to send out an all-college notice regarding a recommended change to the bylaws to ensure that the changes can be voted on at the first all-college meeting in August 22. That started my day-long introduction into wordsmithing an email, carefully describing the voting process regarding the changes in the continuing appointment and promotion process. As someone who was used to just reading announcements and thinking, "Oh, that's interesting," I was thrust into an altogether new role. With each version, I sent it off to my predecessor and waited for a positive reply only to realize that he was suggesting another change. He was truly a patient mentor as I tweaked each version. I was not prepared for the level of editing and attention to detail necessary for an all-college announcement. I quickly realized my summer break was over, and my life (as long as I was College Senate president) was going to be transformed. This started the roller coaster of two years in the office of College Senate president.

Spring 2016: Reflections from Barry

The key to genuine shared governance is constant communication. This requires various groups being kept in the loop with the emphasis on understanding what developments are occurring around particular topics. It is imperative that participants are not only invited into the group from the outset but are active and true contributors to the conversation.

Once we triangulate the many voices (while maintaining one vision), the institution prospers. Because this belief is a key to the environment in which I wanted to work, it was significant in the decision-making process of applying for the position of provost at Morrisville State College.

During my academic career, I had made a conscious effort to learn as much as possible about the field of higher education. As a doctoral student in sociology at South Dakota State University, I was fortunate to have a class titled "Profession of Sociology," which educated me in pedagogical issues, theories, and techniques for teaching and the application of sociology to organizations, occupations, and professions. The work of applied sociology was intriguing, particularly the idea of using sociological theory to produce positive change in society and specifically in organizations. The ideology of crafting positive change by applying theory into practice motivated me to learn as much as I could about any situation prior to making decisions. Making the best decision required collecting information, learning about the topic, and investigating multiple outcomes before coming to a conclusion. As I began my career in higher education, I looked for a job that would allow me to bring positive change to the institution.

I was fortunate to apply for and get a position (assistant professor, coordinator of Criminal Justice Programs) at Keystone College, a private comprehensive college in northeastern Pennsylvania, with the responsibility of developing and coordinating the first bachelor's degree program (criminal justice administration) at the college. This was an exciting opportunity that allowed me to teach and research the development of a program that would ideally respond to the needs of the community and commonwealth.

At a private institution, there was no formal shared governance body to rely on for feedback and guidance when developing the program. It was my sole responsibility to develop and forward the program proposal to the Department of Education for approval. Although there were groups on campus such as the Faculty Senate and Staff Assembly, they met for the purpose of distributing information from the administration to their particular constituents, and not for discussion and institutional decision making. After serving in that role for about four years, I accepted a position at the college as dean of students, which was a Cabinet-level position. Based on the institution moving from a junior college to a four-year college, the Middle States Commission of Higher Education suggested that we have a student affairs representative at the Cabinet level. The influx of different demographics in the residence halls from moving to a four-year institution brought about much conflict on campus in this time. Keystone was a rural, small, private institution, and resources and personnel were not prepared for the type of students and issues that were part of the diverse population now being served. I was selected to serve in the role of dean of students for an interim period while a national search was in progress. The main objective during this time was to reduce the number of behavioral incidents in the residence halls and develop engaging activities for a diverse student body in the hope that a sense of belonging and a safe learning environment could be developed. My background in juvenile justice and the development of residential programs helped me in this task. The results of the national search ended with me being appointed to the newly developed role of dean of students.

As a new Cabinet member, I had the opportunity to suggest and participate in discussions that eventually expanded the role of the Faculty Senate and Staff Assembly to have a voice on the president's Cabinet. Both groups were appointed a Cabinet liaison, which brought their issues and concerns for discussion at the Cabinet meetings. The liaisons (I served as Staff Assembly liaison) met monthly with their respective groups to provide updates about administrative decisions and to collect information or concerns to be discussed at the Cabinet meetings. Although this was not a formal shared governance process, it opened the lines of communication, which was a step in the right direction toward having multiple voices be part of decision making.

Throughout my career, I have had the opportunity to experience different degrees of shared governance, from the lack of it at my first institution to the last one before coming to Morrisville State College. During this time, I was part of an institution with an obvious adversarial relationship to another institution that worked well together. As I served as an associate professor at one school, I saw clear divisions between the administration, faculty, and staff. Monthly meetings were held with administrators, and these tended to focus on decisions that administration made without input from the campus community. On the other hand, as dean of academics at my most recent institution prior to going to Morrisville, we successfully negotiated two contracts. I met monthly with the presidents of the Faculty Association and Educational Support Professionals (groups representing faculty and staff members). These group presidents were also members of the president's Cabinet. This kept the lines of communication open and allowed issues to be addressed as soon as possible. The structure of the Cabinet allowed the interests and voices of all campus members to be represented and heard. The processes regarding decision making allowed time for each Cabinet member to meet with their constituents for feedback prior to a final decision that affected the campus community was made. Cabinet meetings were held twice a month, which provided members with an opportunity to obtain feedback from the campus groups they represented. During the following meeting, action would be taken on the particular topic and be part of the president's weekly newsletter to the campus community. I found this process to be open and transparent and allowed all voices to be heard on important matters that affected the campus. As I looked for my next career move, it was necessary for me to end up at a place that promoted shared governance and the idea that many voices should be heard before making major decisions.

It was evident from the initial phone interview that Morrisville was striving to display shared governance. The search committee was composed of faculty and staff but no administrators beyond the level of director, with the College Senate president serving as a co-chair. Because I viewed the role of provost as one of the more important positions on the campus, I was impressed that the college had put trust in the "glue" of the institution to screen and select their next provost. This was my first indication that my application for this job was the right choice for me.

At the heart of shared governance is the concept of sharing. At its core, the word *shared* offers everyone an opportunity to participate or take a role. In the case of the search for provost, the search committee evaluated applications, established a list of candidates, conducted phone interviews, contacted references, and selected a group of finalists to invite to campus. What I saw at the time, and what became clearer in retrospect, was that the search committee had an important role in the search process, but that did not include making the final hiring decision.

When I arrived on campus to begin the face-to-face interview, the centrality of shared governance's involvement continued. The day and half of interviews provided all constituents on campus an opportunity to participate in the search. Input was sought following three open forums (one each for faculty, staff, and students). Time was set aside for me to visit the Norwich campus and speak to constituents there and for them to provide input. Genuine shared governance gives voice (but not necessarily decision-making authority) to concerns across all constituencies, as well as to issues unique to specific groups. The method used in the on-campus interview process allowed specific groups to question me and allowed issues common to the institution in general to emerge via the open forums and in other smaller group meetings.

A major part of shared governance is trust in the role of the final decision maker, who is responsible for conducting background checks and formally negotiating with the front runner. This individual, normally the president, is ultimately held responsible for the success (or failure) of the appointment. The Morrisville president contacted me and made the official offer. He gave me time to consider the offer and get back to him with my decision. I reflected on my visit to the campus, as well as some of the questions posed by faculty and staff in the open forums. Questions arose that centered on course load, diversity, and inclusivity. Another set of questions related to what one person referred to as "the Ivory Tower," asking if I would be a leader who sat in the tower or if I would interact with the general population. I concluded that the faculty and staff wanted their voices to be heard. My style of management is based on being in the trenches, hearing and seeing issues prior to implementing policies, making decisions, and developing processes. I concluded that Morrisville State College would be a good fit for me, primarily because faculty and staff members wished to develop a dialogue, something with which I felt comfortable.

Summer 2016: Barry's Introduction to Morrisville

In my first 60 days as provost, I set out to be a walking administrator. This meant that I met staff and faculty in their offices, toured the facilities, and asked multiple questions as to why our processes are the way they are and why some seem to be missing. This was a deliberate effort to meet people in their areas and facilities and have the deans give me tours. Not only did I ask many questions, I sought extended answers. I wanted to fully understand the rationale for doing things a certain way or why we don't do other things in a consistent manner. Questions such as how can one student be academically dismissed from the college while their roommate with the same GPA, attempted credits, and earned credits is not. What is the process for granting release time and criteria? Why aren't committee representatives discussing issues during school meetings before decisions are made? I found a lot of inconsistency from school to school, each doing things their own way. Although there was an abundance of questions, I had to narrow my concerns to a few I believed the college could address in the upcoming year or two. Some of the major questions included assessment and enrollment concerns. Why don't we have institutional learning outcomes? Where are the online courses and programs? What is our process for granting prior learning credits? What is the role, charge, and brand of the Norwich campus? What is the process for addressing low-enrollment courses and programs?

As a result of these observations, I began to understand more about what the campus was going through, which essentially was a stabilization process after shared services and the feeling of uneasiness, trust, or being unsettled. I held an open faculty/staff meeting in August and proposed 14 topics that I wanted to explore further, particularly as they relate to processes.

The topics were

- academic review
- writing across the curriculum
- incorporating diversity into curriculum
- field trip process
- faculty load
- Norwich campus
- low enrollment process
- concurrent enrollment
- institutional learning outcomes
- enrollment management/retention
- online programs
- prior learning
- committee representation
- release time

During my first all-campus meeting, I presented these topics as conversations that we would be having over the next nine months. Some items I hoped could be resolved within a few months, and others I knew would take longer. It might take a year or two to gather information before making any new policy and procedure decisions. Although the president felt this was an aggressive agenda, I viewed it as the foundation and building blocks to assess shared governance and campus priorities. I needed to determine whether the campus only gave lip service to shared governance or whether the shared governance leaders had meaningful input into and involvement with the decision-making process.

Years One and Two: Reflections from Margaret

As the newly elected campus governance leader, I found myself at the head of a very young shared governance body. College Senate was less than four years old when I accepted the position of president.

I consulted the previous campus governance leaders, and each had words of wisdom. Their snippets of insight were helpful. One of the conversations was a suggestion to review the precepts written by former SUNY Chancellor Bruce Johnstone and consider what they mean. This helped me shape my thoughts and actions as College Senate president. Each time I consider the validity of a decision, I return to the precepts to ensure that I maintained a student-centered approach to issues. The issues discussed below are examples of how these precepts helped ground me in my decision-making and leadership processes.

1. Begin with a sense of purpose that is positive, not negative; that strives to make things happen, rather than to prevent them; that makes the institution a better and stronger place, rather than merely controls or watches over the administration. (Johnstone, 1991)

As I considered shared governance at Morrisville, I kept returning to the timeline: we had a college president, Dr. Rogers, who was new to the role, but not new to us after four years of uncertainty (during which he had been provost). After President Raymond Cross left in 2010, we had several interim presidents and leaders during the SUNY experiment of shared services and for a period of time we were linked administratively with SUNY Poly. The experience of losing key administrators to shared services eroded the morale of the college community. I felt that we had little trust for system administration and administrators in general. We needed to create a sense of purpose that was positive while trusting in the process, following the precept that we should have a positive sense of purpose. As I continued to return to this precept, I told myself that changes do not happen just because an issue is brought to the attention of the administration. College-wide changes take time. Our faculty and staff needed time to develop a sense of trust, move toward a positive sense of purpose, and work to make the institution a better and stronger place.

One of the early challenges was after my first one-on-one meeting with the president. He shared his frustration with the level of activity of the current Diversity Committee. He believed we needed to create a diversity task force, charged with delivering results related to specific tasks around addressing diversity, equity, and inclusion. After our first all-college meeting, faculty members approached me with several questions asking about the change from committee to task force, and wondering about when and how faculty input had been sought, since the chair of the task force had been announced. I reflected on the first precept and started negotiations with the president. I wanted to have a faculty member co-chair the task force and have the committee members elect this co-chair. The president and I agreed on half of my requests—he agreed to having a co-chair but reserved the right to interview and select that person. Faculty were asked to volunteer their services, and he reviewed the list of volunteers and chose the co-chair.

> 2. Be concerned for the institution as a whole, in its full breadth and depth, rather than for a single part, particularly a single part that you as a faculty representative may most narrowly represent. Be concerned for the institution in the long run, not just for the moment. (Johnstone, 1991)

Creating the Provost Search Committee is an example of one of the earliest times I found myself behaving differently by looking at the college as a whole. Discussions with our president and interim provost focused on leadership and committee makeup, with a desire to keep the committee somewhat small and manageable. However, this did not allow for voices from each area of the college within the provost's job description, nor did it allow for an open selection process. Once again, ultimately determining the size and composition of the committee required a give-and-take negotiation with the administration. We also ensured ongoing communication with the college community and in the end created an inclusive search committee.

> 3. Be comfortable with the principle and essence of collegial governance; a faculty role is advisory and therefore limited, yet it can be real and beneficial and powerful. Remember that it is the exchange of views and the lively interaction that conveys the most information and therefore which influences most greatly, not simply a final tally of votes on a particular resolution. Be confident of your influence and tolerate some ambiguity in the matter of final authority. (Johnstone, 1991)

Example of issues that fit this precept are the "common times" course schedule and the final exam schedule. Our college community had become comfortable scheduling classes and exams in a manner we thought was best for students. However, the new administration pointed out that this belief was not always accurate. They recommended that we establish common start times for classes and a more systematic exam schedule. Once again, the faculty questioned the process: "Where is the shared governance in this decision?" Discussions with the administration, both at the executive committee level and questions during College Senate, did not change the new schedule for classes and final exams. In spite of our input, the administration's decision on common start times stood. As hard as the changes were to adapt to, life at Morrisville State College is still productive and—we must admit—students can now schedule classes with a bit more ease.

4. Be generous and slow to anger. Know that men and women of lively intelligence will differ, perhaps profoundly, even in adherence to similar goals and standards. Do not allow personal agendas onto the governance table and keep the process of governing on the highest road. (Johnstone, 1991)

This precept was particularly challenging, as shown in the next example. Several months into the semester, our executive committee had followed our routine (meeting and discussing tentative agendas for the next few College Senate meetings). While chaperoning a trip to New York City, I received an urgent email from a faculty member. He was concerned about an upcoming space change in his building with which he disagreed. He had learned that the communications team was going to move into the loft of the Design Center. As the coordinator of the Architectural Studies Program, he did not agree with this change and had exhausted every avenue to communicate his concern. He was requesting that his concern be addressed through the College Senate.

As I consulted with the executive committee and agreed to adjust our agenda, I sent out the meeting notice. As had become routine, I also sent an email to the president requesting his presence at the next meeting. I worked hard to listen to the concerns of the administration and faculty and ensure that we had an opportunity to hear each other and be "solution focused." During the College Senate meeting, we learned of the president's rationale for the move: to create a high-functioning space for the communications team. He believed this space would ensure that the team had the resources and space they needed to develop competitive marketing and communications information. The faculty member shared the needs of the architectural studies students and the anticipated impact an active office in the loft of the Design Center might have on his program. As we discussed these conflicting goals, we learned that the building had an underutilized garden level (semi-basement). This space, then used for storage, could be made appropriate for the communications team, but some renovations would be required. Ultimately, the communications team moved to the second floor of another building until a final decision was made. During our follow-up executive committee meeting, we reflected on whether the College Senate had been the best venue for the discussion, and we determined that it was. It had been the only public forum left for the faculty member to address his concerns. Rather than yielding to the emotion involved and becoming confrontational, we were proud that we kept ourselves focused on problem solving. For members of the executive committee, the process and solution were a point of pride for shared governance.

5. Be courageous. Be willing to take difficult stands and to make tough discriminations. (Johnstone, 1991)

The person in the position of campus governance leader can address many challenges. I now have much more experience in this role, but these challenges demand that I recognize that a decision can be both right and unpopular. For example, I find myself facing the difficulty of realigning our common meeting hours of Tuesdays and Thursdays at 1 p.m. with the meeting times for the College Senate standing committees. We are returning to committees meeting the first and third Thursdays at 1 p.m. When I introduced the idea to several committees, it was met with mixed reactions. However, I continued to work with the administration and executive committee to create the schedule.

I am aware that the schedule will cause frustration. However, student representatives will be able to attend in a consistent manner, and the committee members will know in advance of each semester that the first and third Thursdays are reserved for standing committee work. In addition, the provost has agreed to work with the executive committee to assign key members of his team to serve in his place as we create a college of engaged faculty, professionals, and administrators. It might have been easier for me to allow for committees to schedule their own meetings, but I am confident that personal hardships can and should be set aside by the campus governance leader.

6. Work hard at the tasks of governance. These are part of your job. Take pride in the product of your work, whether in the form of written or oral augmentation. Demand the same or higher standards of integrity and of academic quality in governance that you would demand of colleagues in articles you might review for a juried publication, or the academic work of your students for which you are expected to give academic credit. (Johnstone, 1991)

This precept is one where I find mixed results as we move forward. Our college is currently still learning to adjust to a College Senate model after having a Faculty Congress model for many years. In addition, we are considering further expanding representation—from other members of the college community. Concurrently, we partner with the administration to examine the overall perceptions of shared governance.

The introduction of a new provost, chosen by the college community, created a different means of communication. As someone new to our college, Provost Spriggs pointed out that we were not broadly communicating the details of shared governance beyond committee members or College Senate members. For example, when important decisions were made, faculty and staff often lamented a lack of information regarding possible changes in the college prior to the announcement of a change. To address this concern, he created topical discussion groups and ad hoc committees focused on key issues. Since they were co-facilitated by administrators and faculty/staff, the discussion groups created a sense of engagement across the college community. These groups knew that their responsibility was not to resolve the issues. But participation in these groups facilitated the type of dialogue that had been lost over the years.

As Barry's first academic year came to a close, he and I knew we needed to find a way to keep the topics in the forefront of the minds of members of our college community. Once again, I accepted the responsibility for helping address this need. What kind of process could be developed to keep us working together toward a common goal that would address the issues in an inclusive manner with student-centered solutions? Thoughtful conversations with the provost and president have allowed for meaningful dialogue. The results of our discussions have included sharing solution-focused perspectives related to a wide variety of topics, including faculty/staff load and salaries, campus climate, and the communication processes within the college. I am proud of the conversations we have initiated and maintained.

7. Keep governance in perspective. Do not let it crowd out your teaching or your scholarship. Know when to let go. Be able to turn over the reins of governance when the time has come, not just to friends or to those necessarily like-minded, but to others, to new blood. (Johnstone, 1991)

As we continue to reenergize shared governance at Morrisville State College, I find myself strategically reaching out to faculty and staff to join committees. Of course, approaching someone I know to run for office or join a committee is easier, but that will not create the inclusive diverse community we know we need, if we wish to reenergize shared governance.

As I approach my second term and the third year of my role, I realize how far I have come in understanding the challenges and roles of shared governance. I now understand various ways to work on shared goals. I have become better able to engage with the college community in a way that provides a renewed energy. I am hopeful that we are supporting new leaders who will be ready to assume the leadership roles as I and the other members of the executive committee finish our terms. We will work together and all learn to turn over (or take) the reins as our terms end (or begin).

Year One: Reflections from Barry

As the academic year began, I put out a call for volunteers for each conversation I anticipated starting, to measure level of interest. Based on the lack of participation on a few of the College Senate committees, I was not expecting an abundance of people finding the time to join. I was surprised when volunteers for each conversation ranged from a high of 35 people to a low of 11: more people than I expected expressed a desire to be part of a conversation. The next step was to ensure that there was faculty and staff involvement in a leadership role. This was accomplished by requesting (from among those who had expressed interest) volunteers to serve as co-chair, along with an administrator. There were multiple members who volunteered for more than one ad hoc committee, and we had no problem finding multiple people to serve as co-chair. When we had two or more faculty and staff wanting to serve as co-chair, we allowed all to serve. At times, we had multiple leaders in the groups.

Over the course of the fall 2016 semester, I held Friday sessions for an hour to begin conversations and take pulse and direction as to the campus concerns (or lack thereof). I provided my notes to the co-chairs on each ad hoc committee to offer some guidance. I hoped these would be used to set forth agendas for the conversations. We continued focusing on the topics during the opening meeting in January, when we used part of a professional development day to give the co-chairs the opportunities to run their first conversations. These conversations began at the start of the spring 2017 semester and culminated with transitions to College Senate standing committees, task forces/committees (e.g., Diversity, Equity, and Inclusion Committee; Salary and Workload Task Force), and administrative committees.

The next step was to collect information gathered over the course of the year. Depending on the topic, a request was for the co-chairs to submit reports to my office on March 1 or May 1. Upon receiving the reports, I met with College Senate President Margaret Hoose to assign topics for the upcoming year based to either a College Senate standing committee (depending on the College Senate committee's charge) or (if no College Senate committee was appropriate) develop an ad hoc administrative committee with representation from the College Senate. At the closing faculty meeting in May, we presented to the campus our joint reflections on the work accomplished and the next steps for the year ahead. The theme of shared governance continues to be supported at Morrisville State College. We regularly participate in retreats and meet at least twice a month to take the pulse of the institution. The retreat participants include members of the administration (President's Council), College Senate officers, and the chairperson of each College Senate standing committee.

College Senate President Hoose recently introduced me to the Seven Precepts for Campus Presidents (Administrators), which is a useful organizing paradigm for providing a brief synopsis of my reflections of my first year (Johnstone, 1991).

1. Respect your elected faculty senate and seek to involve and strengthen it. View it positively, as a partner and indispensable helper, rather than as a natural adversary or as a body whose enhanced strength or effectiveness need to diminish yours. (Johnstone, 1991)

I have always examined organizational structures based on functional equality—not to be confused with functional organizational structure. Simply put, we must examine issues and consider planning versus implementation. Is one more important than the other, is the engineer more functionally important to a factory than the frontline worker that makes use of the concept and design?

I would suggest administration uses (and needs) shared governance to implement plans, just as the engineer uses the frontline worker to implement the design. Although I had set forth a plan to have 14 conversations over the course of the academic year, it was up to the faculty and staff to carry out my plan.

> 2. Be comfortable with the principle and essence of collegial governance; a faculty role that is advisory and therefore limited, yet that can be real and beneficial and powerful. Do not let honest differences of viewpoint between you and your faculty governance body become tests of will or strength or credibility, either of you or your faculty governing body. Be willing to give and to "lose" at times; be willing, at other times, to hear the faculty and, in the end, to disagree and exercise your necessary authority. Be assured that faculty governance bodies understand that overwhelmingly advisory role and know that presidential decisions from time to time will be made that will not please them. But recognize the faculty's legitimate and strongly felt sense of entitlement to be included in the deliberations that affect the mission and academic character of the campus. (Johnstone, 1991)

As I examine this precept, several situations come to mind that related to it over the course of the academic year. I do not try to "battle wills," but instead ask for the consequences and benefits of the decision-making process. In addition, I seek to find out how a decision under consideration might be best for the total institution. For example, I thought it was a good idea to use the final professional development day to have the College Senate committees to report on what had been accomplished during the year and set forth their agenda for the upcoming year. This idea was met with resistance from the faculty, because traditionally the Professional Development Committee set forth the agenda for the day. My suggestion was initially perceived as being a usurpation of the day by administration.

After an hour of conversation with the executive committee, we concluded that we would compromise. We agreed to have the committees meet a half hour prior to the start of the agenda planned by the Professional Development Committee. During that hour, it was evident to me that the collaborative work accomplished over the course of the year could have been jeopardized if I was not willing to take the "loss" and had insisted on pushing my own agenda.

3. Be generous and slow to anger. Know that men and women of lively intelligence will differ, perhaps profoundly, even in adherence to similar goals and standards. Do not allow personal agendas onto the governance table and keep the process of governing on the highest road. (Johnstone, 1991)

There were lessons to learn in the heart of this precept. College Senate meetings are limited to 50 minutes, so it is crucial that the time be used wisely. All must commit to continued progression of action. I feel we are all in the belief that the administration and the College Senate could use more time to discuss important issues. The way we handle this is to collect as much information (e.g., have as many conversations as possible) to try to resolve issues prior to bringing them to the meeting.

On one occasion, a faculty member (after speaking to numerous people on campus, including me) put an item on the agenda specifically relating to his program and administration's decision to occupy space in the building where his classes were held. Although there seemed to be some difference of opinion as to the appropriateness of this topic for the agenda, the executive committee decided to err on the side of transparency and put it on the agenda for discussion. As I sat at the meeting, observing the nonverbal sentiments of the rest of the group, I got the impression that many members of the Senate thought the issue could have been resolved in a different venue. Although there may not have been another venue in place for the faculty member to voice his concerns publicly, I was aware of another reason to not object to the discussion of the topic in the Senate: this had the potential to set forth an adversarial relationship between the Senate and administration. Fortunately, this was not the case, in that information emerged that allowed unused space in the building to be capitalized on. The precept of being slow to anger was pertinent, and it functioned for both senators and administrators.

4. While democratic principles are laudable, and while students, professional staff, and others can contribute much to the formulation of policies and have voices that need to be listened to, the historic tradition of University governance accords a special role to the teaching faculty. (Johnstone, 1991)

This precept outlines how many institutions have been able to progress through difficult times. While we believe that in the philosophy of "many voices, but one vision," we recognize that some voices are more influential than others. Our College Senate encompasses both faculty and professional staff; our all-faculty/staff meeting includes both faculty and staff; yet in both these settings, much of the discussion is directed toward the academic needs of the campus. During the interview process, it was evident that the questions posed from faculty members were intended to assess each candidate's ability to promote shared governance. As noted earlier, all 14 conversations over the course of my first year emerged out of the academic arena and concerns faculty had posed during both my interview and throughout my first semester of getting to know the faculty and staff.

5. Have high expectations of your faculty governing bodies and convey this to them. Recognize that faculty governance, for a variety of reasons, may not be strong at a particular campus at a particular time, and that an uninspiring quality of faculty leadership or a poor quality of reports and official faculty actions may reflect a widespread lack of faculty interest in the concept of shared governance or in their own governance body—which may, in turn, reflect the faculty's perception of your or your administrative colleagues' lack of interest in, or esteem for, their advice and counsel. Do not gratuitously ignore shoddy or mean-spirited actions if you should observe them in your faculty senate, but demand better—and know that the best way to strengthen weak faculty governance may be to take it more seriously. (Johnstone, 1991)

During my first year, I spent time observing; I found great interest from the faculty governing bodies in participating in making the campus stronger, yet they were hesitant and struggled to trust the process. Just as administrators have to develop stamina to get through obstacles and not allow them to fade away as more pressing issues take our attention, so do members of the faculty governing bodies. I wanted to build trust in the governing bodies that I was a person of action and would work to keep their interests in mind as we were strengthening the campus together.

To maintain our momentum and build on what we started in my first year, we committed to continuing the work to discuss the key issues brought to my attention. We worked on the ad hoc committee recommendations and identified focal points for the upcoming year. We wanted to secure the understanding, in the minds of all, that there was still work to be done and we would continue to work through identified concerns. We took a whole-campus approach to engage the college community in the change process through shared governance and administrative conversations.

In addition, we emphasized the benefits of holding committee representatives accountable for communicating back to their schools. In that way, information from discussions and obtaining feedback will provide a loop through the faculty/staff and back to the committees. This will aid in promoting the expectations we have for our faculty and staff.

> 6. Faculty governance and collective bargaining can co-exist and flourish, even with overlapping membership, but the differences must be carefully respected. The union must be the sole representative of the faculty in matters that properly belong on the bargaining table. By the same token, the faculty, through its governance bodies, both can, and has an academic responsibility to, engage in deliberations and the provision of advice on a wide range of policy matters, both academic and financial. (Johnstone, 1991)

For faculty governance coexisting with collective bargaining, a deliberate attempt from all is required. The brief experience that I had over the past year leads me to believe that the college does a satisfactory job maintaining the boundaries between governance and union. Although representatives from governance and the union serve on college committees, I have yet to see conflicts. I have shared identical concerns with both representatives from faculty governance and collective bargaining (salary and load issues). At times when the issue presented was not the responsibility of a certain body, I have been redirected to resolve the concern.

However, I have also had the experience of sharing a concern with both groups. In some cases, I have seen success with both, when issues are central to all. For example, one of the conversations in the past year was around faculty load/release time. After multiple conversations, we have expanded this issue to encompass faculty and staff salaries. This task force now includes representation from shared governance, administration, and union leaders.

> 7. Insist on a respect for the principles of collegial governance from all of your management team. (Johnstone, 1991)

When I first arrived on campus, I often heard "we already tried that," or "faculty will have a problem with that." I took it upon myself to break down the adversarial walls and deliberately serve as a role model for collegiality within my provost council. As an applied sociologist always searching for positive change in societies and organizations, I wanted to take an approach with the campus community that would show change can occur and be positive for the college. By using a decision-making process I had learned decades ago (and continue to use as a framework to ground myself), collegial governance comes naturally. By addressing and deciding on important issues facing the college, the PISCO plan (deBono, 1971) has been a very effective tool. As an applied sociologist that is always searching for positive change it has

PISCO is a lateral thinking process that follows the steps outlined below. During all meetings, I always ask the group to begin by identifying the Purpose or Problem under consideration. Next, I suggest we obtain as much Input as possible. We consider how to reach out to the whole campus community—those directly and indirectly involved in our decisions. To be comprehensive, and obtain the most crucial input, it is imperative that we query people and groups with access to as broad a base of relevant information as possible.

We then come up with multiple Solutions, understanding that there will always be options. We will try to generate multiple ways to reach our goal. From among the solutions, we will need to make a Choice. We do our best to ensure that we carefully consider the input we previously gathered. The final step is the Operationalization of the choice. This is where the first precept comes back into play. Once again, we realize the functional importance of collegiality and the need for Senate to implement our decisions. Although my team has been at the college longer than I have, this technique has helped us all. We are slowly understanding that for us to be functional, we need to maintain reciprocal respect and a collegial approach to shared governance.

Conclusion: From the Perspectives of Margaret and Barry

As this chapter was being written in 2017, during a critical time in our nation's history, it is important to have administrators and faculty/staff join together to navigate the dangerous shoals imperiling the future of higher education. This can best be done using the paradigm of shared governance. We must stand together. Even though we may see things through multiple lenses and have multiple voices, we must have one vision.

As a campus governance leader, I (Margaret) learned the value of listening to hear the undercurrent of an issue and how to stay solution-focused. I also have found that building a collaborative relationship from trust takes time and respect. Trust that the individuals involved will rise to the occasion and consider solutions that are student-centered and benefit the institution in comparison with individuals protecting the status quo. Respect that we will hold each other's accountable and remain focused on the issues and not the personalities involved.

As the provost and throughout my career as a campus administrator and leader, I (Barry) have realized that understanding the campus culture and the people within the campus is very important for me to make progress and move my vision forward. Just as it is necessary to understand the biographies of one's students for teaching and learning to occur, it is necessary to understand the biographies of the campus and people who are part of it to build a stronger campus. I have found it effective to not only know individuals based on their title as to what they are doing but to know who they are in relation to what role we have them performing. Understanding who we have on campus allows us to capitalize on the total person and not just the structured responsibilities and task on a job description. I have found that by engaging in technical dialogue and having open office hours, I have been able to find faculty and staff to spearhead some of my ideas and objectives. My agenda and desires—such as a consistent academic review process, viewing the School of Liberal Arts beyond just being a service to others on campus, and professionalizing and legitimizing educational support services to become a comprehensive program of student development—have been some goals that have been moving forward with the aid of faculty and staff outside of their designated responsibilities.

References

deBono, E. (1971). *Lateral thinking for management: A handbook*. New York: McGraw-Hill.

Johnstone, D. B. (1991). Academic governance in the State University of New York: Precepts for campus presidents and faculty. In *SUNY University Faculty Senate Governance Handbook* (2013 edition) (Appendix 5). Albany, NY: SUNY.

5

The Rights, Wrongs, and Challenges of Governance Communications

Joe Marren

This chapter offers theoretical and applied considerations on general communication with examples and specific references to governance. Because communication is crucial, it's necessary to start with theory about the why of what we do before venturing down the road that leads to how we do it.

Ludwig Wittgenstein theorized that language contextualizes experiences: "The limits of my language are the limits of my world," he wrote in a bon mot that has been cited in many essays. When we communicate the results, debates, and goings-on (the "stuff") of college senate plenaries and committee meetings, we quite naturally use words. But effective communication is more than words, it's also gestures, sighs, expressions, camera angles, screen captures, and much more. We use all of that (sometimes more, sometimes less) to tell what we know to people we think should also know it or want to know it.

This is reflected in Noam Chomsky's theories on transformative generative grammar that can be found in many textbooks. In a nutshell, what he says is that we all have the need and the ability to communicate (deep structure). This deep and fundamental communicative urge is transformed into the surface structures of grammar that helps an audience comprehend things in a two-way model of communication between a producer (e.g., you) and the receiver (e.g., me).

But there's something else. If communication is just a list of notes, rules, offerings, and so on, then it is efferent communication (think of an index or maybe a syllabus). However, we are human and want to communicate with a bit of personality, or maybe we want to advocate for a specific idea using a plethora of adjectives and active verbs. When we do that, it's aesthetic communication. Humans seem to favor aesthetic communication, and that bolsters Chomsky's theory that because we have the ability and need to communicate, the communicator's job is to use all the nuances of language to help an audience of readers, viewers, scrollers, clickers, or scanners acquire meaning.

Chomsky theorized that we can produce an infinite number of ideas behind words. If we couldn't, we would eventually reach the end of language because we would have run out of signs and symbols for words and expressions. But we are constantly thinking of new things to say, and thus we need to make and understand an infinite number of sentences. Deep structure gives us the desire to communicate; we then generate surface structures such as grammar into coherent messages.

Such creativity leapt through the millennia from cave drawings to hieroglyphics to an alphabet to a printing press to iPads and their online ilk. If people are intimidated by the quirkiness of web writing that has gone from desktops to laptops to tablets and phones in less than a generation, then take a moment to think about Ralph Waldo Emerson when he said there was a need for an original American literature free of European models. Just as he challenged the new American writer to be original, we must think of new ways to capture the essence of our efforts to communicate our ideas to audiences near and far, enthusiastic and apathetic. And if Emerson is not an adoptable reference to build such a model, then turn to poetry. The last line from the Robert Frost poem "Riders" goes like this: "We have ideas yet that we haven't tried."

Implications

Such theories are nice to talk about as we sit around the communication campfire on a wintry night, but the pertinent issue for us is specifically how communication works for those in governance—whether we are at a specific campus or part of a system-wide group at the SUNY level? Part of the answer is obvious (as Chomsky noted): at its core communication between groups makes our jobs easier in all aspects of shared governance. The proof can be found in several chapters in the first volume of the SUNY Press series *Shared Governance in Higher Education: Demands, Transitions, Transformations*, edited by Sharon Cramer.

As several authors in that volume note, open and sincere communication is a deep structure that must be part of effective shared governance (i.e., we have to want to talk to each other). Specifically, Kelley Donaghy, who was the campus governance leader in 2006 at the SUNY College of Environmental Science and Forestry (ESF), wrote: "Major decisions were made by a select group of faculty (not elected, but assigned by department chairs). These decisions were rarely communicated to the community as a whole for input. . . . In most cases, policies just emerged, and the rest of us had to learn to live with them" (Donaghy, 2017, p. 198). Communication was needed at ESF, and governance failed when communication was missing because faculty did not know when meetings were held and did not have an incentive to participate.

Unfortunately, the breakdown in communication divided the campus into administration and faculty sides, with little outreach from either side to the other until Donaghy facilitated a needed change. To really work, shared governance needs a leader who recognizes the need for and makes use of strong communication. As she explained: "The ideal of shared governance that I envisioned was fully based on superior communication. . . . I felt that to be successful I had to start at the top, which meant communicating effectively with the key administrators" (Donaghy, 2017, p. 206). Donaghy had to communicate the drafts of policies and new procedures for reviewing the policies, to a large and sometimes divided audience. The job didn't end with a transformation of internal procedures. She often had the responsibility for communicating SUNY's system-wide decisions and policies (some of them unpopular on local campuses or unfunded for many others). This meant that she had to implement a shared governance culture that depended on communication. As she noted, "The stronger the communication between all members of a campus, the more easily the campus will adapt to change when it comes" (Cramer, 2017, p. 217).

ESF's struggles with bridging the communication gap was not unique. In the same volume, a chapter about CUNY's Medgar Evers College in 2009–13, written by Sallie Cuffee, Owen Brown, and Evelyn Maggio analyzed a similar stalemate but focused on curriculum changes. The lack of a cohesive shared governance culture—and the consequential lack of communication among groups—led to an unfortunate divisiveness. As they contrasted their experiences with those of others, they observed that similar situations arose across campuses: "The battle for control of colleges' and universities' curricula has been the basis of many struggles played out within the context of shared governance" (Cuffee et al., 2017, p. 232).

The authors recognized that although a commitment to effective and open communication may not always work, insufficient communication usually leads to the collapse of shared governance and a consequential lack of focus and cohesion between groups. In such cases, not only does the academic mission fail, the students suffer.

In a more optimistic conclusion to the volume, Norm Goodman provides hope and a solution: get more people involved in the entire process. How? Through long-term and effective communication with stakeholders: "Governance bodies need to identify and then recruit these individuals. Outreach to them should be individualized and emphasize the fact that their involvement in these communities will not only be useful to a well-functioning campus, but to meeting their own goals as well" (Goodman, 2017, p. 246).

The preceding snippets point out that there is a group of faculty and staff who seem to serve on countless committees and task forces known to academia. It's not that those folks necessarily want to be there (although some probably do), it's just that no one else has stepped up. So people leave governance up to others. But all of us have to care, we have to get involved, and we have to speak truth to power. We need to communicate the issues and the reasons why things don't have to be the way they are.

Function

Some French philosophers would have us believe that even though we are born free, we are in the chains of old ways of thinking. Let me use journalism as an example because when we report back to our constituents on our home campuses or to our departments from a local Campus Senate or committee meeting, we essentially function as journalists. The trouble is, we tend to use the prevailing news models of the 19th and 20th centuries rather than the many tools at our disposal in the 21st century. (See the thoughts of Emerson mentioned in the introduction.)

News reporting is not just a traditional one-way street from producer to receiver, today it is more of a conversation between many groups across many platforms in an increasingly nonlinear manner. Current communication strategies and practices—indeed, education itself—is being framed as a disruption to traditional models because of a reliance on social media platforms. To paraphrase Immanuel Kant, we should awaken from our dogmatic slumbers and ask ourselves three things in connection with communication: what should we (and others outside our governance bodies) know? What can we/they do? What might we/they hope?

What should we know? Simply put, all governance bodies from the University Faculty Senate to local senates and every group in between should think about changing how they communicate within and outside the group. As was seen in the previous examples, the more information that is provided, the better the functioning—and sharing—of governance occurs. We must intellectually grasp that the time for kicking the tires of change has passed; it's time to buy the car.

What can we do? Let's talk about more online or innovative delivery. We need to quickly and accurately communicate news and official viewpoints to our immediate constituents, stakeholders across SUNY, and (sometimes) the outside world of legislators, SUNY policy-makers, journalists, public opinion shapers, and the public at large. The old ways still work, but they're somewhat clunky in the new social media world. We must be innovative and not think of technological innovation as a disruption.

What might we hope? When it comes to communicating the ideas and goals of shared governance (as was seen in the examples), not everyone is as outwardly focused as they could be, nor do they communicate as well as they should. Technology gives us new ways of delivering an effective message, and it also can help us create a constituent-focused message. If we effectively get our message out to the target audience, we are likely to see a rise in constituent knowledge about issues and in people willing to participate once they know what our governing bodies are and what they do.

In a speech several years ago before a journalism group, Eric Newton of the Knight Foundation proposed the three questions above and suggested that media companies must adapt to meet changing deliveries and audience expectations/sophistication. That's easily transferable to SUNY because we—at the system level and with local College Senates—can take his message to heart as we strive to tell people in the community and the outside world why and how we do what we do. Creating open lines of dialog shows that we are transparent and consistent in an increasingly divided and complex world.

To be successful, we need to step back and look at our communication options. The most familiar way to approach this self-examination would be to analyze:

1. what we as senators (or other campus representatives) do now, and

2. what we can do better when communicating with our committees or home campuses.

Frankly, the best way to do this analysis is via social media. That means members must talk to one another about issues both trivial and important and with a fair amount of consistency. The advantage to social media is immediacy, but the disadvantage is that we as a governance body can't edit unauthorized posts or tweets before they go from brain to finger to keyboard to live. Each governance body would have to determine who will send out official posts and tweets and when. But also keep in mind the advantage: We can use technology to constantly and immediately clarify context and/or redefine a conversation. For example, a Twitter account could be used to post messages about various presentations at Campus Senate meetings or University Faculty Senate plenaries, and then the SUNY intranet could be used to follow up, post more details, and drive traffic to any site that offers analysis.

As to external communication, what we want is to get our viewpoint out to the public, whether that is the narrowly defined Campus Senate community or the legislators and voters. The specific message and issue du jour would dictate the approach and audience. For example, crafting a digital press release with social media links for stakeholders outside the campuses would be different than an internal message because an external message must include more context. Likewise, an external message should not be politically naive and unintentionally cause a stir. Don't misunderstand: Sometimes causing a ruckus is good if it gets people talking and thinking, but whatever hierarchical mechanism is set up to send external messages should be sensitive to the real politics of the administrations.

So what do we put on press releases? Our viewpoint combined with our strategy. A reporter who would get these releases should be able to get three news stories out of any announcement: the preview (here's what is going to happen), the event (it's happening), and a post-event analytical piece. Our issues would likely concern budgets and academic initiatives, and the trick is to write them in a way that would not lead to conflict that would hinder initiatives.

Form

Let's consider a hypothetical situation. We're in a quandary about how to get colleagues to read our missives. That indicates that it's important for us to think of different ways to get news out to internal and external audiences.

First, some context is required. Many people have heard of the five W's and the H—who, what, when, where, why, and how—that many journalists live by. In truth, most news stories are *what* stories, and so are most of the emails, tweets, and other communication on governance events we send to colleagues (the "here's what happened" approach). We want people to read all the information, so concentrating on sending out the "what" in nuggets will prepare constituents for the news from plenaries and other events. For example:

- **Advance:** An administrator (e.g., the chancellor, provost, or president) is happy or mad or even indifferent about something. (This is a *who* story that can be turned into a *what* advance story by highlighting the issues facing the faculty senate that will come up during the plenary.)
- **The event:** A report on the outcomes of a meeting or event (e.g., responses from the administrator to the members of the governance body, as well as resolutions, committee reports, etc.); this is a *what* story.
- **Follow-up:** Here are *how* things were resolved; or this is *what* will be worked on. This is essentially an analysis piece that would call for thoughts from the main players.

Here are five suggestions for writing press releases, social media posts, and any communication going out to a website that an audience will potentially read.

1. **Know your audience.** The people who read our tweets, posts, press releases, and online reports are in a hurry as they prep for class or glance through things between appointments and committee meetings. Help them out. Although we want to write long, they want to read short.

Jakob Nielsen, a Web usability researcher and engineer, has done multiple studies finding that web readers don't read, they scan (Nielsen, 1997a, 1997b, n.d.). More to the point, they scan when they're in a hurry to glean the pertinent info. That means we only have a few seconds to get and hold their attention. So think about:

- Informative headlines and subheads
- Bold type on proper nouns or important points
- Bulleted lists

- Short paragraphs (single idea per paragraph)
- Pictures or graphics. But take to heart the broadcast maxim: "See cow, don't say cow." If you include a picture of a building, explain the context and significance and do not simply say "Here's a building at home campus." Instead, say something like: "The Communication Building at home campus has been getting attention across the state as administrators praise the proposed new communication plan produced by the folks who work there. Administrators say it can be a model for other state systems to follow."
- Layers—such as links to complementary stories, maps, video, audio, or columns of data—can use elements to explain why the story matters (as a print story would), allow people to hear or see human drama (broadcast stories), and engage readers interactively (online stories).

A few more words about pictures or graphics: some sort of graphic element should be a part of our communicative efforts whenever possible. The challenge is to make sure the graphic complements the story and adds visual meaning in a clear and dynamic way. Rather than settling for a picture of a dignitary shoveling some dirt at a groundbreaking ceremony at home campus, we need to stop and think what the image represents. For example, what departments will be in the building? How will students benefit? What role will the building play in campus culture? When will it open? Where will the professors park? Instead of a groundbreaking picture, perhaps a picture of a full science lab would be better, or an image of a car windshield with lots of tickets.

When using graphics, make sure they do not reproduce verbatim what is in the accompanying story and is easily understandable.

2. **Make news packages tight and bright.** How? Think about these tips:
    - Tell readers the ending right away. ("SUNY will increase reimbursement to campuses.")
    - Use subject-verb-object sentences. ("The campus presidents cheered the news.")
    - Use active voice and action verbs to express connotation and denotation. ("We'll spend the money wisely on fac-

ulty lines.")Avoid overusing adjectives and adverbs, but use them when necessary to add depth. ("~~Beleaguered~~ Professors cheered the ~~wonderful~~ news.")

3. **Explain why what you wrote is important.** For example, why is SUNY being generous with increased reimbursements to campuses? Use deep links (statements from administrators, SUNY press releases, graphics and charts supplied by the fiscal experts, audio, video, etc.) to amplify without writing more words.

4. **Banish gray.** Long gray or black blocks of type are deadly. Think: can the info be better presented in a graph, chart, or table? Can the sentences and paragraphs be shorter? Does it have to be written in an academic style? Can it be cooler? Punchier? People want their info *now*. Web writing should be scannable and splittable.

    - **Scannability:** Highlight key words or phrases to make a point. Briefly repeat such info from time to time in new ways.
    - **Splittability:** Break some information off into links.

Break up long paragraphs because long paragraphs are generally a sure way to get people to stop reading. The goal is to keep eyes moving and minds interested and not have people skip over prose. News people generally strive to write online paragraphs of two or three sentences. We would be wise to follow that example.

One-sentence or one-word paragraphs can help pace the text and capture attention.

Really, it works!

A shift in mood or topic can also help create these one-sentence or one-word paragraphs.

Kapow!

See what I mean?

5. **Link, link, link!** Because the headline will likely be the first line of a link, make sure it is straightforward and succinct. Let people know what they're getting.

    - Use key words that refer to things people will remember.
    - Write it in a conversational tone.

Link deep within a site instead of just to top pages. No one wants to go to the top page of a link and then click through to find the promised information.

If there is a mention of a specific physical location, consider a link to a map to show people where those places are.

Consider using internal links for navigational ease.

A word of caution: technology means change, and sometimes people may think that how we communicate is more important than what we are saying. As social media extends our thoughts to a wider world, it affects perceptions of us and our messages. We should be aware of the effects of the messages we send out. So tweet as if your mother is reading.

References

Cuffee, S. M., Brown, O., and Maggio, E. (2017). A self-critique of shared governance at Medgar Evers College; the recent protest years, 2009–2013. In S. Cramer (Ed.), *Shared governance in higher education: Demands, transitions, transformations*. Albany: State University of New York Press.

Donaghy, K. J. (2017). Governance leadership: A journey. In S. Cramer (Ed.), *Shared governance in higher education: Demands, transitions, transformations*. Albany: State University of New York Press.

Goodman, N. (2017). Conclusion: Working together to share governance. In S. Cramer (Ed.), *Shared governance in higher education: Demands, transitions, transformations*. Albany: State University of New York Press.

Nielsen, J. (1997a). How users read on the web. *Useit.com*. Retrieved October 1, 1997, from http://www.useit.com/alertbox/9710a.html.

Nielsen, J. (1997b). Why web users scan instead of read. *Useit.com*. Retrieved October 1, 1997, from http://www.useit.com/alertbox/whyscanning.html.

Nielsen, J. (n.d.). Writing for the web. *Useit.com*. Retrieved in March 2004 from http://www.useit.com/papers/webwriting.

Part III

Avoiding Governance Quicksand

Pragmatic Considerations

6

The Campus Concept Committee
A Case Study in Shared Governance

Lisa M. Glidden and Deborah F. Stanley

Effective planning demands that the broadest possible exchange of information and opinion should be the rule for communication among the components of a college or university
—AAUP (1966, section 2.c)

This chapter examines SUNY Oswego's integrative planning committee, the Campus Concept Committee, through the lens of shared governance. The committee is built on principles of responsibility and contribution, and it strengthens our understanding of shared governance and its outcomes, although it is embedded in a traditional formal structure where final decision-making authority rests in administrative officers. We analyze the successes and challenges this model of shared governance has for integrative planning that weds academics and facilities. We argue that shared governance works best when it is understood as an ongoing relationship charged with advancing institutional initiatives and working through defined challenges.

This chapter offers an in-depth examination of academic process by exploring a microcosm, the Campus Concept Committee (a key committee at SUNY Oswego, the home campus of the authors) through the lens of shared governance. As will become clear and perhaps familiar to readers, the committee's existence illustrates how members of a campus (while striving to meet the ideal of shared governance) experience the successes and challenges of shared governance. The authors analyze their experiences, arguing that shared governance works best when it is understood as part of an ongoing relationship and its members are charged with advancing institutional initiatives and working through defined challenges. The committee is built on principles of responsibility and contribution; its existence strengthens our understanding of shared governance and its outcomes, even though it is embedded in a traditional formal structure with final decision-making authority resting in administrative officers.

SUNY Oswego's Campus Concept Committee, with representation from faculty, staff, students, and administration, is charged by the Faculty Assembly and the president with overseeing the development of renovations and new construction on campus.[1] The committee provides leadership and coordination for long-range physical space and facilities. It works to acquire an institutional perspective. To that end, many constituencies on campus are represented, and committee members are asked to adopt an institutional perspective instead of only representing their constituency.

The committee engages appropriate constituencies through extensive consultation and recommends priorities for action to the president. The committee is co-chaired by the Faculty Assembly chair and the associate vice president of facilities. The membership includes eight representatives from Academic Affairs, eight presidential designees, and four student association designees. In 2017 we added a voting seat for the director of Campus Technology Services. Votes are weighed equally, and the majority rules, although we work hard to build consensus on decisions. Over the years, we have found that the model can and should be codified within the institution, but to be effective, all members be proactive and engaged. Its continued commitment to communication and consultation contributes directly to its success and ultimately leads to the success of separate stakeholder groups and the institution as a whole.

The next section provides a brief review of shared governance, followed by background on the Campus Concept Committee. The following section shifts to pragmatic considerations. We identify how the committee provides opportunities to strengthen shared governance, as well as challenges that arise even with a continued commitment to shared governance. We conclude with some lessons learned from our experiences.

Principles of Shared Governance

Shared governance is a term that is often invoked but not always clearly defined; across institutions and among scholars, there is not consensus regarding its definition.[2] In 1966 the American Association of University Professors (AAUP) published the often cited statement on governance that refers to interdependence of components of the university (AAUP, 1996, section 1). The question of definition is explored in greater detail elsewhere in earlier volumes in this series (Cramer, 2017a, 2017b). For the purposes of this essay, we are concerned with shared governance as it relates to long-term planning and communication, because of the impact planning (physical resources and budgeting) and communication have on the interdependent components of the university.

A major challenge of shared governance is crafting an understanding of that interdependence and the responsibilities that are associated with each of its roles. "Shared governance is . . . complex; it is a delicate balance between faculty and staff participation in planning and decision-making processes, on the one hand, and administrative accountability on the other" (Olsen, 2009). As evidenced in our case study, configuring that balance was a crucial part of successful long-term planning.

History of the Campus Concept Committee

The Campus Concept Committee was created in 1998 to manage the first multiyear capital plan approved for SUNY by the state legislature since the 1960s-era SUNY build-out. The growth in the 1960s was stimulated by the Baby Boomer generation. As those first Boomers neared high school graduation, the idea of going to college became increasingly rooted in US culture for men and increasingly women. Nationally, there were not enough institutions or institutional space to handle the emerging demand for a liberal arts education. One strategy to solve that dilemma stood out: fast-tracking additional capacity in terms of academic programs and physical facilities. "Normal" schools, that is, teacher training colleges, could fairly quickly and economically be enlarged physically and programmatically.

At SUNY Oswego, "old campus" consisted of the original quad of Oswego Normal School, approximately 517,500 square feet of space of academic and residential buildings dating from 1913 through the 1950s. In the 1960s and 1970s, after acquiring additional land, Oswego built "new campus," adding almost 2.4 million square feet of assignable space in several new buildings, residence halls, the athletic center, an administration building, and a new student union around an adjacent new quad. That infusion of funds ended, and state allocations of capital funds were unseen for almost 30 years. Funding from private sources was also severely limited. Public colleges in New York were discouraged from private fundraising by law and regulation because it was perceived as direct competition with independent institutions for private dollars.

Before 1998, the campus had no comprehensive plan to guide physical space and condition. The college would request capital funds connected to identified projects but without any multiyear conceptual plan. These projects were based on requests that originated from discrete groups from the campus, which had either assessed deterioration or identified a need or wish. Most requests were denied, put on a statewide list, funded incrementally, or underfunded. The result of such deferment was that new requests supervened prior requests. When long-term capital funding became available, it was welcomed, even though it introduced more significant competition and required the development and commitment to a system-approved long-term plan.

Creating the capital plan was indeed a challenge. After almost 30 years without funding for improvements or repairs other than emergencies, deferred maintenance and stymied dreams were everywhere. We had many potential projects for capital improvement, and a related need to raise morale by improving the physical plant. We faced a learning curve on computer cabling and acquiring and locating appropriate technology. Determining the order by which to allocate resources was crucial for creating a comprehensive plan. We realized that in addition to the logic of these decisions, there were also political challenges because decisions would prioritize existing needs. SUNY Oswego was similar to most other comprehensive institutions in that it was (and still is, to some extent) made up of fairly siloed groups. Each was intimately informed about its own needs and wishes but had little understanding or knowledge of others in the college. Each had real needs, which we acknowledged could lead to polarization within the process if they were not handled well.

When the long-term capital funding was announced, the campus was physically uninviting and falling behind in new technology. SUNY Oswego, like public colleges in many Northeastern states, was suffering from years of cuts to operations budgets. These cuts led to personnel reductions, closing of "campus schools" (public K–12 schools on college campuses, which were convenient sites for student–teacher placement), and shelving ideas for new programs. The campus had often tried to buffer faculty and staff from layoffs by reducing other expenditures. In a particularly uninspired moment, an administration in the mid-1980s had pulled individual phones out of faculty offices and stopped mowing much of the grass (on a 700-acre campus). When those actions were reversed in the 1990s, there were cuts that led to retrenchments of programs deemed "nonessential" and faculty/staff experienced reduction in force, a rarely used process for releasing tenured faculty or professional staff members with permanent appointment. To add to budget worries, a more conservative wave of SUNY trustees was inserting political views into curriculum and research. For example, around that time the SUNY Board of Trustees mandated a prescribed General Education Program.[3]

In 1997, after these stressful times for the campus, a new president was appointed (Deborah F. Stanley). By 1998, things were looking up. Enrollment increased overall and in the top part of the student profile because of new presidential scholarships for high-performing applicants and the Oswego Guarantee to contain student costs.[4] We created some new revenue streams in fundraising and external contracts. These resources helped us seed some high-profile program development like an MBA program, which required a state-approved master plan amendment. To meet accreditation standards, the School of Business facilities needed upgrading structurally and technologically. Even so, these items of good news were not enough to shake off a malaise that was due to prior stagnant state funding and difficult personnel reductions.

The new capital plan, however, provided several potential opportunities. Most important, it would allow us to take advantage of technological advances that promised to greatly enhance teaching, research, and collaboration. What was once out of reach was seemingly possible if the plan we established could translate to the real world. There was a great deal riding on formulating a long-term capital plan. The Baby Boomers had graduated, and designing new enrollment plans to recruit students was a challenge. New programs and teaching paradigms had the potential to turn enrollment around if we could provide the space and technology to support an attractive campus along with a compelling mix of programs.

Thinking about the campus outside of silos, in global and connected ways, could help us to define projects and determine priorities. If we could move beyond politics, our shared goal would not be a campus of new and improved buildings but a forward-looking, revamped institution with extraordinary learning environments everywhere. We would all commit to valuing physical spaces that centered on learning and fostered deep learning, whether or not our own buildings, programs, or initiatives were top priority. The Campus Concept Committee was created to achieve that goal. This is an example of an integrated planning model that brought representatives from various constituencies to the table, whose institutional home bridges the administration and Faculty Assembly.

With the exciting legislation of an appropriation for SUNY capital expenditures based on a five-year plan, SUNY Oswego's capital budget went from almost nothing to a possibility of millions of dollars a year for five years (somewhat over $20 million a year). We needed a plan that not only projected expenditures in that range but also was logistically possible. The main condition for receiving the next year's allocation was that we had to move the projects forward on the schedule according to that prescribed by the SUNY Construction Fund. Picking the right projects—those that could be accomplished while advancing the educational quality and reputation of SUNY Oswego—were daunting tasks. The specter of designing a plan that could accomplish those goals but have it met with cynicism or fractured goodwill among "winners" and "losers" on campus was a looming risk. The process for designing the plan had to be one that encouraged campus-wide pride and ownership, even if certain faculty and staff members moved into magnificent new spaces while others "waited" in unrenovated buildings with older technology. It was crucial that all believed their turn would come.

Senior leadership was experienced enough to know that merely informing the campus community about strategy and decision making—the communicate, communicate, communicate idea of shared governance and collaboration—had severe limitations. Usually those types of communications were one-offs (e.g., speaking to faculty groups separately, writing to staff, holding a meeting with other stakeholders). We realized that this approach offered no collaboration, idea gathering, or shared responsibility. To create a shared endeavor, we needed to enfranchise and build a community of experts, involving varied stakeholders on campus. The intention was to include faculty, formal governance, union representatives, students, staff, and administrators. The leadership would be shared between finance administration and academic leadership. We asked for a multiyear commitment in exchange for investing in their knowledge and understanding about capital projects.

The Campus Concept Committee's goal was to integrate silos and build consensus. Its structure reflects this goal. Half its members, representing different constituencies, are elected through the Faculty Assembly, and half are appointed by the president. It is co-chaired by the sitting chair of the Faculty Assembly and the current associate vice president of Facilities Services (see Appendix A for the original members of the committee). Initially, the committee worked from a vision of moving Oswego from a program-centered campus to a learner-centered campus. That vision was the guide for the capital improvements. Physically, the campus was structured with academic programs at the core and student housing, clubs, and dining halls at the periphery. The goal was to be a campus where, in the words of David Hill, an early committee member, students could "bump into knowledge" throughout the campus.

In an era of accelerating disinvestment in higher education, many writers on the topic of quality and value of higher education were developing theories and practices that integrated new knowledge about how students cognitively embed information on a conceptual level, in a lasting way beyond memorization. The strategies they touted were analytical and compelling: deep learning and synthesis of information are more likely to occur when a person is relaxed and open, can apply theory in hands-on experiences in real-world situations, had exposure to interdisciplinarity, and is in supportive nurturing environments that allow conversations with peers and faculty to be easily received (see, for example, Barr & Tagg, 1995; Kuh, 1996). Many of these ideas had seeped into our two recent strategic plans: Engagement in Learning (1996) and Engagement 2000. The change was gradual but constant. Although most higher education was measured in credit hours and seat time (the old teaching paradigm), we began trying to assess what students were learning; we tried to determine if learning could be enhanced by learner-centered environments. By opening breakfast in August 2000, President Stanley acknowledged that the culture of the institution was intentionally changing and the Campus Concept Committee had a vital role in shaping the transformation (see Appendix B for Stanley's remarks).

Prioritizing schools and units to benefit from resources was a formidable political challenge. Given the varied needs and wants across campus, and the necessity of prioritizing projects for the new capital plan, some disappointed constituencies across campus were inevitable. Shared governance was the way to get to unification on campus. In the next section we discuss several of the successes and identify a few challenges addressed via shared governance.

Successes

The committee very quickly took on a life of its own. Its shape and purpose became (and remains) much more active and involved than was initially conceived. The group did a great deal by way of ideas, research, inclusion of the greater campus, and communication and work with architects, vendors, and SUNY. As time went on, committee members increased their hands-on experience and expertise with such topics as construction, safety, equipment, and even landscaping. They dealt with financial realities and space requirements and limitations. As a result of their increasingly sophisticated understanding of relevant issues, capital projects could be staged and concurrent efforts (handling the current endeavor while looking ahead and preparing for the next) became routine.

Without the full complement of the Campus Concept Committee's broad membership, this would not have been possible. Senior administration alone could not have infused projects with the history, understandings, identity, culture, and aspirations of SUNY Oswego. Clearly, the committee's work was of great value, creating an environment of mutual trust and goodwill that positively affected the political climate on campus. In addition, the quality of their work was exceptional, elevating the outcomes of each new or renovated structure. The new academic paradigm was integrated holistically across campus, while ensuring that the particular needs and nuances of separate scholarly disciplines were respected.

Because of the committee's work, funds from the 1998 capital plan were successfully expended in terms of the quality of physical projects, the contribution they made to a new academic atmosphere, and, especially important, demonstrating to the SUNY Construction Fund that the Oswego campus had capacity to apply all the funds on time and on plan. The physical plant of the School of Business was renovated, contributing to accreditation by the Association to Advance Collegiate Schools of Business. The Campus Center, now called Marano Campus Center, was created by renovating two existing buildings and building a superstructure with new elements (an ice rink, lecture halls, classrooms, and spaces for student organizations). Marano Campus Center now perfectly reflects the ideals of having a learner-centered campus. Student organizations, as well as the student-run newspaper and radio and TV stations, are located in the center of the building. The facility also houses some of the humanities departments and interdisciplinary programs, with spaces designed for students to bump into knowledge. Figures 6.1 and 6.2 show the before

Figures 6.1 and 6.2. Before and after renovations of a hallway in Poucher Hall. Illustration by Aslı Kinsizer.

and after photos of a hallway in Poucher Hall, now the home of Modern Languages and Literature in the Poucher wing of Marano Campus Center. The seating area in Figure 6.2 is bordered by faculty offices and language labs.

The whole process of implementing the plan successfully increased trust while decreasing cynicism by engaging members of the campus community. The committee took part in substantive consultation while developing a long-range plan. It held focus groups and polled many campus constituencies. Asking for input invited people to move past cynicism. The committee's structure was not designed to have members represent certain constituencies and "deliver" individual wish lists. Instead, it was intentionally created with broad representation, designed so that the in-depth knowledge of (and intimate experience with) SUNY Oswego could be contributed to all discussions. The background of committee members and their willingness to relinquish their departmental identities in favor of committee membership meant that they approached complex dilemmas in new ways. Thus, they offered rich and informed contributions, which became the basis for consensus and decisions. The structure was specifically designed to enable all to hear each other and accept shared responsibility. As an unexpected benefit, the committee's work style helped create the framework for greater communication and trust across departments and divisions.

The committee endured after the first capital plan because it was institutionalized in the shared governance organization. New members were elected after initial terms were up, and the committee remained active, creating long-term plans even when capital funding was not available. The result was that if the Construction Fund unexpectedly had funds, Oswego was ready with a project to pursue.

Challenges

The Campus Concept Committee had an ambitious charge. To address the primary task of crafting a long-range plan, members had to familiarize themselves with many unfamiliar and intricate topics. In this section, we identify a few challenges in terms of shared governance and meeting the charge of the committee. We also cover some continuing challenges as the committee finishes its second decade.

As identified earlier, one of the challenges of shared governance is the question of accountability—taking responsibility for decision making. In the early days of the committee, members had a steep learning curve about the multiple facets—financial, structural, institutional—of major building projects. As they built up their knowledge and capacity for decision making, the process for moving those decisions out of the committee was not well developed. The committee would come to a decision, but there was no institutional process or final authority in place to sign off on their decision before it moved on to the president. The SUNY Construction Fund required a sign-off by the president for moving all decisions (e.g., processes of bidding and procurements) forward—at the outset and as projects progressed. As a result, the campus was missing deadlines.

To address this, we created a small group with authority to make decisions. The small group included all the vice presidents, the assistant vice president for Facilities, and the president to review the input and choices submitted by the committee and make final decisions. In this way, we balanced the interdependence of the Construction Fund's requirement with the multiple constituents making decisions on the Campus Concept Committee. We ensured that responsibility and accountability for final decisions was met via the small group.

A second challenge we faced was balancing the need to build up expertise and recognition of the amount of faculty service required by committee membership. The Campus Concept Committee was created as an ad hoc committee through the Faculty Assembly. In its early days, faculty members elected to serve on the committee were accepting a position with an undefined term. On one hand, it made sense for faculty or professional staff to serve for multiple years because of the learning curve of being on the committee. On the other hand, the committee was a workhorse. Being a member required a high time commitment during and between its frequent meetings. Two issues of concern arose. First, while faculty service is a component of promotion and retention, it tends to be the least valued component (compared with teaching and research); its value varies greatly from department to department. For faculty members, there was a high opportunity cost of serving on the committee in terms of having less time for research and writing. Second, the committee ran the risk of becoming exclusive and limiting voices at the table. We dealt with this challenge by defining membership and instituting staggered three-year terms for the faculty and professional staff representatives. Student terms for the four student seats are for a single year with an option for reappointment; we have found that reappointed students have the knowledge base to participate more fully in the committee.

A third challenge was maintaining the committee's overarching goal of focusing on long-range planning. During the building phase of the first capital plan (1998–2003), the committee lost this focus of long-term planning and got very involved in the nitty gritty of the current projects. After that, the committee returned to long-term planning. Several years later, when capital funding for a new science complex was received, pragmatic concerns once again took priority. The committee focused on the current building project, instead of maintaining the longer-term perspective. Although the initial long-range plan identified several primary and secondary projects, those plans needed to be reviewed as time passed to determine whether they still met the needs and vision of the campus concept. To address this challenge, the Campus Concept Committee created a new organizational structure: subcommittees deal with the current projects and may include people who are specific to the project under way, while the whole committee continues to maintain a longer-range vision. The benefit of a subcommittee model is that it brings those affected and interested into the governance process, which brings us closer to the ideal of inclusivity. The subcommittee structure also allows the larger committee to stay at the concept level and not get mired in the construction details.

A fourth challenge concerns morale and long-range planning fatigue. The committee is developing plans without regard to available capital funds. Some plans remain shelved for a long time. We may revisit and update a plan without any assurance of it ever coming to fruition.

Happily, the success SUNY Oswego has had in planning, managing, and celebrating funded projects has built a wellspring of confidence in the decision makers within the SUNY Construction Fund, and the new funding is already earmarked to come Oswego's way. In fact, the fund had previously referred to the Campus Concept Committee as a best practice. It is important to educate the campus community about how long-range planning works, as well as how state-funded capital funding works. Having "plans on the shelf" means we are ready. Often state funders ask if any state entities have anything on the shelf so they can be assured of efficient use of funds in real time and in political time. Getting the money spent so there is something to show the public is important, and our proven track record has led to investments in our campus that we might not have received otherwise.

The final difficulty is woven into many of the challenges already discussed—finding and using effective communication strategies. Olson

(2009) notes, "the key to genuine shared governance is broad and unending communication. When various groups of people are kept in the loop and understand what developments are occurring within the university, and when they are invited to participate as true partners, the institution prospers." That is easier said than done. The Campus Concept Committee regularly reports during Faculty Assembly meetings, and presumably the members of the Faculty Assembly report back to their departments, but a lot of information is reported by various councils at each meeting. The committee has a website that is updated regularly, but do people visit it to get information? We continue to work on communication strategies. The campus is currently undergoing a restructuring, including a reconsideration of its marketing and communications strategies, under a new chief communications officer. The website now includes new aspects designed to keep the campus up to date on many issues (e.g., Title IX reporting, safety concerns, and health matters). These new web functions may prove effective for the Campus Concept Committee as well.

Conclusion

As SUNY Oswego had the opportunity to reenvision and transform its campus, we created an integrative planning committee, the Campus Concept Committee, that had an institutional perspective, built on the ideals of shared governance. Half the members are elected through the Faculty Assembly. The other half are appointed by the president. This committee had broad consultation with the campus community. The structure allows for it to hear others and to have shared responsibility. It was tasked with considering strategic, programmatic, facilities, and financial opportunities and solutions. Institutionally, it bridges Academic Affairs, Student Affairs, and the administration. The committee successfully managed two rounds of five-year capital funding and is gearing up for a third. Along the way, it faced several challenges and is striving to identify and use communication strategies to overcome the limitations of previous approaches.

Shared governance works best when it is understood as an ongoing relationship. That relationship can and should be codified in institutions. To be most effective, it is important not to get complacent or believe that the institutional structure alone will suffice. Successful shared governance requires broad constituent input and continued individual commitment to engage, communicate, and consult in an iterative way, across and among all sectors of the campus community. Ultimately, shared governance is undertaking and sharing the responsibility for campus sustainability and success.

Notes

1. The Faculty Assembly is Oswego's shared governance body. Each academic department and the library have one or two representatives, determined by full-time equivalent employees. Representatives of administration (four), professional staff (three), and the student association (four) are also voting members.
2. For more on principles of shared governance, see chapter 1 in this volume. See also chapter 13 in this volume.
3. See K. O'Brien's discussion of the SUNY Board of Trustees' involvement in general education, chapter 9 in this volume.
4. The Oswego Guarantee, promises each student (1) to offer the necessary classes for students to graduate in four consecutive years of study (if courses are not available, the college will enroll the student in them tuition free); (2) continue to offer small classes; and (3) not increase room and meal plans for four consecutive years. More information is available at https://www.oswego.edu/admissions/oswego-guarantee.

References

American Association of University Professors. (1966). *Statement on government of colleges and universities*. Retrieved from https://www.aaup.org/report/statement-government-colleges-and-universities.

Barr, R. B., & Tagg, J. (1995, Nov./Dec.). Teaching and learning—a new paradigm for undergraduate education. *Change: The Magazine of Higher Learning, 27*, (6), 12–25.

Cramer, S. F., Ed. (2017a). *Shared governance in higher education, vol. 1: Demands, transitions and transformations*. Albany: SUNY Press.

Cramer, S. F., Ed. (2017b). *Shared governance in higher education, vol. 2: New paradigms, evolving perspectives*. Albany: SUNY Press.

Kuh, G. D. (1996). Guiding principles for creating seamless learning environments for undergraduates. *Journal of College Student Development, 37*(2), 135–48.

Olson, G. A. (2009, July 23). Exactly what is "shared governance"? *Chronicle of Higher Education*. Retrieved from http://www.chronicle.com/article/Exactly-What-Is-Shared/47065.

Stanley, D. F. (2000). Remarks by the President at the Opening Breakfast [transcript].

Appendix A
Initial Members of the Campus Concept Committee

Name	Constituency	Term
Sue Camp	At large	1998–2001
June Dong	School of Business	2000–2003
Donald Feck	School of Education	2000–2003
Craig Graci	At large	1999–2002
Kristen Gublo	Professional staff	1999–2002
Chris Hebblethwaite	At large	1999–2002
David Hill	At large	1999–2002
Al Lackey	At large	2000–2003
David Sargent	Arts and Sciences	2000–2003
Michael Flaherty	Auxiliary Services	open ended term
Joe Grant	Vice president	open ended term
Carolyn Rush	President's representative	open ended term
Jim Scharfenberger	Dean of Students	open ended term
Sarah Varhus	Provost representative	open ended term
Casey Walpole	CSEA	open ended term
Jerry DeSantis	AVP Facilities, co-chair	open ended term
David King	Faculty Assembly chair, co-chair	open ended term

Appendix B
Deborah F. Stanley's *Remarks by the President at the Opening Breakfast* (2000)

Since 1996, when *Engagement in Learning* began to shape our thinking, we have embraced a culture of learning, encouraging the concept in many of our formal and informal processes. An explicit emphasis on fostering environments conducive to learning has permeated all of the capital projects being coordinated through the Campus Concept Committee. Clearly, goals for learning are driving discussions and integrating with principles of physical design in all our activities in that area. I hope you will have the time to look at the floor plans for the new School of Business at the front of the room. If you read the mission statements guiding the program and design studies for Swetman/Poucher study and the New Campus Center study, I believe you will feel confident that Concept Committee members have done great honor to the trust placed in them on behalf of current and future generations of learners. On a different life span projection is the project on advanced technology classrooms. Meticulously researched and planned as demonstration models for three distinct classroom applications, we have three beautifully appointed classrooms—Lanigan 107, Mahar 215, and Mahar 220, at a cost of about $500,000 ready to go today! Faculty and students will be using and also testing the benefits of the new rooms. This is an important model of an effective feedback loop-consultation leading to action and action leading to consultation, helping to insure a continuum of sustained excellence. You might be interested to know that the total spent on capital projects last year was over $8,600,000. (Stanley, 2000, 6)

7

Reflections on the Process for Developing a Rubric for Assessing Shared Governance

Deborah L. Moeckel

This chapter provides a reflective narrative about the process followed by a subcommittee of the SUNY Council on Assessment (SCoA) in the effort to develop a rubric for assessing shared governance. It describes the rationale for the various steps taken, the source documents used, and the challenges experienced by the working committee. The final section discusses the current status of the project.

What does good shared governance look like? Is it like that trope about pornography that there's no good definition but you "know it when you see it?" Are there essential elements that should appear in specific proportions? How would these elements be affected by things like state regulations and accreditation standards? Can you assess and improve shared governance, or are you stuck with (paraphrasing Longfellow) "when it's good it's very, very good, but when it's bad it's horrid"?

This essay describes an attempt to flesh out the essential elements of good shared governance and create a framework for developing a rubric that could serve as a guide for assessing shared governance at an institution. (Spoiler alert: we do not yet have one.)

Background

I am a member of the SUNY Council on Assessment (SCoA). This group is advisory to the SUNY provost and was formed when SUNY revised its assessment policy in 2010. Initially, the policy was fairly regulatory in nature, in that it required a lot from SUNY institutions, including three components: (1) specific types of assessment at defined points in multiyear cycles, (2) reports that had to be submitted to the system office periodically, and (3) assessment processes that had to be approved by system administration.

SUNY institutions chafed at these expectations, and their representatives successfully made the argument that the processes in the policy were duplicative and unnecessary because institutions were already required to meet the accreditation assessment standards of the Middle States Commission on Higher Education. A task force was convened to streamline the SUNY assessment requirements, resulting in a revised policy that essentially outlined the critical elements of assessment from the SUNY perspective. This revision was completed in 2010. When boiled down to basics, it required (with a few additional stipulations) that SUNY institutions meet or exceed Middle States assessment standards, thus effectively eliminating duplication of effort.

SCoA was a direct outgrowth of the revised policies, designed to provide support to SUNY institutions regarding assessment. Its mandate was to underscore the shift in the role of SUNY system administration, a transition from a policing role to a facilitative one. The primary roles the group has played have been in the development of tools and processes for promoting and supporting effective assessment. To this end, there have been essentially three aspects of SCoA's efforts: (a) annual regional workshops on current assessment topics, (b) two noncredit online certificate programs in the assessment of institutional effectiveness and the assessment of student learning, and (c) the development of rubrics for assessment of institutional effectiveness and degree programs. The council meets twice a year in January and June, and subcommittees do the heavy lifting for various projects in between meetings. The committee has no official budget, and members are supported by their home campuses for any travel costs related to committee work. Time commitment of the council/committee members, as well as the members of the various subcommittees, is voluntary and uncompensated—all the more impressive because the work associated with SCoA is considerable. There are no set terms for membership, and most likely, members remain on the committee because they value assessment and believe they are contributing to efforts that strengthen own institutions and others within the system.

My responsibilities as an assistant provost at SUNY system administration include (among other things) serving as staff liaison to SCoA, coordinating accreditation support for SUNY institutions, and serving as the SUNY liaison on Middle States accreditation team visits to our campuses. In this capacity, I have gained a bird's-eye view of accreditation findings at SUNY institutions. This perspective and the empirical evidence of trends in campus efforts and accreditation status have been invaluable in providing timely and relevant assessment-related information to SUNY campuses. During one of these accreditation visits, it became clear that the shared governance structure of the institution was at the heart of the resulting noncompliance findings. The institution needed a way to assess the current structure's effectiveness, which would provide guidance in making needed improvements as well as empirical evidence about what was or was not working. A rubric would serve the need quite well, but none existed. Solution: SCoA.

The Process so Far

I broached the idea of developing a rubric for assessing shared governance at the January 2017 SCoA meeting, and a subcommittee was formed. Two faculty members from the university-wide governance groups, Jeff Steele (representing the Faculty Council of Community Colleges [FCCC] a member of the FCCC governance committee), and a faculty member at Herkimer Community College, and Janet Nepkie (representing the University Faculty Senate [UFS] and a faculty member at SUNY Oneonta) agreed to serve. It is important to note that the governance committee of FCCC under the leadership of chairperson Diane Bliss (faculty member at Orange Community Colleges), was also in the process of developing a definitive picture of the characteristics of good shared governance. We wanted to make sure that SCoA was not duplicating the efforts of the FCCC and that the groups would work together rather than compete. Steele's participation in our group helped resolve this issue. In addition, we recruited Bill Anderson (then CFO at Dutchess Community College and well versed in accreditation), Karen Ferrer-Muniz (Instructional Student Support Services and Retention at Hudson Valley Community College, representing student interests), Kim Scalzo (director of Open SUNY at system administration and rubric guru). As of this writing, we haven't yet recruited a student member.

The impetus behind our subcommittee and its membership was the easy part. Now what? How should we approach this monumental and politically sensitive task?

The decision to create a rubric had been made, but we had concerns about how this project would be viewed and how the rubric would be used. One concern was that the project not be perceived as pushing an agenda, or a particular model of shared governance, and that the rubric be used as we intended—as a tool for collaborative self-assessment and continuous improvement. We therefore made a commitment to an inclusive process, gathering feedback on our drafts with as many constituency groups as possible. To this end, we developed a framing statement to introduce the rubric. This statement would be used when discussing the rubric project with constituency groups to ensure that the purpose was clearly understood. It follows here in its entirety:

> The potential benefit of developing a tool for assessing shared governance has become increasingly evident given the comprehensive emphasis on effective assessment for all aspects of SUNY institutions, and the reflection of this requirement throughout the new Middle States accreditation standards. In the spirit of self-reflection and continuous improvement, the SUNY Council on Assessment (SCoA) is in the process of developing a rubric which could be used by campuses for this purpose. The rubric will incorporate common aspects of the Middle States standards, the AAUP shared governance principles, and New York State regulations addressing shared governance. The rubric will also be widely vetted for input from as many constituencies as possible. Since this rubric is being designed as an institutional self-assessment tool, it is not intended for use as a means of mandated evaluation, but rather as a way of assisting campuses in identifying elements of their shared governance processes which seem strong, and those elements which may need improvement. This rubric is not being designed to promote any particular model of shared governance. It is being designed in the spirit of effective assessment, for use by institutions for their own self-improvement.

I had done a bit of background work prior to the January 2017 SCoA meeting, when the topic was first raised. Ever since the issue of assessing shared governance had emerged, I had known that SCoA needed to address the accreditation standards. The question had also come up during the accreditation visit as to whether the shared governance structure in question was consistent with New York State regulations regarding respective roles of each constituency group. Also relevant was the matter of good practice in shared governance as described by the American Association of

University Professors (AAUP). I collected these documents and separated the information by the constituency roles in each. I color-coded them so we could keep them straight. These source documents formed the basis of our approach to content (see Appendix A).

With regard to format, SCoA had already developed a well-regarded rubric for institutional effectiveness (see Appendix B) that had been based on Middle States standards and empirical evidence taken from accreditation team reports. This rubric had been previously presented at a Middle States conference and was very well received. The team members felt that this rubric's format could provide appropriate structure for conceptualizing the work.

The final shared governance rubric would be divided into three sections addressing participation, decision making, and communication. Jeff Steele assured us that these sections were consistent with the general categories being discussed by the FCCC group. We added columns for the elements under consideration, such as conflict of interest and responsibilities, and added another column to address the constituency group affected by the elements under consideration. Finally, goal statements were needed to define specific results. Each statement would be evaluated in levels of accomplishment: Level 0, Not Evident; Level 1, Emerging; Level 2, Proficient; and Level 3, Excelling.

At this point, we had an idea of the general content needed, a plan for the format, and an understanding of the vetting process. We divided the work by constituency group. Kim Scalzo took presidents; Bill Anderson took administration; Jeff Steele and Janet Nepkie worked on faculty content; Karen Ferrer-Muniz took the student content; and I took elements addressing governing boards. We had momentum, structure, and division of labor—we thought we were under way.

Then we got stuck. The process of trying to distill the elements common to all three source documents was overwhelming, and we had trouble making any progress. Working together by conference call, we determined that we needed to start with a single source document and then add elements from the others as we progressed. Given that this project had begun with needs identified during an accreditation visit, it seemed appropriate to begin with the Middle States standards. I took the standards and created goal statements. Clarification from state regulations or AAUP principles were added where a connection was evident. The committee then developed these into the format we had used for the institutional effectiveness rubric, describing the goals at the various levels of achievement. A few early draft examples of this approach follow, illustrating the "Participation" section. Elements include Conflict of Interest

(Board Constituency) and Responsibilities (Faculty and Administration Constituency) (see Appendix C).

We extensively discussed all draft goals and proficiencies as they were developed. Several challenges emerged as we proceeded. We had difficulty establishing the content of the upper two levels without imposing our own values and wishes. Ultimately, it was determined that the essential difference between Level 2 and Level 3 was that Level 3 had to incorporate institutional assessment of each goal and the successful use of the assessment results to make improvements. Obviously, given the examples in the sample provided above, Levels 2 and 3 for these goals will need to be revisited with this criterion in mind.

Additional questions were identified as the work progressed.

1. Should there be a different rubric for the SUNY community colleges and the SUNY state-operated campuses? The community colleges have their own governing boards of trustees, and the state-operated campuses, with a few exceptions, have college councils that act in an advisory capacity. The SUNY Board of Trustees serves as the governing body for the state-operated campuses. Does this necessitate two different rubrics, or can a single tool serve both groups?

2. Definitions are needed. One source of confusion was distinguishing between "shared governance" and "faculty governance." Also, for some constituency groups, clarification was needed as to who was included. Does faculty refer to all faculty? Tenure-track faculty? Full-time or part-time faculty? Professional service faculty, such as librarians or counselors? Does administration include all administrative staff, or is the term limited to those of a specific rank or position classification?

We do not yet have answers to these questions. Discussion continues regarding whether specificity in these areas is warranted or whether institutions should determine these clarifications for their own campus cultures.

SUNY Voices

At about this point, Janet Nepkie suggested that we should present the rubric at the SUNY Voices conference in April 2017. I recall saying to her, "But Janet, we don't have a rubric yet!" But she was not to be deterred. She eventually persuaded me that the conference would be a good opportunity to get feedback on what we had done so far and gather suggestions for going forward.

Jeff Steele, Janet Nepkie, and I presented the rubric in its draft format (see Appendix D) and asked attendees for feedback. A rich discussion followed, and Jeff Steele took extensive notes.

We also distributed feedback forms with the following questions:

- What needs further explanation?
- What are we missing?
- Will what we are doing be helpful? If not, what could be more useful?
- Is your campus doing anything currently to assess the effectiveness of shared governance? If so, what?

People who attended our session included faculty, administration, representatives from the SUNY Student Assembly, and a president or two, so we quickly gleaned insights from a variety of perspectives. Attendance at the conference also gave us the opportunity to attend a session by Diane Bliss and the FCCC committee, to see how our respective efforts dovetailed and complemented each other. Feedback from her committee members at our session was also very helpful.

General feedback from the session discussion included the following topics:

1. We need more about students in the rubric, which we might gain if we research source documents on student participation in shared governance in higher education.

2. Student involvement should be incorporated into the levels of assessment (e.g., student participation must be included in assessment items, and students must have been involved, for an institution to receive a rating of Level 2 or 3).

3. Should items like "credentials of administrators, faculty, and staff" be a part of shared governance? The Middle States standards included credentials, so these figured in the rubric.

4. Items should be further divided into not only categories but subcategories. Avoid having too many individual items within

a single category. Possibly have each constituency evaluate the others at some point in the process/for each category.

5. The rubric could be used to educate boards of trustees regarding authority and roles.
6. The Association of Governing Boards should be checked for source materials.

Information from the feedback forms also included the following themes (verbatim responses are included in Appendix E).

- In response to the question "What needs further explanation?," there were many questions requesting clarification of terms, roles, and responsibilities

- In response to the question "What are we missing?," suggestions were made about including dialogue among constituencies, training in shared governance, student involvement, and specifics about curriculum purview.

- In response to the question "Will what we are doing be helpful? If not, what would be more useful?," the responses were uniformly positive. Clearly an instrument of this type is generally perceived by respondents as being valuable and useful.

- In response to the question "Is your campus doing anything currently to assess the effectiveness of shared governance? If so, what?," the responses were generally in the negative. If assessment of shared governance is being conducted, it is not consistent or broadly applied.

The open feedback category yielded many varied suggestions. In brief, the messages received were these:

- Development of such a rubric is necessary and timely.
- The rubric is too long and complex and would be unwieldy to use.
- The rubric is too short and doesn't include enough information about each constituency.
- There is not enough content about student participation in shared governance, and we lack source documents to inform this.

- Don't focus on credentials, but focus on processes and source documents that could be useful.

Going Forward

The June 2017 SCoA meeting provided an opportunity for the group to meet face to face for a more detailed discussion of the conference feedback. In addition, we expanded the group to include the SCoA Rubric Committee, chaired by Ken Kallio from SUNY Geneseo, who led our previous rubric development efforts. It seems clear from the most recent discussion that we need to adjust our thinking about the process for next steps. We had made considerable progress on developing a rubric that partially addressed our needs but probably focused too much on some of the accreditation elements (e.g., credentials of presidents, faculty, and administration). We realized that these were not germane to the shared governance process. We found out (thanks to SUNY Voices conference participants) that we had overlooked valuable source documents that could inform this project in beneficial ways. The following documents were added to our resource base:

- A document from AAUP titled "Evaluation of Shared Governance" (AAUP, n.d.) that provides a list of questions "designed to allow for the immediate evaluation of the state of shared government at institutions of higher education."

- A presentation from a 2015 Middle States conference on assessing shared governance by our colleagues at Finger Lakes Community College (Ortloff & McClean-Scanlon, 2015), which lays out a structure for rubric development.

- A statement from the Association of Governing Boards of Colleges and Universities (2010) on board responsibility for institutional governance.

We are still looking for good source documents on student participation.

Clearly, this is a heavily recursive process, and SCoA has returned to our original task of finding the common essential elements from the source documents. We learned the hard way that this is not likely to be a committee task. It seems clear that someone will have to distill the information and propose the necessary content for revising the rubric.

What is not in question is the necessity of developing such an instrument. The one resounding unequivocal response we received from the

SUNY Voices conference was that such an assessment tool was necessary, timely, and useful. We realize that we may not be able to produce this rubric quickly, given the complex nature of the subject and the unresolved issues. However, there is every reason to believe that, given the engagement and feedback from the conference and possibilities for collaboration as we progress further, we will be able to produce a document that will be of value to our institutions. We will help them achieve their goal, and ours—to assess and improve their shared governance structures and processes effectively and meaningfully.

Epilogue

After the SUNY Voices conference in 2017, the FCCC adapted the general SCoA rubric format and constructed a rubric based on the findings of their governance committee. The resulting rubric was shared at the 2018 SUNY Voices conference. It was subsequently distributed widely for potential use by campuses. It is my understanding that consideration is being given to adapting the FCCC version for use at State Operated campuses. Subsequently, SCoA decided not to pursue construction of a shared governance rubric. An initial review of the FCCC rubric indicates a strong focus on faculty governance in contrast to the more general shared governance version initially proposed by SCoA. At the 2018 SUNY Voices conference, I shared a presentation on the shared governance implications incorporated in the new Middle States standards adopted in 2014 (see Appendix F). If interest remains in developing a more general rubric for assessing shared governance, the references in that presentation may serve as a better initial foundation than Standard 4 of the former Middle States standards, *Characteristics of Excellence*, which informed SCoA's previous efforts.

References

American Association of University Professors. (n.d.). *Evaluation of shared governance*. Retrieved from https://www.aaup.org/sites/default/files/files/Evaluation%20of%20Shared%20Governance.pdf.

Association of Governing Boards of Universities and Colleges. (2010). *Statement on board responsibility for institutional governance*. Retrieved from https://www.agb.org/sites/default/files/agb-statements/statement_2010_institutional_governance.pdf.

Ortloff, D., & McClean-Scanlon, M. (2015). Assessing shared governance. Presentation at Middle States Commission on Higher Education Annual Conference. Retrieved from http://www.msche.org/documents/AssessingSharedGovernance.pdf.

Appendix A: Shared Governance Roles

- Regular text: NYS regulation
- **Bold: MSCHE Standard VII**
- <u>Underlined: AAUP principles</u> (paraphrased where needed)

General Principles

An accredited institution possesses and demonstrates the following attributes or activates:

- **A clearly articulated and transparent governance structure that outlines roles, responsibilities, and accountability for decision-making by each constituency, including governing body, administration, faculty, staff and students.**
- **Periodic assessment of the effectiveness of governance, leadership and administration.**

Introduction

A. <u>In order to respond appropriately to external forces, institutions must have their own generally unified view of the government of an institution.</u>

B. <u>Regard for the welfare of the institution remains important.</u>

C. <u>"Third, a college or university in which all the components are aware of their interdependence, of the usefulness of communication among themselves, and of the force of joint action will enjoy increased capacity to solve educational problems."</u>

Joint Effort

The variety and complexity of the tasks performed by institutions of higher education produce an inescapable interdependence among governing board, administration, faculty, students, and others. The relationship calls for adequate communication among these components and full opportunity for appropriate joint planning and effort . . .

   A. Important areas of action involve at one time or another the initiating capacity and decision-making participation of all of the institutional components.

   B. Differences in the weight of each voice, from one point to the next, should be determined by reference to the responsibility of each component for the particular matter at hand.

   C. Areas indicating a need for joint effort include:

   Determination of General Educational Policy

   Internal Operations of the Institution including

   Framing and execution of long range plans including communications and decision-making

   Decisions regarding existing or prospective physical resources

   Budgeting

   Choice of a new president

Board of Trustees

Establish governing policies and delegate responsibility for executing policies to administration

   A. Appoint presidents (subject to SUNY Board approval)
   B. Approve curricula
   C. Prepare, approve and implement budgets
   D. Establish tuition and fees
   E. Approve sites and facilities

F. Provide for the awarding of certificates, diplomas, and degrees on recommendation of faculty and president

G. Appoint personnel

H. Determine and implement salary and employee benefits schedules

I. Approve the organizational pattern of the college

J. Formulate and record the policies and procedures of appointment and conditions of appointment of the president and professional administrative personnel

K. Establish policies and delegate to the president or designee:

1. Personnel policies:

    a. Appointments, promotions, tenure and dismissals of faculty and staff members

    b. Conditions of employment, leaves of absence and sabbatical leave

    c. Rules and regulations to which faculty and staff are expected to adhere

    d. Statements regarding academic freedom

    e. Subject to local and state civil service regulations, the working conditions for nonacademic personnel and fixed rates f compensation

2. Creations of divisions, departments, and appropriate administrative and academic positions and definition of duties to carry out the objectives of the college

    a. Regulations governing the behavior and conduct of students and guiding the co-curricular program of the college

    b. Authorization and supervision of travel for the purposes of the college

    c. Care, custody, control and management of land, grounds, buildings, equipment and supplies used for the purposes of the college for carrying out its objectives

d. Use of college facilities for outside organizations
   e. Admission of students
   f. Preparation of a budget for operation of the college for submission to and approval by the local sponsor and SUNY Board
   g. Preparation of capital equipment and capital construction budgets
   h. Use of college facilities for research, consultation or other contractual services pursuant to the educational purposes of the college
   i. Make available for inspection all college policies and procedures at the college for the convenience and information of members of the college constituency.

- Serves the public interest, ensures that the institution clearly states and fulfills its mission and goals, has fiduciary responsibility for the institution, and is ultimately accountable for the academic quality, planning, and fiscal well-being of the institution.

- Has sufficient independence and expertise to ensure integrity of the institution. Members must have primary responsibility to the institution and not allow political, financial, or other influences to interfere with their governing abilities

- Ensures that neither the governing body not its individual members interferes in the day-to-day operations of the institution

- Oversees at the policy level the quality of teaching and learning, the approval of degree programs and the awarding of degrees, the establishment of personnel policies and procedures, the approval of policies and bylaws, and the assurance of strong fiscal management.

- Plays a basic policy-making role in financial affairs to ensure integrity and strong financial management. This may include a timely review of audited financial statements and/or other documents related to the fiscal viability of the institution.

- Appoints and regularly evaluates the performance of the president

- Is informed in all its operations by principles of good practice in board governance
- Established and complies with a written conflict of interest policy designed to ensure the impartiality of the governing body by addressing matters such as payment for services, contractual relationships, employment, and family, financial, or other interests that could pose of be perceived a conflicts of interest.

A. <u>Final institutional authority</u>

B. <u>Entrusts the conduct of administration to the administrative officers and the conduct of teaching and research to the faculty. The board should undertake appropriate self-limitation</u>

C. <u>Plays a central role in relating the likely needs of the future to predictable resources; responsibility for husbanding the endowment; responsible for obtaining needed capital and operating funds</u>

D. <u>Should pay attention to personnel policy</u>

College Councils

§ 332.1 Establishment

In accordance with the provisions of the Education Law, there shall be a council at each State-operated institution and, in the case of the State University College of Environmental Science and Forestry, a board of trustees.

§ 332.2 Responsibilities

Individual councils and, in the case of the State University College of Environmental Science and Forestry, the board of trustees, shall exercise such powers as are provided for in the Education Law, subject to the general management, supervision, control, and approval of and in accordance with rules established by the State University trustees. Consistent with the statutory responsibilities of such bodies, they shall develop and foster strong relationships between their institutions and local communities and promote campus and university interests.

President

Provide general educational leadership and promote the educational effectiveness of the institution in all its aspects

- A. Implement, execute and administer all policies of the BOT and SUNY BOT
- B. Formulate and present to the college trustees for their action recommendations on:
    1. Curriculum
    2. Budgets
    3. Salary and benefits schedules for all professional and non-professional employees
    4. Personnel appointments, tenure, retention and retrenchment (unless this has been delegated to the president)
    5. Organizational structure
    6. Planning and management of facilities
    7. Granting of degrees or certificates
- C. Administration of collective bargaining agreements
- D. Submit an annual report on the operation of the college to the trustees and prepare such other reports as the SUNY trustees may require
- E. Assure the preparation of a faculty handbook in which the roe of the faculty on the administration and advancement of the college is described
- F. Assure the preparation of documents needed for orientation and guidance of students attending the college

- **Is appointed by, evaluated by, and reports to the governing body and shall not chair the governing body**
- **Has appropriate credentials and professional experience consistent with the mission of the organization**

- Has the authority and autonomy required to fulfill the responsibilities of the position including developing and implementing institutional plans, staffing the organization, identifying and allocating resources, and directing the institution toward attaining the goals and objectives set forth in its mission
- Has the assistance of qualified administrators, sufficient in number, to enable the Chief Executive Officer to discharge his/her duties effectively; and is responsible for establishing procedures for assessing the organizations efficiency and effectiveness

1. Shares responsibility for definition and attainment of goals, for administrative action, and for operating the communications system that links the components of the academic community
2. Selection of academic deans and chief academic officers with advice of and consultation with faculty
3. Has an obligation to innovate and initiate
4. Ensure that standards and procedures in operational use conform to policy established by the board and to the standards of sound academic practice
5. Ensure that views of the faculty ate shared with the Board and vice versa
6. Responsible for maintenance of existing institutional resources and creation of new resources
7. Responsible for a large area of nonacademic activities
8. Responsible for public understanding and is the main person who speaks for the institution

Faculty

A. Participate in the formulation of policy related to:
   1. Student health, scholarship, standards of admission, attendance and discharge of students, curriculum and other study programs, the granting of degrees, student activities, extra-curricular activities and student discipline

B. Present recommendations to the President regarding
   1. Instructional budget
   2. Appointments, reappointments, tenure, special salary increments, promotions and leaves of absence of members of the instructional staff
      - Has primary responsibility for such fundamental areas as curriculum, subject matter and methods of instruction, research, faculty status and those areas of student life which relate to the educational process
      - On these matters the power of review or final decision lodged in the governing board or delegated by it to the president should be exercised adversely only in exceptional circumstances, and for reasons communicated to the faculty. It is desirable that the faculty should, following such communication, have opportunity for further consideration and further transmittal of its vies to the president or board. Budgets, personnel limitations, the time element, and the policies of other groups, bodies and agencies having jurisdiction over the institution may set limits to realization of faculty advice
      - Sets requirements for degrees offered, determines when the requirements have been set, and authorizes the president and board to grant the degrees thus achieved
      - Have primary responsibility for faculty status and related matters: appointments, tenure, and dismissal. The Board and President should concur except in rare instances and for compelling reasons which should be stated in detail
      - The chair or head of department should be appointed with appropriate faculty consultation
      - Agencies for faculty participation in governance should be established at each level where faculty responsibility is present. An agency should exist for the presentation of the views of the whole faculty. The structure

> and procedures for faculty participation should be designed, approved, and established by joint action of the components of an institution

§ 606.1 Name

- There shall be a Faculty Council of Community Colleges which operates within the program of the State University of New York

§ 606.2 Purposes

- (a) The council shall focus on matters relating to community college faculty and make recommendations regarding academic concerns and issues, policies, and programs. Specifically, the council shall:

- (1) provide opportunity and structure for the faculty of community colleges to formulate positions on policy matters of common interest to the community colleges for transmittal to community college presidents, trustees and sponsors

- (2) provide an opportunity for the faculty of the community colleges to act in an advisory, consultative and planning capacity to the chancellor of the university

- (3) provide a forum for the consideration of matters of common interest to the faculty of the community colleges

- (4) provide means for the interchange of ideas among the faculties of the community colleges and between the faculty and the administration of the university and

- (5) provide an additional channel of communication between the university administration and local governing boards of the community colleges

- (b) The council will work with the Faculty Senate of the State University of New York on matters of common concern in the conduct of university affairs

§ 331.1 Name

- There shall be a University Faculty Senate of State University of New York

§ 331.2 Purposes

- The senate shall be the official agency through which the university faculty engages in the governance of the university. The senate shall be concerned with effective educational policies and other professional matters within the university

§ 334.4 Responsibility

- The faculty of each college shall have the obligation to participate significantly in the initiation, development and implementation of the educational program

§ 330.3 Responsibilities

- The university faculty shall be responsible for the conduct of the university's instruction, research and service programs

Administration

- An organizational structure that is clearly documented and that clearly defines supporting relationships
- An appropriate size and with relevant experience to assist the CEO in fulfilling his/her roles and responsibilities
- Members with credentials and professional experience consistent with the mission of the organization and their functional roles
- Skills, time, assistance, technology and information systems expertise required to perform their duties
- Regular engagement with faculty and students in advancing the institution's goals and objectives

- Systematic procedures for evaluating administrative units and for using data to enhance operations

Students

- Election of a student trustee who is a full voting member of the board. (Community College Rules)
- Election of a student member of the college council (State Operated)

§ 341.2 Purpose

The student assembly shall be the official organization by which State University students participate in university-wide governance. The student assembly shall provide the following:

(a) a forum for consultation and the exchange of information between State University students, the chancellor, and the State University of New York Board of Trustees on matters of a university-wide nature which affect student concerns and

(b a procedure for electing the student member of the State University of New York Board of Trustees

The student assembly shall exercise such other responsibilities as the chancellor or the State University of New York Board of Trustees refer to it.

A. Student desire to participate responsibly in institutional governance:
   1. Opportunity for educational experience
   2. Involvement in institutional affairs
B. Ways should be found to permit significant student participation within the limits of attainable effectiveness
C. Students should be given the opportunity:
   1. To be listened to in the classroom without fear of institutional reprisal for the substance of their views

2. To be free to discuss questions of institutional policy and operation
3. To be accorded due process when charged with serious violations of institutional regulations
4. To be accorded the same right to hear speakers of their choice as is enjoyed by other components of the institution

Appendix B. SUNY Council on Assessment, Assessing Institutional Effectiveness

Background

The SUNY Council on Assessment (SCoA) was established to support SUNY campuses in their efforts to assess institutional effectiveness and student learning outcomes. In fulfillment of that charge, SCoA has developed this self-assessment rubric focused on institutional effectiveness. The idea to design a rubric for this purpose took inspiration from a self-assessment rubric designed by Linda Suskie, and grew out of a compilation study of commendations, suggestions, and recommendations of Middle States accreditation reviews of SUNY campuses between 2010 and 2012. In all, 26 decennial team visits, 6 follow-up visits, and 9 Periodic Review Reports were examined for appraisals of how these institutions were addressing the assessment of institutional effectiveness. From that study, it became clear that campuses would benefit from having a tool that they could apply to their own institutions in order to gauge how they were doing in this area. An analytic rubric seemed the best way to present the various aspects of assessing institutional effectiveness. Since this rubric was designed as an institutional self-assessment tool, it is intended to serve more in a formative function rather than a summative one. It can be used to shine a spotlight on areas of institution-level assessment that may need improvement in order to advance overall institutional effectiveness. The rubric may also reveal how well an institution is "closing the loop" by questioning how well assessment findings are used in planning and resource allocation. This rubric was not designed for the comparison of institutions, either within or outside of SUNY. Nor was it designed to ensure that an institution has achieved the standards set forth by Middle States. It was designed in the spirit of the assessment movement, for the use by institutions for their own self-improvement.

Interpretative Notes

The language used throughout the rubric was intended to be applied flexibly to the very different parts and levels of organization that form the structure of colleges and universities. Thus, the terms "area" and "unit" were meant as a generic terms for any institutional organizational entity (e.g., different divisions, programs, departments, etc.). Similarly, the term "outcome" must be understood as relative to the particular area or unit that is being examined. In some instances, depending on the department or unit, the term "outcome" may refer to student learning outcomes. In other instances, outcomes other than student learning outcomes may be the focus. The intended meanings of the terms attached to the four levels of the scale also warrant comment. These labels were chosen to convey degrees of institutional progress toward assessment-related goals, and the labels are approximations at best. "Not evident" suggests assessment-related work is mostly or entirely absent. "Emerging" implies such work is underway, possibly newly created, but still largely piecemeal in its manifestation and with no overall institutional coordination/support. "Proficient" means the institution is doing a competent job with assessment, but there are still slight gaps/deficiencies. "Excelling" is meant to capture the point at which an institution has a thorough and accomplished process in place. Of course, to say that it is "accomplished" does not mean assessment is done. We are all well aware that assessment is a recurring process in the service of continual institutional improvement. In that same spirit, this rubric is likely to be a continually evolving document. Suggestions for improvement can be directed to the developers via www.sunyassess.org.

Directions: For each row in the rubric, select the level (0, 1, 2, or 3) that most accurately describes the current state of your institution. Optimal results may be obtained by requesting that a broad range of campus constituencies complete the rubric, and then using the results for discussion and planning.

Aspect	Element	Goal	Level 0: Not evident	Level 1: Emerging	Level 2: Proficient	Level 3: Excelling
Design	Plan	The institution has a formal assessment plan that documents an organized, sustained assessment process covering all major administrative units, student support services, and academic programs.	There is no overall institutional plan for assessment. Assessment may be conducted at the institution, but when it occurs, it is completed on an ad hoc basis, perhaps in response to specific challenges.	Some, but not all functional areas/units conduct assessment systematically and these have policies and plans that pertain to assessment within the area/unit; there is no coordination of or standards for assessment set by the institution.	All functional areas/units conduct assessment systematically and may have written policies to guide the process. There is no overall institutional plan that serves to coordinate use of assessment data to improve institutional effectiveness.	There is a written plan that specifies responsibility for conducting assessment at both unit and institution levels and that identifies reporting timelines and procedures. The plan also indicates how assessment data is channeled into the strategic planning and budgeting process.
Design	Outcomes	Measurable outcomes have been articulated for the institution as a whole and within functional areas/units, including for courses and programs and nonacademic units.	Outcomes either have not been written, or where they do exist, they are not stated in ways that directly suggest how to measure them.	Some but not all units have their own outcomes statements. For example, academic affairs may have identified student learning outcomes, but no other units have identified outcomes.	All units have outcomes statements, but not all of these are stated in terms that link to measurement operations.	All units within the institution and the institution as a whole have clearly stated and measurable outcomes.
Design	Alignment	More specific subordinate outcomes (e.g., course) are aligned with broader, higher-level outcomes (e.g., program) within units and these are aligned with the institutional mission, goals, and values.	Course/program or other functional area outcomes, when present, are not mapped to or aligned with higher level outcomes nor are they shown to be related to institutional mission, goals, and values.	Alignment of outcomes has been achieved in some but not all areas/units.	Alignment of lower level outcomes to higher level outcomes within areas/units is mostly complete. Alignment of higher levels unit outcomes to institutional mission, goals, and values is not complete.	All units indicate how their outcomes are aligned with institution mission, goals, and values. Alignment within units is specific and appropriate to the unit and its role in the institution. Alignment of outcomes indicates a strong sense of shared purpose within the institution.

Implementation	**Resources**	Financial, human, technical, and/or physical resources are adequate to support assessment.	No resources are available to support assessment.	Resources to support assessment are handled on an ad hoc basis.	There is budgetary support of assessment activities within units that conduct assessment, but there is no overall institutional plan for providing the full range of resources to support assessment.	The institution and each area/unit has made a commitment to assessment and provides all necessary resources for assessment.
	Culture	All members of the faculty and staff are involved in assessment activities.	Assessment, if occurring, is done by lone individuals charged with assessment responsibilities.	Some units involve faculty/staff in assessment planning and collection and review of data.	All units involve all faculty/staff in some aspect of assessment, planning data collection, and/or review of data.	All members of the university community are involved in assessment activities in their respective units. Institution leaders frequently articulate assessment as an important value/activity of the institution.
	Data focus	Data from multiple sources and measures are considered in assessment.	Assessment data are not collected.	Assessment data are collected in one or more units but consists primarily of survey results and/or anecdotal evidence.	All units collect some combination of direct and indirect evidence to assess performance.	Assessment is based on, where appropriate, multiple measures of performance, including direct and indirect measures and quantitative and qualitative data.
	Sustainability	Assessment is conducted regularly, consistently, and in a manner that is sustainable over the long term.	The institution cannot document that there is sustainable assessment activity occurring within any functional responsibility areas (academic, student services/support and administrative offices).	The institution can document that sustainable assessment activity is regularly occurring within several units of the institution, but assessment practices are either not universal or not sustainable for the long term.	Assessment is routinely conducted in most, if not all, units. The sustainability of the assessment activity varies in terms of how regularly it occurs or in how systematically outcomes/goals are assessed. Assessment activity is becoming a regular part of each unit's functioning.	Assessment is routinely conducted in all appropriate units. The sustainability of the assessment activity is evident in that assessment occurs regularly and systematically and has been ongoing for many years. Assessment activity is a regular part of each unit's functioning.

continued on next page

Aspect	Element	Goal	Level 0: Not evident	Level 1: Emerging	Level 2: Proficient	Level 3: Excelling
	Monitoring	Mechanisms are in place to systematically monitor the implementation of the assessment plan.	There is little or no evidence that the institution has in place or is developing effective systematic monitoring of the quality and implementation of assessment activities within and across units.	Assessment plans are in place. Systematic monitoring of the quality and implementation of assessment activities is occurring within some units, but not others. There is little evidence of institutional level monitoring of assessment activities.	Systematic monitoring of the quality and implementation of assessment activities is occurring within most, if not all, units. The institution has begun establishing a means for ensuring that all units regularly conduct and report assessment activities.	There is evidence of systematic monitoring of the quality and implementation of assessment activities within all units. The institution has an established mechanism for monitoring unit compliance with institutional assessment policies.
	Communication	Assessment results are readily available to all parties with an interest in them.	Assessment results, if they exist, "live" in the individual unit and are not broadly communicated.	Assessment results are owned by the functional area and are shared with others on an as-needed basis.	Units within the institution share assessment results routinely with each other or make them accessible to others within the institution. Public disclosure of appropriate assessment data is limited.	Assessment results are disseminated to appropriate audiences at appropriate times; data appropriate to external audiences are available in easily accessible public domains; data needed for internal decision making are readily accessible to decision makers.
Impact	Strategic planning and budgeting	Assessment data are routinely considered in strategic planning and budgeting.	Assessment data stay within the area in which they were collected. They do not factor into institutional strategic planning and budgeting.	One or more units use assessment results in budgetary requests and/or to inform strategic planning.	Assessment data are used in strategic planning and budgeting, but there is no clear mechanism in place to ensure this is accomplished routinely.	Institution is able to demonstrate that strategic planning and budgeting processes have routinely used assessment data in decision making.

Closing the loop	Assessment data have been used for institutional improvement.	There is little or no evidence that assessment results are used for institutional improvement.	There is evidence that assessment results are occasionally used for institutional improvement.	There is evidence that all units regularly use assessment results to inform improvements.	There is an institutional commitment to using assessment results to inform improvements; all units regularly use assessment data to close the loop; the institution presents evidence that assessment results, including student learning assessment, are routinely used for institutional improvement, effectiveness and planning.

Appendix C. Shared Governance Assessment Early Draft

Constituent group	Goal	Level 0: Not evident	Level 1: Emerging	Level 2: Proficient	Level 3: Excelling
Board of trustees	The board has a clearly written policy statement defining conflicts of interest which all board members support and adhere to.	No such statement exists.	A statement exists but lacks definitions and has not been updated.	A clear statement with definitions exists and board members sign an annual statement acknowledging and affirming compliance.	A clear statement with definitions exists. Yearly compliance is affirmed. Board members review the content and assess their compliance annually.
Faculty	Faculty have primary responsibility for such fundamental areas as curriculum, subject matter, methods of instruction, research, faculty status and those areas of student life that relate to the instructional process.	Faculty do not have any responsibility regarding decisions made in these areas. All decisions are made by others without input.	Faculty are nominally considered to have responsibility, but not primary responsibility. Faculty input is provided, but it is not meaningful, and decisions are really made by others with only a token show of faculty input.	Faculty are considered to have primary responsibility. Their recommendations are meaningful and respected. All faculty input is provided through mutually established structures, processes, and procedures.	Faculty are considered to have primary responsibility. Their recommendations are meaningful and respected. All faculty input is provided through established processes and procedures. Any rejection of faculty recommendation in these areas is

		automatically coupled with a formal explanation of the reasons why. The effectiveness of these characteristics is regularly assessed for the purpose of continual improvement.	
		Any rejection of faculty recommendation in these areas is automatically coupled with a formal explanation of the reasons.	
Administration	The institution has an organizational structure that is clearly documented and clearly defines reporting relationships.	The organizational structure is either unknown or changes frequently and is not documented.	An organizational structure shows reporting relationships in place.	A functional organizational chart exists showing the roles of each unit and responsibilities of people in each unit.	A functional organizational chart aligned to support the mission and goals of the organization is in place and identifies the roles of each unit tied to specific goals.

Appendix D. Shared Governance Self-Assessment Draft

The potential benefit of developing a tool for assessing shared governance has become increasingly evident given the comprehensive emphasis on effective assessment for all aspects of SUNY institutions, and the reflection of this requirement throughout the new Middle States accreditation standards. In the spirit of self-reflection and continuous improvement, the SUNY Council on Assessment (SCoA) is in the process of developing a rubric which could be used by campuses for this purpose. The rubric will incorporate common aspects of the Middle States standards, the AAUP shared governance principles, and New York State regulations addressing shared governance. The rubric will also be widely vetted for input from as many constituencies as possible. Since this rubric is being designed as an institutional self-assessment tool, it is not intended for use as a means of mandated evaluation, but rather as a way of assisting campuses in identifying elements of their shared governance processes which seem strong, and those elements which may need improvement. This rubric is not being designed to promote any particular model of shared governance. It is being designed in the spirit of effective assessment, for use by institutions for their own self-improvement.

Directions

For each row in the rubric, select the level (0, 1, 2, or 3) that most accurately describes the current state of your institution.

	Element	Constituent Group	Goal	Level 0: Not evident	Level 1: Emerging	Level 2: Proficient	Level 3: Excelling
Participation	Governance structure	Board of trustees President Administration Faculty Staff Students	There is a clearly articulated and transparent governance structure that outlines roles, responsibilities, and accountability for decision making for each constituency.				
		Board of trustees President Administration Faculty Staff Students	There is a process for the periodic assessment of the effectiveness of governance, leadership, and administration, and the results of these regular assessments are used to enhance shared governance.				
	Conflict of interest	Board of trustees	The board has a clear written policy statement defining conflicts of interest which all board members support and adhere to.	No such statement exists.	A statement exists, but lacks definitions and has not been updated.	A clear statement with definitions exists and Board members sign an annual statement acknowledging and affirming compliance with it.	A clear statement with definitions exists. Yearly compliance is affirmed. Board members review the content and assess their compliance annually.
	Responsibilities	Board of trustees	The legally constituted governing body serves the public interest, ensures that the institution states and fulfills its mission and goals, has fiduciary responsibility, and is accountable for the academic quality, planning, and fiscal well-being of the institution.				

continued on next page

Element	Constituent Group	Goal	Level 0: Not evident	Level 1: Emerging	Level 2: Proficient	Level 3: Excelling
	Board of trustees	The board has sufficient independence and expertise to ensure the integrity of the institution.				
	Board of trustees	The board ensures that neither the board nor its members interferes in the day-to-day operations of the institution.				
	Board of trustees	The board oversees at the policy level the quality of teaching and learning, approval of degree programs and awarding of degrees, the establishment of personnel policies and bylaws, and the assurance of sound fiscal management.				
	Board of trustees	The board plays a basic policy making role in financial affairs to ensure integrity and strong financial management.				
	Board of trustees	The board appoints and regularly evaluates the performance of the chief executive officer.				

	Standard				
	The CEO is appointed by, evaluated by, and reports to the governing body but does not chair it.	CEO position is vacant and temporarily filled with an interim.	A CEO appointed by and reports to a governing body but no evidence of a structured evaluation process.	An established CEO reporting to the governing body with evidence of a structured evaluation process.	An established CEO reporting to a governing body with documented evidence of a regular annual performance evaluation with established goals and community input.
President (CEO)	The CEO has appropriate credentials and professional experience consistent with the mission of the organization.	Meets minimum credentials with no relevant experience.	Meets or exceeds minimum credentials and possess limited appropriate professional experience.	Meets or exceeds minimum credentials and possess broad professional and leadership experience appropriate for the position.	Exceeds minimum credentials and possess extensive professional and leadership experience at multiple levels within an educational institution.
President (CEO)	Has the authority and autonomy required to fulfill the responsibilities of the position including developing and implementing institutional plans, staffing the organization, identifying and allocating resources, and directing the institution toward attaining the goals and objectives set forth in its mission.	President lacks the authority and autonomy to lead the institution without required internal or external input or approval.	President is leading the institution but is required to seek internal or external input or approval on some operational activities.	President has the authority and autonomy to lead the institution effectively. May experience occasional undue influences which will affect the institution.	President has the authority and autonomy to lead the institution free of undue influences. The president works closely with internal and external stakeholders in fulfilling the mission.

continued on next page

Element	Constituent Group	Goal	Level 0: Not evident	Level 1: Emerging	Level 2: Proficient	Level 3: Excelling
	Administration	Has the assistance of qualified administrators, sufficient in number, to enable the CEO to discharge his/her duties effectively; and is responsible for establishing the procedures for assessing the institution's efficiency and effectiveness.	Insufficient capacity, skills, or defined roles within the administration to enable the CEO to discharge his/her duties effectively and/or responsibility for establishing procedures for assessing efficiency and effectiveness is not clear or does not exist within the current roles of the administration.	Some administrative roles exist and are defined to lead specific functions, but there may not be enough capacity or the structure may prohibit them from carrying out their responsibilities, and/or some procedures may exist for assessing efficiency and effectiveness, but not comprehensively and/or not systematically.	A sufficient number of qualified administrators are in place with clearly defined roles and an appropriate organizational structure to allow them to carry out their responsibilities effectively, and a comprehensive set of procedures for assessing efficiency and effectiveness against a set of institutional metrics are documented and carried out systematically.	A sufficient number of highly qualified administrators are in place and work interdependently as a self-directed team to help lead the institution with a performance-driven culture based on systematic assessment of effectiveness and efficiency, which shows improvement toward institutional metrics over time.
	Administration	An organizational structure that is clearly documented and that clearly defines reporting relationships.	The organizational structure is either unknown or changes frequently and is not documented.	An organizational structure showing reporting relationships is in place.	A functional org chart exists showing the roles of each unit and responsibilities of individuals within each unit.	A functional org chart aligned to support the mission and goals of the organization is in place and identifies the roles of each unit tied to specific goals, and individuals as well as unit leaders can articulate how their role supports the goals and mission of the broader organization.

		Minimum required credentials and experience are not well defined for administrators and/or credentials and experience of administrators are inconsistent with the mission of the organization or their functional roles.	Minimum required credentials and experience of administrators are defined and they have only some level of experience and may or may not have the credentials expected for their roles or the mission of the organization.	Required credentials and experience of administrators are defined and administrators in place meet all of those requirements.	Required credentials or experience of most administrators exceed minimum expectations for their roles and the mission of the organization and the team of administrators represent a comprehensive set of strengths, skills, and experience with close alignment to the mission and goals of the organization.
Administration	Has credentials and experience consistent with the mission of the organization and their functional roles.				
Administration	Has the skills, time, assistance, technology, and information systems expertise required to perform their duties. (Add skill with technology to bullet?)	Administrators fall short in carrying out their duties on a regular basis due to lack of skills, capacity, expertise, or access to good technology infrastructure.	Administrators are able to carry out some of their duties effectively, but fall short on a regular basis due to lack of skills, capacity, expertise, or access to good technology infrastructure.	Administrators are able to consistently and effectively carry out their duties in support of the mission and goals of the organization.	Administrators are able to consistently and effectively carry out their duties in support of the mission and goals of the organization, and regularly leverage current as well as new or emerging technologies to improve the efficiency and effectiveness of the overall organization.

continued on next page

Element	Constituent Group	Goal	Level 0: Not evident	Level 1: Emerging	Level 2: Proficient	Level 3: Excelling
	Administration (defined as at the director level or higher)	Has regular engagement with faculty and students in advancing the institution's goals and objectives as appropriate to the role.	There is minimal to no engagement between faculty/students and the administration.	There is some engagement between the administration and faculty and/or students, but it is not effective in helping to advance the institution's goals and objectives.	There is sufficient and regular engagement between the administration and both faculty and the faculty/student perspectives are considered important to advancing the institution's goals and objectives.	There is ongoing engagement between the administration and both faculty and students, and both faculty and students have a clearly defined and active role in advancing the institution's goals and objectives.
	Administration	Has systematic procedures for evaluating administrative units and for using assessment data to enhance operations.	No procedures are in place to evaluate administrative units or use assessment data to enhance operations.	There are some procedures in place to evaluate the effectiveness or impact of administrative units and/or assessment date is collected in some cases to enhance administrative operations.	Procedures are in place to ensure systematic evaluation of administrative units on a regular cycle using a comprehensive set of assessment data to improve administrative operations in all areas.	Procedures are in place to ensure systematic evaluation of administrative units on a regular cycle using a comprehensive set of assessment data to improve administrative operations in all areas. Evaluation and assessment outcomes show improvements in efficiency and effectiveness of multiple units over time.

	Board of trustees President Administration Faculty Staff Students	All constituencies utilize sufficient opportunities, resources, and support for professional growth (professional development, training) and innovation? Or do we want to say something like "demonstrate continual efforts to develop themselves professionally."			
	Board President Administration	Faculty and staff are provided with sufficient opportunities, resources, and support for professional growth and innovation.			
	Faculty (defined as both full-time and part-time faculty?)	Have credentials and experience consistent with the mission of the organization and the requirements of their discipline.	Minimum required credentials and experience are not faculty and/or credentials and experience of faculty are inconsistent with the mission of the organization or the requirements of their discipline.	Minimum required credentials and experience of faculty are defined and they have some level of experience and may or may not have the credentials expected for the mission of the organization or the requirements of their discipline.	Required credentials and experience of faculty are defined and faculty in place meet all of those requirements.	Required credentials or experience of most faculty exceed minimum expectations for the mission of the organization and the requirements of their discipline.
	Faculty	Faculty are rigorous and effective in teaching, assessment of student learning, scholarly inquiry, and service, as appropriate to the institution's mission, goals, and policies.			

continued on next page

Element	Constituent Group	Goal	Level 0: Not evident	Level 1: Emerging	Level 2: Proficient	Level 3: Excelling
	Faculty	Faculty participate in the formation of policy related to: Student health, scholarship, standards of admission, attendance and discharge of students, curriculum and other study programs, the granting of degrees, student activities, extra-curricular activities and student discipline.	There is no evidence that the faculty provide meaningful participation in these areas.	There is evidence that the faculty body provides input into, and participates in, some of these areas, but not others, or their input is inconsistently meaningful in the formation of policy in all of these areas or this is done informally or it is done by individual faculty members but not the body.	There is evidence that the faculty body, through established and formal processes and procedures, consistently provides input into, and participates in, the formation of policy in all of these areas and their input is consistently respected.	There is evidence that the faculty body, through established processes and procedures, proactively and regularly engages in the formation of policy in each of the areas, and, based on periodically assessment of the effectiveness of this engagement, makes improvements to the processes and procedures.
	Faculty SUNY/ UFS	The faculty of each college shall have the obligation to participate significantly in the initiation, development implementation and assessment of the educational program.	Faculty are not engaged in initiating, developing or implementing the educational program.	Structures, policies, and processes for faculty engagement exist but do not effectively allow for initiation, development or implementation of the educational program.	Structures, policies, and processes for faculty engagement exist and effectively allow for initiation, development and implementation of the educational program.	Structures, policies, and processes for faculty engagement exist and effectively allow for initiation, development and implementation of the educational program. Such engagement is evident prior to formal consideration of educational proposals by administration.

		There is no evidence that faculty are involved in curriculum approval, research or service.	There is some evidence that faculty are involved in curriculum approval, research or service.	There is evidence that faculty are responsible for curriculum approval, research, and service, and measure student learning through effective assessment.	There is evidence that faculty are responsible for curriculum approval, research, and service; measure student learning through effective assessment; and use assessment results to improve teaching and learning.
Faculty SUNY/UFS	The faculty are responsible for the implementation of the institution's instruction, research and service programs.				
Board of trustees President Administration Faculty Staff Students	Methodology and criteria used for decision making are clearly stated and transparent to the college community and are grounded in assessment data as well as other objective sources.				
Board of trustees President Administration Faculty Staff Students	All constituencies are actively engaged in the shared governance process according to their defined roles.				
Faculty	Faculty are aware of campus policies for decision making and strive to fulfill their committee responsibilities.				
Faculty	Faculty present recommendations to the President regarding the instructional budget, appointments, reappointments, tenure, special salary increments, promotions and leaves of absence of members of the instructional staff.				

continued on next page

Element	Constituent Group	Goal	Level 0: Not evident	Level 1: Emerging	Level 2: Proficient	Level 3: Excelling
	Faculty	Faculty have primary responsibility for such fundamental areas as curriculum, subject matter and methods of instruction, research, faculty status and those areas of student life which relate to the instructional process.	Faculty do not have any responsibility regarding decisions made in these areas. All decisions are made by others without input.	Faculty are nominally considered to have responsibility, but not primary responsibility. Faculty input is provided, but it is not meaningful and decisions are really made by others with only a token show of faculty input.	Faculty are considered to have primary responsibility. Their recommendations are meaningful and respected. All faculty input is provided through mutually established structures, processes and procedures. Any rejection of faculty recommendation in these areas is automatically coupled with a formal explanation of the reasons.	Faculty are considered to have primary responsibility. Their recommendations are meaningful and respected. All faculty input is provided through established processes and procedures. Any rejection of faculty recommendation in these areas is automatically coupled with a formal explanation of the reasons why. The effectiveness of these characteristics is regularly assessed for the purpose of continual improvement.
	Students	There is a student representative on boards of trustees and college councils. Their roles are clear to them and they participate actively and appropriately, receiving the opportunity for educational experience and input into institutional affairs.				Faculty encourage administration to make faculty governance the first avenue of administrative consultation.

		There is no evidence that the faculty body provides meaningful recommendations in these areas.	There is evidence that the faculty body makes recommendations in, some of these areas, but not others, or their recommendations are inconsistently meaningful in all of these areas or this is done informally or it is done by individual faculty members but not the body.	There is evidence that the faculty body, through established and formal processes and procedures, provides recommendations in all of these areas and their input is consistently respected.	There is evidence that the faculty body, through established processes and procedures, proactively and regularly makes meaningful and respected recommendations in each of the areas, and, based on periodically assessment of the effectiveness of this engagement, makes improvements to the processes and procedures.
Administration	The organizational structure of the institution is clearly communicated and readily available to the college community.				

continued on next page

Element	Constituent Group	Goal	Level 0: Not evident	Level 1: Emerging	Level 2: Proficient	Level 3: Excelling
Decision making	Faculty Multiple constituencies Authenticity of communication?	Faculty governance encourages transparency and regular communication among all parties on every campus. (Need definition or explanation of faculty governance)	Faculty do not have any responsibility regarding decisions made in these areas. All decisions are made by others without input.	Faculty are nominally considered to have responsibility but not primary responsibility. Faculty input is provided but it is not meaningful and decisions are really made by others with only a token show of faculty input.	Faculty are considered to have primary responsibility. Their recommendations are meaningful and respected. All faculty input is provided through established processes and procedures. Any rejection of faculty recommendations in these areas is automatically coupled with a formal explanation of the reasons.	Faculty are considered to have primary responsibility. Their recommendations are meaningful and respected. All faculty input is provided through established processes and procedures. Any rejection of faculty recommendations in these areas is automatically coupled with a formal explanation of the reasons, and, based on periodically assessment of the effectiveness of this engagement, makes improvements to the processes and procedures.

Communication	Communication is accomplished through announcement rather than discussion. Decisions are not communicated at all. Communication doesn't exist or has broken down entirely.	Communication is one-sided rather than interactive. Some communication exists but it isn't clear, consistent or through formal and established channels or lines of reporting.	All communication is open, transparent and interactive in an atmosphere of mutual respect and professionalism. Regular and clear lines of communication and reporting have been established between the different levels and components of the campus. There is an archive kept of all written communication and reports, accessible to everyone. All meetings open to campus members are advertised to attend along with an agenda of items.	Faculty governance ensures that governance issues and actions are shared regularly among all its constituents. Faculty governance is a voting member of the campus president's Cabinet.

Appendix E: Responses to Draft Rubric

Verbatim responses are from SUNY Voices participants in response to the question "What needs further explanation?"

1. What do the following statements mean?
    a. "Board has sufficient independence and expertise to ensure the integrity of the institution."
    b. "President has authority and autonomy to lead the institution free of undue influences."
2. Indicate if rubric items are directly linked to outside regulation or requirements such as NYS, Middle States etc.
3. Are representatives elected?
4. Students: Are they represented within the shared governance structure outside of the Board of Trustees? Are they voting members at College/faculty Senates? Are they elected by students or? appointed by the governing body?
5. There is an inconsistency in the activeness of the constituency group column, i.e., is this the group that controls the outcome or goal, or the one impacted by it? Or should both be included in each one?
    a. Board/President/Administratio0n/Faculty/Staff are provided with sufficient opportunities . . .
    b. Students: There is student representative on Boards. One provides the opportunity, but in the other case is provided the opportunity. Isn't it the responsibility of the Board to make sure students are included, and of students to seek these roles?
6. How does the Board "ensure" the integrity of the institution and that Board members do not interfere in the day-to-day activities of the institution?
7. Change CEO wording to College President.
8. Who will be the audience for this rubric? How will the results be interpreted and used for the future?

In response to the question "What are we missing?"

1. A piece on dialogue, not one-sided communication between shared governance groups.
2. More feedback re: students.
3. We have a stand-alone shared governance policy. This could be incorporated into the structure section on p. 1.
4. Training/orientation for new members of the shared governance process, including representatives and college councils/boards of trustees. This should include how decisions are made at the institution and who is involved.
5. Should there be guidelines for "sufficient number of administrators"?
6. Administration: does the "functional chart" include the organizational chart? How often is this updated?
7. At the Community College level, definitely use "All Faculty" for input.
8. Define the involvement of groups outside the Board, President, and faculty, since this varies campus to campus (e.g., students, professionals and clerical staff).
9. Curriculum needs to be addressed specifically: *is* there a curriculum committee comprised of faculty either elected or appointed by shared governance and does this committee bring curricular matters (courses, programs, etc.) to the Senate to be voted on?
10. Box for college council needs to be added for four-year institutions that have them. The question is whether they are advisory or governing.
11. Do the Faculty assess the Administration; i.e., is this evaluation a two-way street?
12. When the President says there is faculty involvement, are the faculty elected or appointed?
13. Need more regarding student participation in shared governance: voice in all shared governance bodies and student assembly as part of shared governance.

In response to the question "Will what we are doing be helpful? If not, what would be more useful?"

1. Yes.
2. Yes, it is really helping me to think about areas of our structure that are either vaguely defined or not defined at all.
3. Yes, but remove stuff that is not too relevant to faculty governance but more of a Middle States requirement.
4. Yes, but it seems that it could be simplified somehow. This is the longest rubric that I've ever seen!
5. Yes, we were considering applying for the shared governance award but didn't know if what we were doing was "good enough." This would have been great!
6. Yes, I plan to modify this for assessment of our Senate.
7. Yes, the fact that this matrix may become available for future Middle States reviews.
8. Also, possibly eliminate the levels since each "element" may be more open to a different scale with a section for disclosure.
9. Use this rubric to rate each governing constituency back and forth and then have a general session to reflect on the overall rating.

In response to the question "Is your campus doing anything currently to assess the effectiveness of shared governance? If so, what?"

1. Not yet, but we are restructuring shared governance now . . . with plans to begin assessing next year. A SUNY rubric will be a big help.
2. No.
3. No, but it's a good idea.
4. We have a shared governance association group that meets twice per semester and includes the Faculty Senate, the Professional Staff Senate, Graduate Student Organization, and Student Association.

5. No, but we tell Middle States that we do. ☺

6. There is no procedure set on our campus.

7. As Campus Governance Leader (CGL), I review the annual minutes and create a list of open items, address the originating parties of these items, provide this list and request these parties to reply with follow-up and ultimately with resolution.

Open Comments from Written Feedback:

1. For Administration, there should be a section on "are there enough and are they qualified?" There should also be a section on understanding and technological skill.

2. For all constituencies, there should be an opportunity for professional growth, rather than actual utilization of opportunities as there is not an intent to evaluate individuals.

3. For faculty expectations, there needs to be an expectation for a sufficient number of full time faculty, as well as an expectation for service in the area of assessment committees and other assessment related activities.

4. In parts of the rubric indicating "obligations" for faculty, contractual requirements should be considered.

5. For faculty, being aware of campus policies for decision making is contingent on having ready access to them.

6. The Board cannot change policy vetted through shared governance. They may accept or reject.

7. For the faculty goals of primary responsibility for curriculum and instruction, I would like to see the level 2 and 3 to include there is a curriculum committee comprised of faculty, appointed by faculty? College Senate, and reporting to the Senate and shared governance.

8. With regard to Administration, maybe add a category specifically directed to understanding of technology, and realistic expectations of what can and cannot be done to move the campus forward.

9. For use of sufficient resources for professional growth and development, we should be assessing whether the campus provides these opportunities. Evidence of Faculty/Staff participation could be the supporting evidence.

10. Whether or not faculty are "rigorous and effective in teaching, assessment of student learning, scholarly inquiry and service" is covered by the assessment of student learning.

11. Sufficient number of faculty should be included as it is with administration.

Appendix F: Shared Governance and Middle States: Sources in the Standards Moeckel Power Point Presentation at SUNY Voices 2018

From the 2002 Middle States Standards (excerpted)

Standard 4 Leadership and Governance outlined the following expectations:

- a well-defined system of collegial governance including written policies outlining governance responsibilities of administration and faculty and readily available to the campus community;
- appropriate opportunity for student input regarding decisions that affect them;
- periodic assessment of the effectiveness of institutional leadership and governance;
- written governing documents, such as a constitution, bylaws, enabling legislation, charter or other similar documents, that:
  - delineate the governance structure and provide for collegial governance, and the structure's composition, duties and responsibilities.
  - assign authority and accountability for policy development and decision making, including a process for the involvement of appropriate institutional constituencies in policy development and decision making.

From the 2015 Standards (excerpted), the following expectations are outlined:

Standard 7 Governance Leadership and Administration

- A clearly articulated and transparent governance structure that outlines roles, responsibilities, and accountability for decision making by each constituency, including governing body, administration, faculty, staff and students.
- Periodic assessment of the effectiveness of governance, leadership, and administration.

Comment:

- New standards are less precise.
- Old standards provide additional context about expectations.
- Neither is prescriptive about models of shared governance, although sometimes the reference to governance is not clear as to whether it is the Board or the shared governance structure which is being referenced.
- Both contain additional information regarding responsibilities of the governing board and the Chief Executive Officer.
- Both contain an expectation that assessment of governance will take place.

Implications for shared governance are present throughout the remainder of the current standards, excerpts of which follow.

Standard 1: Mission and Goals

An accredited institution possesses and demonstrates the following attributes or activities:

Clearly defined mission and goals that:

- are developed through appropriate collaborative participation by all who facilitate or are otherwise responsible for institutional development and improvement;

- guide faculty, administration, staff, and
- governing structures in making decisions related to planning, resource allocation, program and curricular development, and the definition of institutional and educational outcomes;
- include
  - support of scholarly inquiry and creative activity, at levels and of the type appropriate to the institution;
  - goals that focus on student learning and related outcomes and on institutional improvement; are supported by administrative, educational, and student support programs and services; and are consistent with institutional mission; and
  - periodic assessment of mission and goals to ensure they are relevant and achievable.

Comment:

There is an expectation for appropriate participation in the development and review of mission and goals, particularly in areas related to student learning.

Standard 2: Ethics and Integrity

An accredited institution possesses and demonstrates the following attributes or activities:

- a commitment to academic freedom, intellectual freedom, freedom of expression, and respect for intellectual property rights;
- a climate that fosters respect among students, faculty, staff, and administration from a range of diverse backgrounds, ideas, and perspectives;
- honesty and truthfulness in public relations announcements, advertisements, recruiting and admissions materials and practices, as well as in internal communications;
- compliance with all applicable federal, state, and Commission reporting policies . . . ;

- the full disclosure of information on institution-wide assessments, graduation, retention, certification and licensure or licensing board pass rates;
- periodic assessment of ethics and integrity as evidenced in institutional policies, processes, practices, and the manner in which these are implemented.

Comment:

- Academic freedom, respect, truthfulness in communications, and transparency in reporting are integral components of Ethics and Integrity.
- Regular assessment of these is expected.

Standard 3: Design and Delivery of the Student Learning Experience

An accredited institution possesses and demonstrates the following attributes or activities:

- Certificate, undergraduate, graduate, and/or professional programs leading to a degree or other recognized higher education credential, of a length appropriate to the objectives of the degree or other credential, designed to foster a coherent student learning experience and to promote synthesis of learning;
- student learning experiences that are designed, delivered, and assessed by faculty (full-time or part-time) and/or other appropriate professionals who are:
  - rigorous and effective in teaching, assessment of student learning, scholarly inquiry, and service, as appropriate to the institution's mission, goals, and policies;
  - qualified for the positions they hold and the work they do;
  - sufficient in number;
  - provided with and utilize sufficient opportunities, resources, and support for professional growth and innovation;

- reviewed regularly and equitably based on written, disseminated, clear, and fair criteria, expectations, policies, and procedures;
- sufficient learning opportunities and resources to support both the institution's programs of study and students' academic progress;
- at institutions that offer undergraduate education, a general education program, free standing or integrated into academic disciplines, that:
  - offers a sufficient scope to draw students into new areas of intellectual experience, expanding their cultural and global awareness and cultural sensitivity, and preparing them to make well-reasoned judgments outside as well as within their academic field;
  - offers a curriculum designed so that students acquire and demonstrate essential skills including at least oral and written communication, scientific and quantitative reasoning, critical analysis and reasoning, technological competency, and information literacy. Consistent with mission, the general education program also includes the study of values, ethics, and diverse perspectives;

Comment:

- This standard perhaps more than any other is quintessentially about faculty. There are both governance and labor implications; however, faculty involvement and ownership is essential to meeting the criteria of this standard.
- Regular assessment is expected.

Standard 4: Support of the Student Experience

An accredited institution possesses and demonstrates the following attributes or activities:

- clearly stated, ethical policies and processes to admit, retain, and facilitate the success of students whose interests, abilities, experiences, and goals provide a reasonable expectation for success and are compatible with institutional mission, including:

- a process by which students who are not adequately prepared for study at the level for which they have been admitted are identified, placed, and supported in attaining appropriate educational goals;
- orientation, advisement, and counseling programs to enhance retention and guide students throughout their educational experience;
- processes designed to enhance the successful achievement of students' educational goals including certificate and degree completion, transfer to other institutions, and post-completion placement;
- policies and procedures regarding evaluation and acceptance of transfer credits, and credits awarded through experiential learning, prior non-academic learning, competency-based assessment, and other alternative learning approaches;

Comment:

- Remediation/developmental education, advisement, transfer, placement, evaluation of credit, policies which promote student success and provide for due process are all aspects of standard.
- Regular assessment is expected.

Standard 5: Educational Effectiveness Assessment

An accredited institution possesses and demonstrates the following attributes or activities:

- clearly stated educational goals at the institution and degree/program levels which are interrelated with one another, with relevant educational experiences, and with the institution's mission.
- organized and systematic assessments, conducted by faculty and/or appropriate professionals, evaluating the extent of student

achievement of institutional and degree/program goals. Institutions should:

- define meaningful curricular goals with defensible standards for evaluating whether students are achieving those goals.

Comment:

- Assessment of educational effectiveness is inherently owned by faculty.
- Assessment of the assessment process is expected.

Standard 6: Planning, Resources and Institutional Improvement

An accredited institution possesses and demonstrates the following attributes or activities:

- institutional objectives, both institution-wide and for individual units, that are clearly stated, assessed appropriately, linked to mission and goal achievement, reflect conclusions drawn from assessment results, and are used for planning and resource allocation;
- clearly documented and communicated planning and improvement processes that provide for constituent participation, and incorporate the use of assessment results;
- fiscal and human resources as well as the physical and technical infrastructure adequate to support its operations wherever and however programs are delivered;
- well-defined decision-making processes and clear assignment of responsibility and accountability;
- periodic assessment of the effectiveness of planning, resource allocation, institutional renewal processes, and availability of resources.

Comment:

- Planning, resource allocation, and decision making based on assessment results, as well as participation of relevant constituencies is an integral part of this standard.
- Regular assessment is expected.

Summary

- Although Middle States is not prescriptive about models of shared governance, the standards provide considerable guidance for determining its effectiveness, as well as guidance for the types of elements for which inclusion of shared governance processes would be appropriate.
- All of the standards include implications for shared governance.
- The SCoA draft rubric was initially based on Standard 4 of the 2002 standards and included the criteria for this standard. The above analysis could provide a more meaningful basis for rubric development going forward.

8

Back to the Past

Imagining the Future of Academic Governance

Michael DeCesare

Taking the AAUP's 1966 Statement on Government of Colleges and Universities *as a starting point, this chapter examines current challenges to traditional academic governance. Specifically, it explores political interference, structural and economic factors, and cultural shifts. After presenting recent cautionary tales of breakdowns in institutional governance, the chapter offers suggestions for strengthening academic governance and, in the process, returning to the model outlined in the 1966 Statement.*

One of the most significant shifts in US higher education in recent decades has been in the government of colleges and universities. Attempts to implement new managerial approaches go back at least a century, but as Gerber points out in his definitive history of faculty governance, "the early 1970s marked a turning point in the scope and magnitude of such efforts" (2014, pp. 121–22). Nearly 50 years later, board members and administrators—and increasingly state legislators and governors—are demanding that institutions of higher learning be run with a business-like efficiency. "Priority alignment," "strategic planning," and "measurable outcomes" are among the catchphrases of the day.

What Is Traditional Academic Governance?

At the same time, many board members and presidents take every opportunity to profess their belief in what has come to be called shared governance. Roughly, this is the idea that an institution's components—especially the governing board, administration, and faculty—must work together to advance the educational mission. I say "roughly" because there is little consensus about what shared governance means in practice (AGB, 2017b, p. 4), nor who must be included for it to be truly "shared."

I prefer the traditional term *academic governance* to *shared governance*, partly because it has been much more clearly conceptualized and operationalized. In fact, there is a definitive statement on academic government: the 1966 *Statement on Government of Colleges and Universities*, which the American Association of University Professors (AAUP) jointly formulated with the American Council on Education (ACE) and the Association of Governing Boards of Universities and Colleges (AGB). More than 50 years after its endorsement by the AAUP and its commendation by the ACE and the AGB to their member institutions, the statement remains the AAUP's central policy document on academic governance. It is the cornerstone of countless institutions' governance structures, including SUNY's University Faculty Senate. The principles and standards it outlines constitute traditional academic governance.

One central principle is this: "The variety and complexity of the tasks performed by institutions of higher education produce an *inescapable interdependence* among governing board, administration, faculty, students, and others. The relationship calls for *adequate communication* among these components, and full opportunity for *appropriate joint planning and effort*" (AAUP, 2015b, p. 118, emphasis added). An inescapable interdependence, adequate communication, appropriate joint planning and effort—these, along with shared responsibility, constitute the foundation of traditional academic governance.

The statement elaborates specifically on joint effort among the institution's components and points out that it will naturally take various forms: "In some instances," for example, "an initial exploration or recommendation will be made by the president with consideration by the faculty at a later stage; in other instances, a first and essentially definitive recommendation will be made by the faculty, subject to the endorsement of the president and the governing board. In still others, a substantive contribution can be made when student leaders are responsibly involved in the process." No matter what forms the joint effort takes, the statement instructs that "important areas of action involve at one time or another the initiating capacity and decision-making participation of all the institutional components, and differences in the weight of each voice, from one point to the next, should be determined by reference to the responsibility of each component for the particular matter at hand" (AAUP, 2015b, p.

118). In emphasizing the "differences in the weight of each voice," the statement introduces a model that offers the opportunity for dialogue, rather than a monologue of pronouncements from the group with the highest rank in the decision-making process.

The rest of the statement outlines the respective roles and primary responsibilities of the governing board, the president, and the faculty. The board's special obligations include relating the institution to its chief community, ensuring the codification of institutional policies and procedures, obtaining capital and operating funds, and operating as the final institutional authority. Although the board maintains a general overview, it "entrusts the conduct of administration to the administrative officers . . . and the conduct of teaching and research to the faculty." As such, the statement also warns that "the board should undertake appropriate self-limitation" (AAUP, 2015b, p. 120).

The college president has special obligations, such as representing the institution to its many publics. The president is responsible for "see[ing] to it that the standards and procedures in operational use . . . conform to the policy established by the governing board and to the standards of sound academic practice. It is also incumbent on the president to ensure that faculty views, including dissenting views, are presented to the board in those areas and on those issues where responsibilities are shared." Generally the president's role is "to plan, to organize, to direct, and to represent" the institution (AAUP, 2015b, p. 120).

The faculty's areas of primacy are too numerous to list here, but it is well worth noting several: "curriculum, subject matter and methods of instruction, research, faculty status, and those aspects of student life which relate to the educational process." On these matters, in particular, the statement notes "the power of review or final decision lodged in the governing board or delegated by it to the president should be exercised adversely only in exceptional circumstances, and for reasons communicated to the faculty," and "the faculty should, following such communication, have opportunity for further consideration and further transmittal of its views to the president or board." The faculty also "should actively participate in the determination of policies and procedures governing salary increases." This is perhaps even more important on nonunionized campuses, where the protections of a collective bargaining unit (i.e., a negotiated contract regarding salary, benefits, and arbitration) are absent. Finally, it is important to highlight the faculty's role in institutional government: "Agencies for faculty participation in the government of the college or university should be established at each level where faculty responsibility is present. An agency should exist for the presentation of the views of the whole faculty" (AAUP, 2015b, pp. 120–21).

I refer to all of this as *traditional academic governance*. This is what has been under attack.

Structural Threats

As a sociologist by training, I tend to focus on structural forces and cultural shifts rather than individual actors when I reflect on threats to academic governance—although I certainly do not ignore the reality that there are some bad actors out there. It's just that we can't fully understand an individual's thinking and behavior without understanding the broader contexts in which they occur.

Structurally, what are we facing? Generally speaking, fewer board members and presidents seem to believe in or even understand joint effort, seeking instead to escape whenever possible from their "inescapable interdependence" with the faculty (see Cowen, 2018, who misunderstands fundamental aspects of traditional academic governance). This approach makes sense to board members—and an increasing number of presidents—who come from the corporate world and are accustomed to primary goals of increasing organizational efficiency and maximizing profit. Even presidents and boards at public institutions are concerned with balancing budgets and increasing endowments, so "profit"—although differently defined—has resonance throughout institutions of higher education. There is little time or space in that world for discussion, deliberation, and debate. There is even less time and space for dissent. Bosses simply make the decisions and instruct the workers to execute them. With its commitment to dialogue and attentiveness to multiple components (e.g., board, administration, faculty), academia must seem like an alternate universe to them.

This should in no way be understood as an apology or excuse for board members' overreach or administrators' encroachment into areas of faculty primacy. For there was no excuse for what happened with the University of Iowa's 2015 presidential search, which was, according to the report of the AAUP's investigating committee, "structured and engineered by the regents' leadership from the outset to identify a figure from the business world congenial to its image of 'transformative leadership.' Once such a person was identified, the rest of what followed was only an illusion of an open, honest search" (AAUP, 2016d, p. 63). There was also no excuse for the president of New Jersey's Union County College unilaterally eviscerating the faculty governance structure or for the University of Missouri board firing Melissa Click from her tenure-track position, both of which happened in 2015 (see AAUP 2015b, 2016c).

Obviously, board overreach and administrative encroachment represent structural threats to traditional academic governance. There are several other structural factors at work as well: shamefully low levels of state funding for public universities, administrations' blissful overreliance on non-tenure-track faculty, the growing insistence that faculty use academic technology in conducting their courses, and administrative bloat. These trends have been well documented in a number of recent books and articles in the AAUP's *Journal of Academic Freedom* and *Academe* magazine.

Cultural Shifts

My primary focus here is on the cultural changes that threaten traditional academic governance. Perhaps the most significant is the growing public belief that the sole purpose of higher education should be job training. If faculty are to impart the habits of mind necessary for citizens to participate in a democracy, we need a central role in the governance of our institutions. But if we are to simply train obedient workers to participate in a ruthless labor market, we do not.

The public equating of "higher learning" with vocational training has manifested itself in any number of ways. On campus, for example, we have been witnessing a growing insistence on providing students with experiential learning opportunities as part of the subject matter curriculum. This insistence is a natural outgrowth of the establishment and expansion of career development centers and the job fairs, panels, on-campus interviews, and professional development opportunities they sponsor for students. Although some of these features have long been present on many campuses, their recent growth has been rapid.

My institution, Merrimack College, has the O'Brien Center for Career Development, which is responsible for "expanding students' horizons while educating and inspiring them to make informed career decisions; providing access to experiential learning and full-time employment opportunities; and linking employers to campus resources" (O'Brien Center for Career Development, 2017). Regarding the last responsibility, the center's website has a link specifically for employers; it takes visiting employers to six links tailored just for them: post a job/experiential learning opportunity, employer resources, career events, on-campus interviews, additional branding opportunities, and finally, become our partner, which promises "to help [the employer] meet your recruiting goals" (Become our partner, 2017).

The page devoted to additional branding opportunities begins: "At the O'Brien Center for Career Development, our goal is to provide employers value-added services that streamline your recruiting efforts. We rely on the support of employers like you to help fulfill these initiatives, and to provide your company or organization with access to top Merrimack College talent" (Additional branding opportunities, 2017). Aside from the mention of the institution's name, one would have no idea from that description that the center resides on a college campus.

Employers who visit the page are asked to consider participating in some initiatives as they "look to attract new talent." These include employer panel discussions, an employer in residence program, industry-specific fairs, and internship, externship, and co-op experiences. The final one is "ask an employer," which provides "direct contact to Merrimack talent in an informal setting. Build your organizational brand on campus while also providing career advice to students" (Additional branding opportunities, 2017).

Merrimack College is not unique. Virtually every college and university has something equivalent to the O'Brien Center—something that trains students for the labor market. The public's belief that colleges and universities should be preparing and developing not intellectually mature, inquisitive, and critically minded students but good workers, led to the rise of campus career development centers and their various initiatives. In a sort of society-level feedback loop, these centers have legitimized and enhanced the belief that college should be primarily—if not solely—about training future employees.[1]

Politicians have picked up on this and are posing their own threats to traditional academic governance. As of this writing, these have recently manifested as political litmus tests for hiring faculty, bills in two states to eliminate tenure, and, in Kentucky, the governor's unilateral abolition and reconstitution of a state university's board of trustees. Political interference in academia has reached the point where it is frighteningly easy to imagine President Donald Trump himself meddling in an institution's governance, perhaps by tweeting at faculty who displease him, "You're fired!!!"

Another significant but less visible cultural shift can be found if we look closely at the language we use. To return to the beginning of this chapter, I deliberately use the terms *academic governance* and *institutional governance* rather than *shared governance*. The AAUP's 1966 statement does not use the term *shared governance*; it refers instead to academic government and institutional governance. Yet shared governance somehow became the preferred term. It is not clear when or how this happened, but it seems that faculty lost a great deal with that tacit substitution, for *shared* could suggest that administrators and trustees are entitled to a share in all decisions, perhaps including those in areas of faculty primacy.

Indeed, administrators are often the most vocal in claiming that they support shared governance. But if you listen closely to what they say and carefully read what they write, you realize they are often not talking about traditional academic governance. Many times, they offer alternative definitions.

One example is a brief 2014 book written by Augustana College president Steven Bahls. *Shared Governance in Times of Change* outlines three traditional—and misguided—approaches to shared governance held by board members and presidents: shared governance as equal rights, as consultation, and as rules of engagement. None of these are consistent with the principles outlined in the AAUP's 1966 statement. The statement does not assign equal rights or an equal voice to each institutional component. Its principles do not include mere consultation. So-called "rules of engagement" also don't constitute academic governance, as the preface to the statement makes clear: "It is not intended that the statement serve as a blueprint for governance on a specific campus or as a manual for the regulation of controversy among the components of an academic institution" (AAUP, 2015b, p. 117).

Bahls's formulation of academic governance—as a "system of aligning priorities"—is just as wide of the mark as the traditional three he rightly criticizes. "Boards, presidents, and the faculty," he asserts, "must get beyond a rulebook and develop an approach that truly aligns priorities, measures outcomes, and holds each other accountable" (2014, p. 26). From this perspective, an approach to governance is needed "in which faculty, board members, and administrators actively engage to share responsibility for identifying and pursuing an aligned set of mission-driven sustainable outcomes and priorities" (Bahls, 2014, p. 27). This is not traditional academic governance. Instead, it appears to mean shared governance in the sense that the board, administration, and faculty desire institutional outcomes and priorities. It is concerning, therefore, that a 2016 AGB report titled "Shared Governance: Is OK Good Enough?" indicated that nearly 60 percent of presidents and board members favor this new "aligning priorities" definition of academic governance.

Equally concerning is a 2017 AGB white paper, "Shared Governance: Changing with the Times," that continues the narrative about the supposed need to redefine academic governance. The introduction says: "While AGB agrees that the AAUP's 'Statement on Government of Colleges and Universities' remains an important touchpoint more than 50 years after its creation, it is important to understand the ways in which shared governance is practiced today" (AGB, 2017b, p. 3). The insinuation is clear: while the 1966 statement is still a "touchpoint," it is limited in its ability to speak to "shared" governance as it is practiced today. Bahls made this point explicitly in his book: "In today's world of transformative change," he wrote, "[the Statement] does [not] foster effective and efficient practices that are necessary for aligning the board, faculty, and administration around priorities that will propel the institution forward" (2014, p. 42).

Where does the statement supposedly fall short? The AGB claims that participants in its focus groups—or what it called "listening sessions"—pointed to three concerns about the statement's relevance today. First, although it mentions student participation in governance, "it does not provide much guidance for dealing with contemporary student demands for a greater role in institutional decision making." Second, "the statement has nothing to say about the role of staff." Third, it "does not address the significant presence of contingent faculty in our colleges and universities" (AGB, 2017b, p. 8).

I do not share these concerns. Giving students and staff a role in institutional decision making is not necessarily dictated by the principles of academic governance; it is, however, dictated by a system of shared governance in which the primary purpose is to "break down silos" and give all "constituents" a "seat at the table"—a share in the process. The third complaint, that the statement does not address non-tenure-track faculty's role in governance, strikes me as more serious. However, as the AGB report itself points out, the matter was "noted in separate AAUP guidance"; that is, in subsequent policy statements (AGB, 2017b, p. 8). Such derivative statements were necessary as the ranks of non-tenure-track faculty swelled in the decades after the publication of the 1966 statement.[2]

As I mentioned, I do not share any of the three concerns laid out in the AGB's 2017 white paper.[3] I do not share the perception that the 1966 statement is analogous to a black-and-white television: a quaint but largely useless artifact of a bygone era. Quite the contrary: I believe the statement is more important than ever. If it is perceived to be irrelevant, it is because faculty have not adequately enforced it, publicized it, discussed it, and insisted that our institutions follow it. Furthermore, we allow redefinitions of traditional academic governance to begin taking hold by sometimes misusing the term *shared governance*.

This is not to suggest that simply changing the words we use will immediately halt the erosion of the faculty's traditional role in academic government. Rather, it is to remind us that language has a deceptively powerful ability to shape—and reshape—our reality, to transform what we perceive and how we think and act.[4] Moving the discussion from shared governance back to academic governance will hopefully begin to return us to the traditional model outlined in the 1966 statement.

Academic Governance and Academic Freedom

The return to the traditional model has implications for academic freedom because violations of it almost always are precipitated by or occur at the same time as governance violations. This was a point that the AAUP suggested nearly 25 years ago. The association's 1994 statement, "On the Relationship of Faculty Governance to Academic Freedom," asserts that "sound governance practice and the exercise of academic freedom are closely connected, arguably inextricably linked" (AAUP, 2015a, p. 125) and that "a sound system of institutional governance is a necessary condition for the protection of faculty rights and thereby for the most productive exercise of essential faculty freedoms" (AAUP, 2015a, p. 123).

One reason the statement offers for why the faculty's voice should be authoritative in its areas of primacy is that this is "a necessary condition for the protection of academic freedom within the institution" (AAUP, 2015a, p. 124). This is particularly important when it comes to authority over faculty status. For "it is the faculty—not trustees or administrators—who have the experience needed for assessing whether an instance of faculty speech constitutes a breach of a central principle of academic morality, and who have the expertise to form judgments of faculty competence or incompetence" (AAUP, 2015a, p. 125). Whenever such decisions are not in the hands of the faculty, there will be not only the potential for board and administrative overreach but the actuality of it.

Evidence of this can be seen in the recent high-profile cases of Steven Salaita at the University of Illinois Urbana-Champaign and Melissa Click at the University of Missouri. Two more examples come from the College of Saint Rose in New York and Spalding University in Kentucky. In late 2015, the president of the College of Saint Rose announced the summary dismissal of nearly two dozen tenured and tenure-track faculty as part of something called a "strategic academic program prioritization process." That action resulted in an AAUP investigation, the report from which concluded (among other things) that the administration and board had created governance conditions that could only be described as deplorable and had rendered tenure virtually meaningless, thereby severely undermining academic freedom at the institution (AAUP, 2016a). The college was subsequently censured by the AAUP's 2016 annual meeting. During the fall 2016 semester, a tenured full professor with 18 years of service to Spalding University was summarily dismissed by the administration. The report of the investigating committee points out the utter lack of due process and violations of academic freedom and tenure that characterized the case. The report also argues that academic governance cannot—indeed, does not—function at an institution at which the president can unilaterally fire a tenured full professor without formally stated cause. It concludes that the future of governance at Spalding is bleak (AAUP, 2017).

Countering the Threats

What strategies and tactics might faculty use to fight these threats and effect a return to the traditional principles of academic government?

Sporadic, individual activism will not be able to counter the structural and cultural trends outlined above. As sociologist Allan Johnson (2008) points out, individual solutions cannot solve social problems. Only collective action can. First, we must take every opportunity to emphasize, promote, and make visible the 1966 statement. Organize events around it. Provide administrators with copies of it. Incorporate it into your faculty handbooks if it isn't there already. In so doing, faculty will become better informed about their responsibilities in academic governance. They will also become attuned to subtle linguistic shifts and might become engaged in active and open resistance of the multiplying alternative conceptualizations of academic governance.

Widespread understanding of the statement is crucial, as recent controversial presidential searches suggest. At Kentucky State University in 2016, the faculty objected that the popular interim president was not among the finalists. The ultimate result was the faculty passing a vote of no confidence in the board. According to an article in the *Chronicle of Higher Education* "The situation at Kentucky State reflected broader anxiety in higher education about how much shared governance extends to the picking of presidents" (Harris, 2017). It is difficult to understand why there would be any confusion, let alone anxiety, over "how much shared governance extends to the picking of presidents." As it is on so many other subjects, the AAUP statement is quite clear about the principles that should underlie a search for a president: "Joint effort of a most critical kind must be taken when an institution chooses a new president. The selection of a chief administrative officer should follow upon a cooperative search by the governing board and the faculty, taking into consideration the opinions of others who are appropriately interested" (AAUP, 2015b, p. 119).

There was just one faculty person on Kentucky State's nine-member presidential search committee. The faculty's written request to the board for greater representation was denied. This hardly qualifies as a "cooperative search by the governing board and the faculty." It is worth noting that the Kentucky State search came on the heels of the controversial presidential appointment at Kennesaw State University in 2016. In that case, the university system's board of regents didn't even bother to appoint a search committee. Without any faculty involvement—let alone a "cooperative search"—the board simply appointed Georgia's attorney general as the new president (Pieper 2017).

This section of the 1966 statement continues: "The president should be equally qualified to serve both as the executive officer of the governing board and as the chief academic officer of the institution and the faculty" (AAUP, 2015b, p. 119). At least the Kentucky State search resulted in an appointee who had prior academic-administrative experience. The appointee at Kennesaw State had no experience working in higher education; likewise, the controversial 2015 appointee at the University of Iowa had never held an academic-administrative position (Pieper, 2017; AAUP, 2016d). Based on these facts alone, neither candidate was qualified to serve as "the chief academic officer of the institution and the faculty."

Finally, the statement says that "the president should have the confidence of the board and the faculty" (AAUP, 2015b, p. 119). At Iowa and Kennesaw State, the president arrived without the confidence of the faculty. It is not clear, at the time of this writing, whether that has also proven to be the case at Kentucky State.

Even a limited understanding of the 1966 governance statement leads to the inevitable conclusion that normative principles of academic governance were compromised in the presidential appointments at Kennesaw State, Iowa, and Kentucky State. That is ammunition that faculty can and must use to object to these kinds of searches at the outset. Without understanding what's in the statement, we don't have that ammunition—or an understanding of the limitations and shortcomings of our own institution's regulations.

Every sociologist knows the Thomas theorem: when people define situations as real, they become real in their consequences. If faculty allow academic governance to be redefined in ways that negate or minimize faculty strength, we face the very real consequence of a weaker faculty voice. Eventually, it will fall silent. On the other hand, if we define academic government on our terms and advocate that definition, the consequence will be a stronger faculty voice, one that is consonant with our special status in our institutions. As members of a profession, this will be one of our primary tasks over the next 50 years. We must undertake it everywhere and in every way we can: in working with our institutions' boards and administrations, to be sure, and in working with our faculty colleagues; in the classroom with our students—perhaps especially those in our doctoral programs who will one day be faculty members; and in the public domain.

Another task is to build sound governance systems at institutions where they don't yet exist and strengthen them where they do. We would do well to keep in mind, though, that a good governance system does not guarantee good governance practices. Those practices depend on us, as the statement on the relationship between governance and academic freedom warns: "A governance system is merely a structure that allocates authority, and authority needs to be exercised if even the most appropriate allocation of it is to have its intended effects." Therefore, "faculty members must be willing to participate in the decision-making processes over which a sound governance system gives them authority. . . . If they do not, authority will drift away from them, since someone must exercise it, and if members of the faculty do not, others will" (AAUP, 2015a, p. 125).

What this points to is the need, when it comes to academic governance, for faculty to collectively go on offense instead of playing defense all the time. The SUNY Voices initiative is a good example of such an approach to institutionalizing faculty governance (Tamrowski et al., 2017). We must also realize that local activism, and even state-wide activism, may not be enough. Faculty must be willing to publicly call out a board, a president, a chancellor, a provost—and even a governor or state legislators—on bad behavior. These parties all have a common fear: negative press. Faculty should play on that fear when necessary. Especially in the age of social media, doing so can be a quick and effective strategy. Scholars of social movements learned a great deal from the Arab Spring of the early 2010s, including just how effective activists can be in using social media for the purposes of getting their message out, mobilizing themselves, and publicizing objectionable actions by their opponents. Why should faculty not use the same techniques?

We have allies. One ally group is students, who are fed up with exorbitant tuition, ballooning debt, and campus injustice. Accrediting bodies are potentially another ally. In one sense, it was encouraging that the Southern Association of Colleges and Schools (SACS) saw fit to put the University of Louisville on probation in 2016 because of Governor Matt Bevin's unilateral action in abolishing and then reconstituting the board of trustees (Jarosi & Kolers, 2017). Perhaps SACS's decision will encourage other regional accrediting agencies to sanction institutions that blatantly disregard normative governance principals.

Faculty will bear the heaviest burden going forward. If we fail to do the work required by academic governance, our role in it will slowly but surely disappear. If we allow academic governance to be redefined, our role in it will slowly but surely disappear. And if we watch quietly as boards overreach and administrators encroach into areas of faculty primacy, our role will slowly but surely disappear. Then we will have lost everything: due process, what remains of tenure, our academic freedom, and ultimately our special, professional, and central place within this country's institutions of higher education.

Even after more than 50 years, the AAUP's *Statement on Government of Colleges and Universities* remains the starting point for faculty-led efforts to counter threats to traditional academic governance. Collective action and political activism will be our most effective tools over the next 50 years.

Notes

This chapter is based on the author's keynote address at the 2017 SUNY Voices Shared Governance conference. A preliminary version appeared as DeCesare (2017).

1. Although such initiatives are typically part of MBA programs and law schools, to take just two examples, I find their recent shift to the undergraduate level troubling.
2. See Monnier (2017) for thoughtful reflections on the role of non-tenure-track faculty in academic governance.

3. Interestingly, a subsequent statement on shared governance by the AGB's board of directors highlighted the continuing significance of the 1966 statement, noting that "specific reference" to it "in the institution's governing documents is an important foundation" for the institutional commitment to shared governance (AGB, 2017a, p. 12).
4. For a discussion of the ramifications of using the term *service* to refer to governance-related faculty work, see Jafar, Feldman, and Chrisler (2017).

References

Additional branding opportunities. (2017). *Merrimack College*. Retrieved July 1, 2017, from http://www.merrimack.edu/obrien-center/increase-visibility.php.

American Association of University Professors (AAUP). (2015a). On the relationship of faculty governance to academic freedom. In *Policy Documents and Reports*, 11th ed. (pp. 123–25). Baltimore, MD: Johns Hopkins University Press.

American Association of University Professors (AAUP). (2015b). Statement on government of colleges and universities. In *Policy Documents and Reports*, 11th ed. (pp. 117–22). Baltimore, MD: Johns Hopkins University Press.

American Association of University Professors (AAUP). (2016a). Academic freedom and tenure: The College of Saint Rose (New York). *Bulletin of the AAUP, 102*, 8–24.

American Association of University Professors (AAUP). (2016b). Academic freedom and tenure: University of Missouri (Columbia). *Bulletin of the AAUP, 102*, 25–43.

American Association of University Professors (AAUP). (2016c). College and university governance: Union County College (New Jersey). *Bulletin of the AAUP, 102*, 44–51.

American Association of University Professors (AAUP). (2016d). College and university governance: The University of Iowa Governing Board's selection of a president. *Bulletin of the AAUP, 102*, 52–68.

American Association of University Professors (AAUP). (2017). Academic freedom and tenure: Spalding University (Kentucky). *Bulletin of the AAUP, 103*. https://www.aaup.org/file/Spalding.pdf.

Association of Governing Boards of Universities and Colleges (AGB). (2016). *Shared governance: Is OK good enough?* Washington, DC: AGB.

Association of Governing Boards of Universities and Colleges (AGB). (2017a). *AGB Board of Directors' statement on shared governance*. Washington, DC: AGB.

Association of Governing Boards of Universities and Colleges (AGB). (2017b). *Shared governance: Changing with the times*. Washington, DC: AGB.

Bahls, S. C. (2014). *Shared governance in times of change: A practical guide for universities and colleges*. Washington, DC: AGB.
Become our partner. (2017). *Merrimack College*. Retrieved July 1, 2017, from http://www.merrimack.edu/obrien-center/employers/become-our-partner/.
Cowen, S. (2018, Aug. 13). Shared governance does not mean shared decision making. *Chronicle of Higher Education*. https://www.chronicle.com/article/Shared-Governance-Does-Not/244257.
DeCesare, M. (2017). Reaffirming the principles of academic government. *Academe, 103*(1). https://www.aaup.org/article/reaffirming-principles-academic-government.
Gerber, L. G. (2014). *The rise and decline of faculty governance: Professionalization and the modern American university*. Baltimore, MD: Johns Hopkins University Press.
Harris, A. (2017, March 6). Presidential search has faculty members fuming at Kentucky State. *Chronicle of Higher Education*. http://www.chronicle.com/article/Presidential-Search-Has/239411.
Jafar, A., Feldman, S., & Chrisler, J. C. (2017). Hang together or hang separately. *Academe, 103*(3),15–19.
Jarosi, S., & Kolers, A. (2017). Louisville, slugged. *Academe, 103*(3), 10–14.
Johnson, A. G. (2008). *The forest and the trees: Sociology as life, practice, and promise*. Philadelphia, PA: Temple University Press.
Monnier, N. (2017). "One faculty and academic governance. *Academe, 103*(3), 25–28.
O'Brien Center for Career Development. *Merrimack College*. Retrieved July 1, 2017, from http://www.merrimack.edu/obrien-center/.
Pieper, A. (2017). Weathering a presidential pseudo-search. *Academe, 103*(3), 29–32.
Tamrowski, N., Good, T., Knuepfer, P., & O'Brien, K. (2017). SUNY Voices. *Academe 103*(3), https://www.aaup.org/article/suny-voices.

Part IV

Lessons Learned

9

Chancellor Nancy Zimpher and SUNY's Shared Governance

Kenneth P. O'Brien

This chapter recalls the early years of Nancy Zimpher's tenure as SUNY's 12th chancellor, with special focus on the changes she initiated to the shared governance practices. By concentrating on three crucial issues—the development of a strategic planning process, the rocky road to increased funding, and the creation and implementation of a system of seamless transfer across SUNY's 64 campuses—the chapter tells an inside story of dramatic changes the chancellor initiated during her first four years (2009–2013). The author, an academic historian of US higher education, served as president of the SUNY University Faculty Senate during these years.

Assessing Nancy Zimpher's tenure as SUNY's 12th chancellor is both professional and personal for me. This chapter allows me to share my recollections of the chancellor's first four years with SUNY, the years I served as president of the University Faculty Senate (UFS). As a historian (of SUNY), I know it is too early for a full scholarly assessment of Zimpher's accomplishments, but my professional training and direct experience together offer the basis for an interesting preliminary judgment on her service. For the purposes of this volume, I focus on the changes the chancellor brought to SUNY's traditional system of shared governance.

To paraphrase Charles Dickens's *A Tale of Two Cities*, my years as UFS president were "the best of times" and "the worst of times." The "worst" because at the beginning (June 2009), when Chancellor Zimpher assumed the responsibility of leading SUNY, it was a deeply troubled system. The "best"? June 2009 marks the beginning of the tenure of

SUNY's most effective chancellor in decades. In support of her vision, she assembled an administrative team committed to making shared governance work.

In February 2009, SUNY announced Zimpher's appointment as chancellor. She had been serving as the president of the University of Cincinnati (2003–2009), her second presidency of a major Midwestern public university. A distinguished scholar of education and educator preparation, she had extensive experience in public higher education and academic administration, rising through the faculty ranks at The Ohio State University to chair a department and then become dean of the School of Education. In addition to her record of scholarship and administration, she brought an abiding commitment to public higher education, especially when it addressed intractable societal problems. For example, she had been instrumental in organizing StriveTogether, first in Milwaukee and later in Cincinnati. By 2009 it had grown into a nation-wide series of campus–community coalitions dedicated to bringing together all interested and relevant parties in a region to improve the educational outcomes for its preK–20 students, especially those of the inner cities. StriveTogether worked to better prepare the students for success in either college or work.

Several years before the announcement of Zimpher's appointment, two colleagues (W. Bruce Leslie, a distinguished SUNY service professor, and John Clark, the interim SUNY chancellor at the time and now president of Western Connecticut University) and I began organizing a two-day conference to examine the history of the State University of New York, which since its founding in 1948 had grown into the nation's largest comprehensive public university system. Today's SUNY encompasses 64 campuses: 30 community colleges, 5 colleges of technology, 5 contract colleges, 3 specialized colleges, 12 master's level comprehensive colleges, 4 academic medical centers (3 with teaching hospitals), and 5 doctoral institutions, 2 of which are members of the Association of American Universities.

Our conference, SUNY at Sixty, took place two months after the board announced Zimpher's appointment, and the conference was designed to explore SUNY's relatively unknown yet remarkable history. It attracted over 100 participants, including nationally recognized scholars of higher education, former SUNY chancellors, and professors and professional staff from across the system that with their varied experiences and expertise reflected the complexity of SUNY itself. Throughout the conference, Zimpher (then a designee, because her term did not start until June 1) was running from one of the 20 panels to the next, taking over 20 pages of notes on yellow legal pads. In addition to providing her with a deeper understanding of SUNY's unique history, she later said this conference was when she "detected her first whiffs of [SUNY's] poor self-image" (Bryant, 2017).

Shortly after the conference, I was elected president of UFS, the body that represents SUNY's faculty and professional staff at the 34 baccalaureate and doctoral institutions. Zimpher and I had our first one-on-one meeting in early June, during which we discussed SUNY's checkered history and academic governance in general. She invited me to join what she called the "cabinet," a group of senior administrators that would meet monthly, with the caveat that the discussions had to be considered confidential. The trade-off was that I was expected to speak my mind openly. She extended similar invitations to my counterparts in the SUNY Student Assembly (SA) and the SUNY Faculty Council of Community Colleges (FCCC). In effect, she offered SUNY's governance organizations seats at the administrative table, an offer that Norman Goodman (2017) later called a "clear signal of the importance she attributed to shared governance." In addition, we agreed to schedule regular meetings, with the promise of access beyond our schedule whenever I thought it necessary, a promise she and her staff kept faithfully.

The chancellor had committed to visiting each of SUNY's geographically dispersed campuses in her first year, a journey that covered thousands of miles. I was invited to accompany her when my schedule permitted, and fortunately I was able to join the small traveling band for 10 of the visits, with my position as an observer, rather than as a member of her team. In the process, I learned a good deal about her and SUNY's variety of postsecondary institutions, each with its own history and mission.

At our first meeting, I had invited her to meet with the UFS's executive committee in the summer. She cleared her schedule and made the short trip from Albany. In an informal dinner setting, she and the UFS leadership established what proved to a lasting pattern of frank yet cordial discussions of the many problems the system faced before and during her tenure.

In the previous two decades, shared governance at SUNY had had its contradictions. On one hand, it has been embedded in the policies of SUNY's Board of Trustees, Article VII, which names the UFS, founded in the 1953, as "the official agency through which the University Faculty engages in the governance of the University. The Senate shall be concerned with effective educational policies and other professional matters within the University" (SUNY, 2019, p. 4). That is a fairly broad mandate, with the phrase "other professional matters" giving the UFS a stake in all

SUNY policies and system-mandated practices. Shortly before Chancellor Zimpher took office, a significant change in the board membership had taken place—first the SA president (voting) and then the UFS president (nonvoting) became members of the board. In 2011, the president of the FCCC joined the board, and like the UFS president, the position carried representation with nonvoting status. These board positions offered the governance organizations' presidents the opportunity to participate in the earliest discussions of policy formation.

Despite the clarity of policy and the inclusion of representatives of the three governance organizations on the board, in 2009 shared governance could fairly be described at best as one of mutual wariness. A bit of history is necessary to provide context.

In the late 1990s, many faculty believed that a significant number of board members, particularly those recently appointed by the new governor, were antagonistic and even hostile to the broader public mission of SUNY and especially to its faculty and staff. The sentiment became much more generalized after the board imposed, without consultation with governance leaders, a system-wide General Education Requirement in December 1998. In response, SUNY's governance organizations on the system and campus levels issued numerous votes of no confidence in the board.

After the battle over the common curriculum had settled into a series of skirmishes regarding policy implementation, a number of subsequent issues (system-wide assessment, system-wide seamless transfer, system-wide budgeting, and strategic planning, to name a few) generated continuing distrust between the representatives of the faculty, professional staff, and students and SUNY's board of trustees and senior administrators in the first decade of the new century. Union leaders on campuses and at state-wide meetings often referred to members of the administration as "management," a language choice that reflected the reality that some administrators at the highest level increasingly came from outside academia and hence, had little experience with or appreciation for campus cultures.

The fight over the General Education Requirement had poisoned the atmosphere for shared governance in another way. The rising demands for university accountability appeared to be based on a deep-seated belief on the part of some board members that faculty members too often were pushing a specific political agenda (generally regarded as "liberal"), conducting research that was poorly designed and not very relevant to the "real" world, and teaching too little to too small an effect. Several of the board's newer members who had been appointed by the recently elected Republican governor, George Pataki, spoke publicly, and often, and were quoted frequently in the Albany papers and increasingly in national conservative media. Rather than working together to examine the most appropriate roles for a modern public university at a time of dramatic shifts in the economy, knowledge, technology, and sociocultural mores, governance became mired in a continuing series of often ugly skirmishes.

The new chancellor understood the enormity of the task before her, in terms of the SUNY-specific issues with shared governance and the broader problems faced by public higher education. In 2009, in the midst of the national economic crisis, SUNY faced several difficult, seemingly intractable, budget issues. In looking back at this period, a former president of one of the campuses alluded to SUNY as a "dysfunctional family," one from which many actively sought to distance themselves (Vancko, 2017). According to an article in the February 11 *Chronicle of Higher Education*, "The university faces a severe financial crisis, and the state government has trimmed $210-million from the system's budget in the current fiscal year. Furthermore, SUNY has long had a reputation as contentious and politicized, leading some observers to speculate that the system is ungovernable" (Fain, 2009). That last budget cut amounted to a cumulative 30 percent loss of state support for the operating budget in three years, a devastating excision of hundreds of millions of dollars from SUNY's campus budgets.

Politicized? Indeed. Even during the glory days a half-century earlier, Governor Nelson Rockefeller's singular commitment to build a great state university system is what finally persuaded state politicians to fund a growing public alternative to the state's outstanding private colleges and universities. In return, SUNY remained a state agency, subject to legislative oversight and crippling regulations. In 1984, Chancellor Clifton Wharton empaneled a distinguished commission to address the "overregulation" that "pervades every aspect of SUNY operation, in ways large and small" (*The challenge and the choice*, 1985, pp. 33–35). Many of the commission's recommendations were subsequently adopted by the legislature, but many were not, leading 20 years later to another commission (New York Commission on Higher Education) to repeat the charge: state regulations constrained SUNY's ability to deliver the educational services needed by the state. According to the commission report, New York State's "public institutions of higher education are hampered by too little revenue, too little investment and too much regulation" (New York State Commission on Higher Education, 2008, p. 1).

The long-term, nation-wide process that began in the 1980s of states "disinvesting" in public higher education had been exaggerated in New York by the twin crises that had so severely shaken Wall Street, first the terrorist attacks on September 11, 2001, and then the global financial crisis in 2008–2009. Each delivered devastating blows to the state's finances, because New York State "received about 20 percent of its tax revenue from Manhattan's securities industry, and the collapse of several banks led the state to lose more money than it did after the terrorist attacks of September 11, 2001" (Kelderman, 2009). Following the crash of the subprime mortgage bubble, the tax base in New York shriveled, which for SUNY resulted in a countercyclical rise in enrollment, dramatically reduced levels of state support, and the legislature's refusal to increase tuition and student fees.

Instability in the system's leadership also contributed directly to SUNY's problems. Since Chancellor Bruce Johnstone left in 1994, no chancellor other than Robert L. King (2000–2005) had served more than three years. From the time of King's sudden departure to Zimpher's appointment, there had been one briefly serving chancellor, two interim chancellors, and one officer-in-charge. The uncertain leadership at the system's center allowed campus presidents to assume greater independence in working with their area legislators to further their campus's ambitions, often disregarding the needs of other schools in the system, which further compounded the problems faced by the new administration.

This was the state of SUNY in June 2009 when Nancy Zimpher assumed the duties of chancellor: a dire financial position for the system, a web of regulations that many thought stifled the creativity needed for innovation, a number of specific programmatic issues that needed system-wide solutions, and an immediately preceding record of weak central administrative authority, all made more difficult given the condition of shared governance processes. To better understand how the chancellor called on shared governance to help address these problems, I focus on three issues: strategic planning, state support, and seamless transfer.

Issue: A Strategic Plan for SUNY

One of the first tasks the board of trustees assigned the chancellor called for the creation of a new strategic plan for the system. In Nancy Zimpher, they found someone with extensive experience designing inclusive planning processes. At both the University of Wisconsin, Milwaukee and the University of Cincinnati, she led the development of ambitious plans (the Milwaukee Idea and UC 21, respectively) for each institution (Kelderman, 2010).

With the notes from the SUNY at 60 conference and the information gathered through her 64-campus tour across the state, Chancellor Zimpher and her staff designed a distinctive strategic planning process for SUNY. "Inclusive" is a fair characterization, with approximately 200 participants who were drawn from SUNY's administration, faculty, professional staff, and students designated by the governance organizations and their campus administrations, plus distinguished members of the larger community and invited guests who met six times over six months in locations spread all across the state. Each meeting focused on a specific issue facing SUNY and the larger society, with the resulting conversations and ideas synthesized into a workable plan by a small steering committee that included leaders of the system's representative governance organizations.

The inclusive nature of the process stood in stark contrast to that used for the previous strategic plan nine years before, a plan that had been produced by a small group of SUNY administrators. Given the chancellor's experience with Midwestern public universities—and the large number of community representatives among the 200—it comes as no surprise that the resulting 2010 plan, "The Power of SUNY," offered a dramatic "reboot" of SUNY's relationship with the state. Adopting the spirit of the Wisconsin Plan and the teaching-research–public service ethic of land-grant universities, SUNY committed itself to developing and using knowledge to address six of the state's most pressing problems. Each specified concern included a section titled "Diversity Counts" that highlighted the long-term historical patterns of discrimination attendant to that concern. Infusing diversity as an issue in the specified issues identified both its importance to the university and its breadth in American social patterns (http://www.suny.edu/powerofsuny).

Too often, academic communities employ countless people, organized in countless committees that hold countless meetings, that finally produce a new strategic plan, orchestrated by a new administration, only to have the plan languish on office shelves, gathering dust. This planning process was different. For each of the six areas of abiding social concern, a working implementation group was organized. Led by senior administrators and composed of faculty, professional staff, students, and administrators from SUNY's campuses, each group identified specific goals and produced plans for achieving them. Similarly organized groups addressed a number of issues that focused on the internal operations of the university, including a group on shared governance, cochaired by the presiding officers of FCCC and UFS. The faculty, professional staff, and student representatives to these working groups were nominated by the FCCC, the SA, and the UFS, which was consistent with the often disregarded principle that governance organizations should select those who represent them.

In the largest sense, the plan provided a roadmap "to revitalize the economy and enhance the quality of life" for all New Yorkers. While the emphasis on SUNY as New York's "engine for economic growth" disquieted many faculty in the university, it proved to be attractive to politicians looking for solutions to the dreary economy in 2010. This was particularly true in the upstate region, which had lost a significant number of industries over the previous three decades, creating chronic unemployment and turning much of the fabled Erie Canal route from Albany to Buffalo into a Rust Belt. SUNY's promise to organize itself more efficiently and use public support more effectively also appealed to lawmakers. But what level of resources would New York State offer in return? For an answer, we turn to PHEEIA and NYSUNY2020.

Issue: PHEEIA/NYSUNY2020

In January 2010, Governor David Paterson presented the Public Higher Education Empowerment and Innovation Act (PHEEIA), which had largely been designed in coordination with SUNY staff to provide new funding through modest tuition increases over five years (without the reductions in state aid that often accompanied past tuition increases) and greater administrative flexibility for the state's two public university systems, CUNY (the City University of New York) and SUNY. To a great extent it was modeled after UB2020, a proposal that had been introduced in the previous legislative session with similar elements—differential tuition for research campuses, campus tuition-setting authority, relief from state regulations, and the ability to create public–private partnerships. Whereas UB2020 had been designed by and for one campus (University at Buffalo), PHEEIA was applicable to most SUNY and by extension CUNY campuses.

Ultimately, the legislature's reluctance to cede control to SUNY or its individual campuses killed the bill. Many argued that the depth of the worst recession in decades was not the time to raise tuition at public institutions, which would impede access to education, especially for students coming from lower-income groups. Part of the legislative reluctance mirrored the strong opposition from the system's academic unions, the New York State United Teachers in most community colleges and the United University Professions (UUP) in the 34 state-operated campuses.

According to union leadership, the legislation would further "privatize" the public system by forcing current state employees to be transferred to private payrolls through public–private partnerships. This would result in a loss of pay, benefits and union membership. Furthermore, the unions expressed consistent and genuine concern about the impact that higher tuition would have on student access, especially for students of lower economic status. In any event, the unions' opposition helped kill the bill. At the time, Chancellor Zimpher publicly noted her surprise at the fierce union resistance; later she came to understand that part of the problem was the administration's failure to discuss the initiative with the union (or the UFS leadership for that matter) well before its public introduction.

For the governance organizations, PHEEIA posed a number of problems, including the possibility of creating a division between UFS and UUP, as well as deep fissures among the UFS's five sectors, each of which had representatives from a specific type of institution. The politically powerful union leadership opposed the legislation and expected the UFS to follow its lead. Although the two groups represented many of the same faculty and professional staff, it was in two distinct realms, university governance in one case and the "terms and conditions of employment" in the other.

In addition, the two constituent bodies were organized quite differently. In the UFS, the four university centers' representatives, attracted by the possibility of higher tuition for their campuses as well as the promise of more easily creating public–private partnerships to commoditize basic research, strongly supported the legislation. The representatives of the four other sectors remained divided, to some extent reflecting a concern that if the freedoms promised in the legislation were enacted, it would result in students moving to the higher-priced, more prestigious university centers, once the enrollment restrictions SUNY had previously negotiated with each campus were removed.

The UFS leadership met with union leaders and SUNY administrators, including the chancellor and the vice chancellor for finances, pressing each party for greater clarity in addressing specific concerns. To prepare the senators for an upcoming vote at the UFS spring plenary, the executive committee conducted an educational campaign that cataloged the advantages and disadvantages of the proposed legislation, using the words and language of the union and the administration. These documents intentionally failed to take a position on the issue, given their educational purpose. But out of the resulting dialogues came a clearer understanding of what the legislation meant for SUNY and the guarantees the membership needed to gain their support. In the end, despite the union opposition, the UFS strongly supported PHEEIA in principle, an act that resulted in a rift between the union leadership and that of the senate that was not repaired until each group elected new leadership in 2013.

In 2011, newly elected Governor Andrew Cuomo introduced NYSUNY2020, which has been called PHEEIA "Lite." With several changes to the original PHEEIA, it passed handily without union opposition. The legislation offered SUNY a larger measure of administrative autonomy and the authority to raise tuition modestly, subject to legislative approval, for each of the next five budget years. In addition, the state promised that at a minimum it would maintain its current level of support, breaking the traditional cycle of reduced state support to match each tuition increase.

There were many reasons for the different legislative results in 2010 and 2011, but one that is overlooked is the role played by the UFS in 2010. By identifying the issues that had to be addressed in PHEEIA, it provided early guidance for what became NYSUNY2020. Although it failed to resolve all budget problems for SUNY, NYSUNY20220 provided the first meaningful infusion of funds in more than a decade and guaranteed fiscal stability for the next years.

On several occasions at UFS plenary meetings, the chancellor identified the new realities facing public higher education, both in New York and across the nation: traditional state support that had leached from public higher education in the preceding decades would be partially restored at best, and at worst would be further eroded during the next economic downturn. Increases in university finances, then, would have to come from sources other than the public treasury—principally from students and their families and greater entrepreneurial activities of the university community. That partially explains the strategic plan allying the university system's goals and activities with those of the larger society and economy. In other words, the Ivory Tower no longer stood alone; in truth it never did. "Learning for its own sake," which was always more a myth than reality for higher education, was increasingly perceived as a luxury that few students could, or taxpayers would, afford. Instead, SUNY publicly drew on the long-standing tradition of US public higher education to propose solutions to current social ills, in New York's case, economic failures, and presented itself as an engine critical to the state's economic revitalization.

Zimpher often told audiences—any audience—that New York's public university had to be one of the major building blocks for the state's economic recovery and future prosperity. This was the message she carried to the UFS and to the campuses across the state. The chancellor used the structures of shared governance to create a larger consensus within the university about the transactional arrangements between the state and its public university that had always been implicit in public support for public higher education, as demonstrated by the histories of teachers colleges and land-grant universities.

What made this especially telling was the history of SUNY itself, with its century-old network of 5 small colleges aimed at fostering agriculture and a range of technical and technological expertise, as well as the 11 comprehensive colleges, the oldest of which had been founded and supported by the state for almost two centuries as teaching training institutes and colleges. Certainly the development of the SUNY network of community colleges, with their comprehensive shared missions of preparing students for the world of work and/or further education underlined the realization that postsecondary education could not be divorced from how women and men worked in their communities, their businesses, their farms, or their schools and medicals centers.

Issue: "Seamless" Transfer

If NYSUNY2020 ultimately offered SUNY a degree of financial stability by creating a predictable pattern of modest tuition increases and the state's promise of "maintenance of effort," "seamless transfer" was a problem with a name but few apparent solutions. From the beginning of the "modern" SUNY in the mid-1960s when the State Teachers Colleges became "comprehensive colleges" (and almost every county wanted its own community college), SUNY's master plans emphasized the need to accommodate the rapidly growing number of transfer students who sought baccalaureate degrees. Thousands moved from one campus to another, risking the loss of credits in the process.

Since the early 1970s, the board of trustees had passed no fewer than seven resolutions declaring "seamless transfer" one of the core principles for SUNY. Yet the deep-seated tradition of each campus—or program—faculty exercising the final authority over its curriculum and degree requirements meant that the policy was largely dead-letter law.

Students who transferred from one institution to another often found different degree requirements for general education, different requirements for lower division courses in an academic major, and inconsistent decisions made in their chosen programs by faculty who jealously guarded the gates of their majors. Sometimes, the denial of credit became apparent only after a student had arrived on the next campus. The actual extent of the issue was never really determined, but the anecdotal evidence continued to mount, with community college faculty and administrators claiming (often with justification) that students received unfair treatment at the hands of the bachelor degree–granting faculty.

The transfer credit problem had been highlighted in the New York State's Commission on Higher Education's 2008 report. Ironically, the then president of the Student Assembly, a commission member as well as a member of the board of trustees, had been denied credit for a core course in his major when he had transferred from a SUNY community college to one of the university centers. Even though he earned an A, his new campus insisted he retake the course. This case became the most visible of the many anecdotal reports of students being denied credit after transferring. In 2008, the board insisted that the often enunciated policy of seamless transfer be implemented once and for all.

The chancellor, whose experience with a state-wide transfer system in Ohio had prepared her for many aspects of these difficulties, accepted this challenge. But the Ohio system was not SUNY, either in the number of institutions or the range of differing institutional missions. Understanding the extraordinary complexity of the problems, she insisted that the solutions emerge from a process that put faculty governance at the center of decision making. Simply stated, Zimpher believed that faculty were responsible for making the curricular decisions governing program and degree requirements, but in this case, the "faculty" were to be chosen from a range of SUNY campuses, substituting system-wide decisions for what traditionally had been campus-based.

In November 2010, the board passed a resolution that mandated that any course designed to fulfill one of the 10 SUNY general education categories on one campus would be accepted by all other SUNY campuses as fulfilling that requirement. Board policy and system mandates first covered those 10 general education areas, but what of the academic majors? Subsequently, in her "State of the University" address in January 2011, the chancellor vowed that SUNY would "break the mold around student mobility" and would allow students to transfer up to five courses in their major to another SUNY campus. In saying that, she pointed to the presidents of the two faculty governance organizations and indicated that this had to be accomplished within the year.

With the appointment of David Lavallee (former provost at SUNY New Paltz, 1999–2009) as provost in 2009, she found a senior administrator who had great experience with the student mobility issue and the respect of faculty governance leadership. He became a willing partner with faculty governance representatives to the critical implementation processes that would govern much of SUNY transfer practice in the future. Provost Lavallee and his staff worked diligently with faculty governance leadership to create a system-wide process that would ultimately engage faculty from more than 50 academic disciplines to guide decisions about specific classes of courses within system-wide transfer.

After more than four years, and two separate review processes in which 1,200 faculty drawn from every campus participated, the goal was achieved. Eventually the faculty groups created more than 50 discipline-based curricular paths that identified the foundational coursework (the specific number varied by discipline) that students should take in their first two years to be able to complete the major in two additional years. What this meant was that credits earned in either approved general education or academic major path courses on one SUNY campus were guaranteed transfer across the system, as long as students earned a C in the major courses. The resulting "major transfer paths" of three to eight courses have been widely distributed and are currently available on the SUNY website for students, advisors, and interested parties to consult (https://www.suny.edu/attend/get-started/transfer-students/suny-transfer-paths/).

The centrality of shared governance in the process was highlighted in two ways. First, a 2009 Memorandum of Understanding signed by the provost and the presidents of FCCC and UFS established an advisory committee composed of faculty appointed by the faculty governance organizations and administrators chosen by the provost and chaired in alternate years by the presidents of the FCCC and UFS. That group, the Provost's Student Mobility Advisory Committee, continues to function today, serving as the primary policy recommending group and a preliminary board of review for any transfer issues that emerge. Second, the campus governance leadership had identified the faculty who served on the discipline-based working groups.

I have concentrated on the three issues above because they were the most compelling of the first years of Chancellor Zimpher's tenure, and in each case, governance leaders were engaged early in the process and able to guide the deliberations. The one case (and there were others) where that failed, PHEEIA, proves the value of shared governance, because it was the one where the administration did not engage either union or governance leadership in the early stages of policy formation. Generally, however, a pattern of including faculty governance leadership in system-wide decisions and initiatives persisted throughout Zimpher's eight years as chancellor; if anything, they became more evident and more routine with time. Today, the presidents of the FCCC, UFS, and SA are critical to any and all discussions about system policy. Clearly, the recommendations of the governance leaders were not always heeded, but then, the governance organization did not necessarily speak with a single voice on every issue. But it is clear that their voices were heard.

Finally, as Chancellor Zimpher left the SUNY chancellor's office, she bequeathed to the future SUNY Voices, a multifaceted initiative funded by the SUNY system. This support led to four summer leadership training institutes for new faculty-staff-student presiding officers of campus governance organizations across SUNY, funding for three annual conferences on Shared Governance, support for a UFS-initiated SUNY Shared Governance Award for campuses exemplifying excellence, as well as a series of books published by SUNY Press on the subject.

Concluding Thoughts

If real estate success is determined by location, location, location, then good governance can only occur when there is access, access, access. No matter what we as faculty/professional staff/student leaders think *should* be the case, college and university administrators serve as gatekeepers to seats at the table when policies and special initiatives are in formative stages. By that measure, the Zimpher administration earns high marks for its willingness to engage governance-selected leadership in meaningful early consultation. Although it did not always work as smoothly as we would have liked, shared governance during Zimpher's time was dramatically better than what came before; in fact, during her tenure governance representatives assumed leadership for system policies and initiatives, such as a new university-wide diversity policy and a system-wide service learning initiative.

From conversations with colleagues across the nation at the AAUP national conferences on shared governance, we have been reassured that the contemporary SUNY practice of shared governance is significantly more fully developed than that on almost any other campus or in other systems. None of this happened by coincidence; rather, it resulted from the support given to collaboration that began with the appointment of Chancellor Zimpher.

Our governance organizations have a central place in academic governance, a fact that Chancellor Zimpher understood. The UFS meets in plenary sessions three times annually at campuses across the state on a rotating basis. Wherever we met, she regularly attended (21 of 24 plenaries was the final count), offering her views on the latest administrative initiatives and taking questions from the five campus sectors and the campus governance leaders. Following her lead, the other senior system administrators did the same, taking unscripted questions from the floor. The tone and passion of the questioning varied, sometimes sharp, other times poignant, and on occasion humorous. Sometimes the chancellor, provost, and CFO left the meeting a bit more bruised than they or we had anticipated, but they returned again and again. For her support of meaningful shared governance and the changes in practice during her administration, Zimpher justly received the Friend of the Senate Award, the highest honor the senate can bestow on a nonsenator.

When faculty governance leaders think of shared governance, which the AAUP now wants to call "academic governance" (see "In Praise of Traditional Academic Governance," by Michael DeCesare, chapter 8 in this volume), we often fail to see it in its genuine complexity. In truth, it involves more than the relationship between the administration and faculty and staff governance organizations. Students are and must be integral to the governance process, however difficult that may be given their transitory status. The same is often true for outside stakeholders, such as taxpayers, legislators, and alumni, that public colleges and universities depend on for necessary external support.

Finally there are the university governing boards, which have the final fiduciary and presidential appointing authority. The governing boards of public institutions, whose members are most often political appointees, have additional burdens. Distinguished women and men—certainly the case for the SUNY Board of Trustees—board members not only volunteer their time, expertise, and experience unstintingly to meet their fiduciary and appointing responsibilities, but they are also frequently called on to serve as defensive buffers against mounting politically-charged criticism from external sources. As indicated previously, the 15-member board included 3 representatives from the university's governance organizations, who in time were more fully integrated into the work of the board. Even though presiding officers of the FCCC and UFS were nonvoting members, they were each asked to chair a board committee. As I left office and my membership on the board, I took with me a deep appreciation for the women and men with whom I served on the SUNY board and their willingness to engage in the messy business of setting policy and overseeing the nation's largest and most comprehensive public higher education system.

Last, I have learned that personalities matter. By that, I do not mean the necessity of becoming friends (however debased that word has become in the age of Facebook) with those with whom we are professionally engaged. Nor would I argue that personal relationships trump the practice and structure of shared governance within academic communities. Although personality should not be the determining factor upon which good university governance rests, I think it is essential to break down the stereotypes we too often use to categorize one another. If nothing else, the 2016 presidential election and the disputatious administration that resulted, has reminded us of the important roles comity, consideration, and respect play if we are to successfully bridge the divides of experience, responsibilities, interests, and differing personal styles that complicate the success of governance in a pluralistic democratic culture.

Chancellor Zimpher's long years as a campus academic administrator and her earlier service as a faculty member and governance leader led her to value faculty concerns and understand that the real work of any university community or system occurs in its classrooms, labs, and studios rather than in committee meeting rooms, however necessary the latter may be. Her frequently voiced search for what she called the "sweet spot" in a deliberation, that place where those at the table could find something they valued in the result, speaks volumes about her willingness to genuinely engage in the sometimes messy, always complicated, ever contested, but essential arena that is university shared governance.

Note

This essay is a major revision and extension of a paper presented in April 2017 at the SUNY Conference on Shared Governance, which I revised for publication as "Nancy Zimpher and shared governance, a comment," *University Faculty Senate Bulletin*, Spring/Summer 2017.

References

Bringsjord, E. L., Knox, D. J., Lavallee, D., and O'Brien, K. P. (2017). SUNY seamless transfer policy and shared governance. In S. F. Cramer (Ed.), *Shared governance in higher education, vol. 1: Demands, transitions and transformations*, pp. 153–78. Albany: SUNY Press.

Bryant, A. (2017). Nancy L. Zimpher on setting a bold vision. *New York Times*, July 28. Retrieved from https://www.nytimes.com/2017/07/28/business/corner-office-nancy-zimpher-suny.html.

The challenge and the choice. (1985). Report of the Independent Commission on the Future of the State University of New York.

Fain, P. (2009). Nancy Zimpher tackles a big challenge as SUNY's new chancellor. *Chronicle of Higher Education*, February 11.

Goodman, N. (2017). Nancy Zimpher, one big audacious idea. *Faculty Senate Bulletin*, Spring/Summer, pp. 13–14. Retrieved from http://system.suny.edu/media/suny/content-assets/documents/faculty-senate/bulletin/FacultyBulletin_Spr-Smr17_V2_final.pdf.

Kelderman, E. (2009). Northeast: Colleges feel ripples of Wall Street Woes. *Chronicle of Higher Education*, August 24.

Kelderman. E. (2010). Shaping SUNY into a whole greater than its parts. *Chronicle of Higher Education*, April 18.

New York State Commission on Higher Education. (2008). *Final report on findings and recommendations*. NYSCHE.

State University of New York. (2019). *Policies of the Board of Trustees*. SUNY.

Vancko, C. (2017). Nancy Zimpher, chancellor extraordinaire. *Faculty Senate Bulletin*, Spring/Summer, p. 17. http://system.suny.edu/media/suny/content-assets/documents/faculty-senate/bulletin/FacultyBulletin_Spr-Smr17_V2_final.pdf.

10

Lessons in Process

"It's Not Just about Transparency, It's about #SharedGovernance"

Philip L. Glick and Domenic J. Licata

Transparency, the essential competency that meaningful shared governance is built around, is insufficient on its own to lead to shared governance best practices. A new paradigm, introducing a set of essential competencies, is used to analyze a 2016 governance meeting at the University at Buffalo, where issues related to the lack of transparency were evident. The chapter illustrates how the meeting was the catalyst for a transformation at the institution and in the UB Office of University Shared Governance: Faculty Senate and Professional Staff Senate in the office's efforts to move toward true shared governance.

Inspired by the championing of shared governance by SUNY Chancellor Nancy Zimpher and Board of Trustees Chair H. Carl McCall, and by the example set by the SUNY University Faculty Senate (UFS), the chairs of the University at Buffalo Faculty Senate (FS) and the Professional Staff Senate (PSS) have endeavored to inculcate the spirit and the process of shared governance into every aspect of University at Buffalo (UB) governance and decision making. On the topic of shared governance, Chancellor Zimpher at the 2015 SUNY UFS Fall Plenary and Chairman McCall at the 2016 SUNY UFS Winter Plenary have declared, "We have got to get this right!" We took the chancellor and chairman at their words.

Shared governance is the name commonly given to the collaborative processes by which most immediate stakeholders—faculty, staff, students, administration, and councils (the five pillars of shared governance)[1]— express and exercise their governance authority and responsibilities in support of the institution's mission. It is a distribution of authority to various campus and system constituencies, based on state laws, the campus's and senate's bylaws, charter, and standing orders that mandate the degree to which each constituency is engaged in that particular area of institutional governance. The competencies of this collaboration include (but are not limited to) the following capacities: trust, collegiality, dialogue, mutual respect, sharing perspectives, listening, a shared sense of purpose, and shared accountability; always being mindful of diversity and inclusion; always remembering some of us have certain privileges and experiences of life that others do not; remaining humble; and recognizing differences while remaining open to finding common ground and transparency of information (see Figure 10.1). It boils down to effective and constructive engagement by the administration and councils with the faculty, staff, and students, which must also be timely. Our collaboration needs to be proactive, not reactive, on issues that impact the campus. We all need to be at the table.²

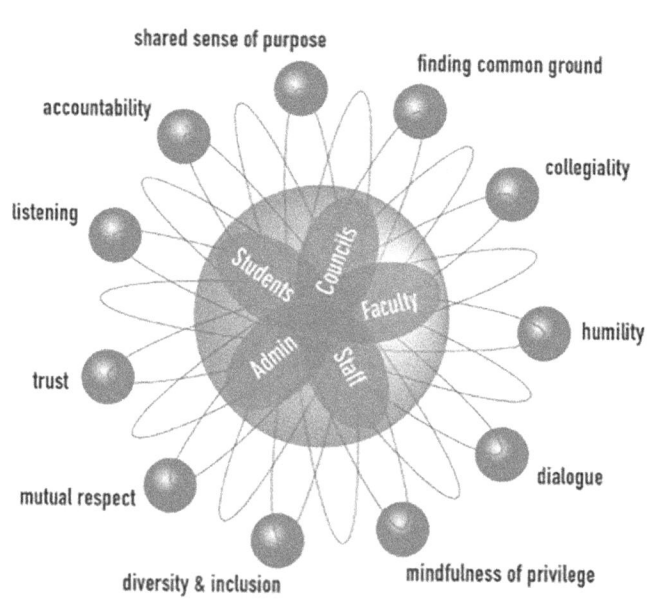

Figure 10.1. The shared governance nuclear competencies of transparency that many institutions with great shared governance are built around.

This chapter describes the first few steps—and missteps—taken by new chairs of the UB FS and PSS in their attempts toward achieving meaningful and inclusive shared governance.

Shared Governance Litmus Test and Joint Initiatives

As the newly elected chairs of the FS (Glick) and the PSS (Licata), we were inspired by passionate advocates of shared governance at the June 2015 SUNY Voices Campus Governance Leaders Leadership Institute to embark on an ambitious collaborative venture to position the University at Buffalo as a leader in shared governance. The FS and the PSS are housed together in what was known as the UB Office of University Governance. UB is among the few SUNY campuses that includes a PSS (ratified in 1972) among its recognized governance bodies (Binghamton is another). In one of our first official acts of the new term as chairs, we asked that each senate resolve to add the word "Shared" to the name of the Office of University Governance, reflecting a commitment to the core principle that "shared governance is a foundational concept in American higher education and describes how institutions of higher education are formally organized and managed when the participation of all parties is included."[3] Through an October 2015 resolution passed by the FS and PSS, supported by Provost Charles Zukoski, and signed and promulgated by President Satish Tripathi, the name is now officially known as the Office of University Shared Governance: Faculty and Professional Staff Senates (see Appendix).

In addition to the initiatives and resolutions brought forth by the senates on behalf of their constituents, we set about maximizing collaboration among all five pillars of shared governance. We devised a litmus test to enable the determination of whether a particular initiative qualified as a shared governance matter. If an activity directly engaged two or more of the five pillars, it qualified. As each issue appeared on our collective agendas, we would ask, "Is this an issue that involves our own constituents, or can it become more impactful if we brought it to students, faculty, staff administration or council?" The faculty, professional staff, and students applauded these actions. This was not always true for the administration. We were not infrequently asked by the provost, the president, and the UB Foundation, "What does this have to do with the faculty or professional staff?" It was usually easy to explain why there was interest in the various matters. It had been nearly impossible to interface with the UB Council, as the chairs of the two senates are not members but only attend council meetings as observers. It has been explained that the chairs were not to have any direct contact with the UB Council or its members. This led to a resolution at the UB FS and the SUNY UFS to request a change in the state education law to allow the chairs of the FS and the PSS at all SUNY campuses to become members of their campus's council (see Appendix). This matter is now sitting on the SUNY chancellor's desk. As of this writing, its fate is uncertain.

Shared Governance Day

In spring 2016 the FS and PSS jointly declared by resolution that the first Tuesday of March be known as "University at Buffalo Day of Shared Governance," which was renamed at the request of President Tripathi the following year to Shared Governance Day, emphasizing that the event was sponsored by the FS and PSS, not the university. The first event brought together faculty, professional staff, senior SUNY UFS leaders, campus administrators, and Chancellor Nancy Zimpher (via video conference) to celebrate the spirit of shared governance, recognize our accomplishments, and set aspirational goals to increase the impact of true collaboration on realizing the mission of the university (see Appendix).

The second annual Shared Governance Day featured a keynote address by SUNY Fredonia President Virginia Horvath. As the president of a campus that won the first SUNY Shared Governance Award, Horvath taught us, among other things, that "building in the buy-in" by inviting the voices of all stakeholders at the beginning, is much more valuable than attempting to sell an idea after the fact to those who had no part in its inception.[4] The third Shared Governance Day took place in March 2018, and the fourth, on March 5, 2019, featured a call-in appearance by SUNY Chancellor Kristina Johnson and Provost Tod Laursen.

To further ensure that all voices were represented in shared governance discussions, the FS and PSS amended their bylaws to include the chair of the other's senate and the leader of the student Council of Advocacy and Leadership (COAL) board to be *ex officio* nonvoting members of their respective executive committees. (COAL is composed of the presidents of the seven student associations, the chief justice of the Student-Wide Judiciary, and the UB Council student representative.) In addition, the FS and PSS reaffirmed that all committees of each senate were open to both professional staff, faculty, and student membership.

Over the term, the FS and the PSS organized several other major joint initiatives, examples of which are provided below.

- Greening the Commons: Partnering with the Student Environmental Network and Students for Sustainability campaign to petition the vendors in the privately managed UB Commons. The goal was to end the use of containers made from expanded polystyrene foam (commonly known as Styrofoam). The partnership led to a resolution by the PSS, passed in 2015 (subsequently endorsed by the FS) to begin educational outreach and request that vendors use a more sustainable, recyclable, and healthy alternative to Styrofoam. The campaign is ongoing (see Appendix).

- Breathe Free: With the support of UB's president, the Office of University Shared Governance (under the endorsements of the FS and PSS) charged a committee to review the Breathe Free smoke-free-campus policy (signed in 2009, amended in 2010). Recognizing that the policy has been largely ignored and not enforced, the committee's charge was to "examine the status of the Breathe Free policy and recommend improvements and strategies to maximize compliance, helping UB become a truly Smoke-Free, Tobacco-Free and Vape-Free Campus." A committee of more than 40 members of the faculty, staff, student body, senior leaders, and Western New York health experts were formed to gather data and present a report, which was to include proposed revisions to Breathe Free, with a focus on education, compassion, fair and equitable enforcement, and community support. The report and proposed policy draft were delivered to President Tripathi in December 2017 and endorsed by the FS, PSS, and the Student Association executive board. (The 36-page report can be found at http://bit.ly/BreatheFreeUB.)

- Shared Governance Continuing Education Series: Early in 2015, the Office of University Shared Governance launched the Shared Governance Continuing Education Series to educate and inform faculty, staff, and students on the tools and processes of shared governance. Topics and speakers have included parliamentary procedures by Sharon Cramer; writing resolutions by Brian White; effective meeting skills by Drucy Borowitz; social media by Robin Sullivan, Phil Glick, and Caroline Lojacono; Safe Zone and Cultural Competency training with Steve Jagord, manager of the Pride Center of Western New York; and "Stop the Bleed" tourniquet training with Lieutenant David Urbanek, UB Police.

- UB Campus Governance Leaders Group: Continuing the tradition established by the previous chairs of the FS and PSS, Ezra Zubrow and Ann Marie Landel, respectively, the Office of University Shared Governance convenes periodic meetings with governance and labor leaders from an array of organizations, including United University Professions (two local chapters), Civil Service Employees Association, UB Police, Research Foundation, Graduate Student Employee Association, Council of Advocacy and Leadership, and others. The charge of the group is to disseminate information to improve communication, collaboration, and completion of shared goals.

Activities of the Two Shared Governance Bodies

In addition to the shared governance initiatives, which in each case brought together at least two of the pillars, the FS and the PSS conducted many effective initiatives in support of UB's mission.

The UB Faculty Senate

The Faculty Senate participated in the following shared governance initiatives:

- Four decanal searches (Public Health, Management, Dental, and College of Arts and Sciences)

- Two decanal reviews (School of Architecture and Planning and Jacobs School of Medicine and Biomedical Sciences)

- The reorganization of the libraries (from an academic to an administrative unit) with the retention of all the rights and privileges of the faculty librarians

- Debated the newly proposed SUNY intellectual property, copyrights, and patent policy. The UB Faculty Senate contributed to the discussion, along with UUP, to carve out the intellectual property and copyright issue (unchanged), and the SUNY Patent Policy has now been passed by SUNY trustees.
- Resolved Educational Opportunity Center faculty members status as full voting members of the FS
- New FS website launched September 6, 2016, with new additions/updates weekly
- A new emphasis on social media (@UBFacultySenate, #SharedGovernance)
- Sustainability matters (Breathe Free campaign, Greening of the Commons, going paperless at meetings, and in other ways—e.g., encouraging all senators to bring a smart device to Executive Committee and FS meetings
- A change in the shared governance office: all artwork from UB's impressive museum collections was returned and replaced with work from faculty and staff
- Develop policies and procedures for retired and emeritus faculty
- Perform a faculty survey by Collaborative on Academic Careers in Higher Education (COACHE); completed for both full-time and adjunct faculty
- Increase/improve FS and its executive committee's "liaison role" on relevant committees and communication with constituents regarding information obtained
- Resolution reconciliation; build in the buy-in of all constituents from the beginning rather than a hard sell at the end
- Gender Equity in Salary Study for full-time faculty
- Adopt a contemporary freedom of expression statement for UB and UB Faculty (see Appendix)
- Access to independent legal opinions for UB FS (see Appendix)

The UB PSS

SUNY recognizes the role of professional staff as crucial members of shared governance (Chancellor Zimpher's comments during the 2016

Day of Shared Governance at UB). Sitting separately from the faculty, however, creates unique challenges in understanding our role. As academic issues, curriculum, tenure and promotion, and budgets are clearly in the realm of the faculty, the PSS has worked to codify its place at the table, representing the concerns of the professional staff in areas such as professional development, quality of work/life, defining shared values, celebrating diversity, contributing to a sustainable environment, and promoting wellness.

In a 2016 amendment to the Constitution of the Professional Staff, Article I, the responsibilities of the PSS were enumerated and strengthened. Notably, paragraph six states:

> The Professional Staff Senate shall be a fact-finding, deliberative, and consultative body, with authority to make studies, reports, and recommendations on all governance matters which have a significant bearing on professional employees. The PSS shall operate, in accordance with the policies set forth by the Board of Trustees of the State University of New York, as a recognized part of the University's shared governance system, and shall, as appropriate, work jointly with others within the five pillars of shared governance: faculty, staff, students, administration and councils.

In spring 2017, President Tripathi approved the amendments, marking a major move forward for the professional staff.

The PSS has also worked diligently to advocate for including professional staff on senior leadership search committees and reviews. Asking the PSS to submit names for consideration rather than the administration appointing staff represents a significant change—now, the process much more strongly exemplifies a spirit of shared governance. The PSS was successful in being invited to offer candidate names for inclusion on decanal reviews for the School of Architecture and Planning and the Jacobs School of Medicine and Biomedical Sciences.

In addition to its focus on shared governance, the mission of the PSS incudes promoting professional development opportunities, fostering collegiality, and celebrating UB culture. Included among the activities of its many committees in 2015–2017 were:

- Potluck picnics and dessert socials
- Annual sustainable living fair

- New employee welcome reception
- Workshop on using LinkedIn as a career success tool
- Narrated tour of Buffalo Niagara Medical Campus
- Educational advisory workshop
- Earth Week celebration luncheons
- Electronics and clothing recycling events
- Annual awards luncheons
- Biannual staff development conference
- First biannual inclusion and diversity conference

These shared governance initiatives and programs would not be possible without the generous efforts of a dedicated and skilled faculty and staff, recognizing the benefits that service to the university's governance brings to the individual and the institution. We are grateful for the support of senators and committee members who continue to push the practice of shared governance forward in each senate, across governance bodies, and in collaboration with the administration.

Working with the Administration Toward Shared Governance

How has administration fostered shared governance? In an example prior to the beginning of the 2015–2016 fiscal year, the provost's office initiated a process involving the outgoing and incoming officers of both senates in the first-ever transparent fiscal planning for the Office of University Shared Governance. The shared budget allowed for new joint initiatives, balanced by the individual needs of the FS and PSS.

Previously, the amount of funding available for senate activities was never disclosed. The senates and their committees had not been given the opportunity to identify strategic objectives and plan accordingly. This new, collaborative process enabled the officers and committee chairs to think proactively about upcoming needs. Underwriting costs of the Shared Governance Continuing Education Series was made possible through this process. It also became apparent that the PSS could support a staff-centered conference on a regular basis: the biannual staff development conference now alternates with the new inclusion and diversity conference on a two-year cycle.

Recognizing the need to accommodate members who have difficulty attending senate meetings in person, the provost agreed to the request of the FS and PSS and provided funding outside of the Office of University Shared Governance budget for video conferencing upgrades at the Center for Tomorrow.

Also at the request of the Office of Shared Governance, the provost launched a review of the outdated UB Faculty and Staff Handbook, supporting a task force of faculty, staff, and administrators to explore the purpose, usefulness, and accuracy of the handbook and to suggest revisions. The work of the task force led to the establishment of an updated digital repository of policies and guidelines previously found in the Faculty Staff Handbook, approved by Provost Charles F. Zukoski in March 2018. The new format will make available the most current and relevant information for easy access by faculty and staff, without the challenges of updating obsolete paper copies. The repository may be found at http://www.buffalo.edu/provost/universitypolicies.html.

In a continuing push toward greater transparency and shared governance, we requested that President Tripathi add the chairs of both senates to his cabinet. The president declined but offered to invite the chairs to fall and spring semester meetings with senior leaders to have focused discussions about shared governance issues. The chairs will also be included in senior leadership retreats. The provost has supported including a senior leader (vice provosts and vice presidents) to sit on every FS committee to act as liaisons between the senate and the administration, to make resolutions easier to endorse and promulgate by the president and become UB policies.

Less successfully, we have requested that the senate chairs be given seats on the UB Council (to join the governor-appointed student representative) and on the board of directors of the UB Foundation. These requests were denied. Undeterred, we wrote UFS resolutions to have faculty and staff at all SUNY campuses to be official members with a vote on their local campus's council. These passed the UFS and are awaiting the chancellor's and trustees' approval prior to being sent to state Education Department to change state educational law. The New York State educational law would need to be modified to include faculty and staff governance leaders on campus foundation boards, which are considered private corporations (see Appendix).

Our Commitment to the "No Surprises" Rule and How We Broke It

Throughout our movement to achieve true and transparent shared governance, we realized the importance of the "no surprises" rule. The idea was presented at a SUNY plenary meeting: just as governance bodies would consider it unfair for the administration to reveal decisions that have already been made without any input from faculty and staff, so too would it seem unfair for the administration to hear of senate actions without having had the opportunity to be involved or at least updated on the activity. This was reinforced when hearing President Horvath's advice, that up-front build-in is preferable to post-completion buy-in. We took her words to underscore how especially important this is if those asked to join the buy-in were not aware that the activity/policy was already decided, or even underway. Another shared governance mantra to live by, for new ideas or programs, is "build-in the buy in up-front, rather than try to hard-sell it at the end!"

The Office of University Shared Governance was successful in involving and informing our senators, constituents, and administration throughout most of our initiatives, including Breathe Free, Greening the Commons, resolutions on UB Foundation divestment from fossil fuels, modified duties after FMLA leave, statements on freedom of expression, and more. These accomplishments prompted us to begin the process of applying for the 2016–2017 SUNY Shared Governance Award. With President Tripathi's support, a committee of faculty, staff, and administrators was formed to prepare the application materials. Several pages of individual and joint senate accomplishments were gathered, and we realized that we still had work to do before achieving true shared governance. Still, we were confident that our progress would be seen by others in SUNY as noteworthy.

Several days prior to the deadline for application, major events had a very negative impact on our university community. These caused us to reflect on the wisdom of concurrent celebration of our progress with shared governance, given what was happening. With a majority of the committee supporting the chairs' recommendation to withdraw from the application process, we prepared a letter to President Tripathi explaining our decision and delivered it to him at a scheduled shared governance meeting without prior notice.

Disregarding our "no surprises" mantra, we did not have the foresight to understand that this tactic would be met with consternation and disappointment. Had we included the president and his staff in our decision-making process, we likely would have gained valuable mutual understanding by sharing concerns. Instead, we damaged the trust they had been striving to construct. In service to UB, the faculty and the professional staff, we regret these events, but we learned many lessons.

Postmortem: Lessons Learned

Writing this chapter enabled us to reflect on our experiences. We thought it would be convenient to have a succinct list of lessons learned thus far as senate chairs.

- Be mindful and celebrate the growth of the competencies of true shared governance: trust, collegiality, dialogue, mutual respect, listening, a shared sense of purpose, accountability, being mindful of diversity and inclusion. We strive to remember that some of us have had the benefit of privileges and experiences that others have not. We work to remain humble, recognizing differences while remaining open to finding common ground. We have learned the power of transparent and timely sharing of information.
- Always err on the side of inclusion.
- Readily acknowledge mistakes and shortcomings.
- Accept blame and seek understanding.
- Learn from mistakes and move ever more strongly forward.

In reality, the most important lesson is that there is no single correct way of achieving true shared governance. It involves flexibility, adjustment, and empathy. It is a process, not an end.

Postscript: The Doctrine of Shared Governance

On March 5, 2019, at the Fourth Annual Shared Governance Day at UB, the FS and the PSS jointly affirmed the adoption of the Doctrine of Shared Governance incorporating many of the ideals discussed in this chapter. As stated in the "Resolution to Adopt 'The Office of University Shared

Governance at UB Doctrine of Shared Governance,'"[5] it is intended to serve as "a legacy mechanism for UB Faculty Senate (FS) Chair Philip L. Glick (2015–2019) and UB Professional Staff Senate (PSS) Chair Domenic J. Licata (2015–2019) as advocates for enthusiastic, relentless and sincere support for shared governance throughout the UB and SUNY system at all levels." It is our hope that "this shall provide a prospective reminder and accountability to their successors to support and strengthen the principles of shared governance at the campus level, at the system level, and between and among the campuses and SUNY System Administration."

The Doctrine of Shared Governance

Shared Governance is a collaboration between faculty, staff, students, administration and governing boards in carrying out the paradigm of shared governance. This collaboration includes but is not limited to: trust, collegiality, dialogue, mutual respect, sharing perspectives, listening, a shared sense of purpose, and shared accountability; always being mindful of diversity and inclusion; always remembering some of us have certain privileges and experiences of life that others have not; remaining humble, recognizing differences while remaining open to finding common ground and transparency of information. In essence, it boils down to "effective and constructive" engagement by the administration and trustees with the faculty, staff and students. Not just effective and constructive engagement, but also timely engagement. We need to be proactive, not reactive on important issues. We all need to be at the table, with a voice and a vote.

Notes

1. See "What is shared governance?," SUNY, https://www.suny.edu/about/shared-governance/sunyvoices/cgl-toolkit/shared-governance/.
2. See Philip L. Glick, chair, Faculty Senate; Domenic J. Licata, chair, Professional Staff Senate; James A. Corra, Student Representative; UB Council, Letter to the editor: Shared governance will assist UB in leading the way in higher education, *UB Spectrum*, October 12, 2016.
3. "Unionization and shared governance at historically black colleges and universities," National Education Association, see http://www.nea.org/home/65416.htm.

4. Remarks by SUNY Fredonia President Virginia Horvath at the 2nd Annual Shared Governance Day at UB, see http://www.buffalo.edu/facultysenate/SharedGovernance/shared-governance-day-2017.html.
5. "Resolution of the Faculty Senate and Professional Staff Senate to Jointly Adopt 'The Office of University Shared Governance at UB Doctrine of Shared Governance,'" March 5, 2019, see http://bit.ly/SharedGovernanceDoctrine.

Appendix

1. University at Buffalo (UB) Faculty Senate (FS) and Professional Staff Senate (PSS) resolution to change the name of UB's Faculty Senate and Professional Staff Senate Offices to: "The UB Office of University Shared Governance." http://bit.ly/2sGjfXD

2. SUNY UFS "Resolution on Faculty and Professional Staff Membership on College/University Councils." http://bit.ly/2DK4sgt

3. UB FS and PSS Resolution: Declaration of "University at Buffalo Day of Shared Governance." http://bit.ly/2Ye77Zl

4. UB PSS resolution (subsequently endorsed by the UB FS) to begin educational outreach and request that vendors use a more sustainable, recyclable and healthy alternative to Styrofoam: "The Greening of the Commons." http://bit.ly/34DM19f

5. UB FS Resolution on "Freedom of Expression Statement." http://bit.ly/2DGh5cK

6. UB FS Resolution to "Address Asymmetry of Legal Counsel in Matters of UB Shared Governance." http://bit.ly/2qedShn

11

Nassau Community College at a Turning Point

Valerie H. Collins

This chapter provides a historical context relative to events of interest to shared governance at Nassau Community College. The role and importance in the process of two organizations—the American Association of University Professors and the Middle States Commission on Higher Education—are discussed. The study builds on a prior study by Collins (1997) and Henry Mintzberg's (1983) theories on organizational power in higher education.

No duty of the faculty outside of instruction ranks higher than intelligent participation in the formation of educational policies and programs and in the governance of the institution. Self-Study provides an opportunity for an institution to evaluate the formal structures it employs to facilitate faculty participation. (MSA Commission on Higher Education, 1991, p. 39)

Nassau Community College (NCC) is the largest single-campus community college in the State University of New York system (SUNY). NCC completed the self-study process for reaccreditation by the Middle States Commission on Higher Education (MSCHE) in 2016. The subsequent Middle States visiting team report noted the failure of 7 of the 14 standards for accreditation and resulting in a significant challenge for the college. Although at times the following study of events provides cause for concern, the ultimate outcome is very positive, reflected by the regional accreditor and the majority of the members of NCC constituencies.

This study provides a historical context relative to events of interest to shared governance at NCC; discusses the role and importance in the process of two organizations—the American Association of University Professors (AAUP), the faculty professional association, and the MSCHE, the regional accrediting body that oversees NCC; and builds on a prior study (Collins, 1997) on Henry Mintzberg's (1983) theories on organizational structure and power in higher education.

Following submission by NCC of the self-study report in March 2016 to the MSCHE and team visit in April 2016, MSCHE placed NCC on probation due to the lack of compliance with half the standards of accreditation (planning, resource allocation, and institutional renewal; institutional resources; leadership and governance; administration; integrity; institutional assessment; and assessment of student learning). A MSCHE small team visited the campus in August 2016. In fall 2016, NCC submitted a monitoring report to MSCHE. This was followed by a November 2016 MSCHE team visit and report that noted compliance with one of the seven failed standards (integrity) but expressed continued concern with the remaining noncompliant standards.

A permanent college president, the first since 2012, arrived on campus in August 2016. In September, the first vice president for academic affairs at NCC in six years was appointed. Filling these long-vacant positions brought a sense of stability to campus that the April 2016 MSCHE team had found lacking, noting "a prolonged period of instability at the senior levels of institutional leadership" (MSCHE Team Report, 2016a, p. 10)

During the spring 2017 semester and the following summer, new initiatives were introduced at NCC, such as the Institutional Planning Committee. A plan was developed and implemented to address the failed standards. Many significant changes occurred, such as the development of the first Academic Master Plan and college-wide plans linked to the 2017–2021 Strategic Plan. These corrective measures resulted in the positive outcome previously noted (NCC, 2017b; MSCHE, 2017).

By the time the September 2017 monitoring report was submitted to MSCHE, followed by a team visit in October, the college, with members of all constituencies working in concert, had reversed a dire situation and turned it into an opportunity to move forward in a positive way. At the next meeting of the MSCHE, NCC was removed from probation and found to be in compliance with all of the accreditation standards of accreditation.

A Historical Perspective: NCC in the 1960s and 1970s

The process of history is unique, but nonetheless intelligible. Each situation and event is distinct, but each is connected to all the foregoing and succeeding ones by a complex web of cause and effect, probability and accident. The present may be the consequence of accidents, or of irresistible forces, but in either case the present consequences of past events are real and irreversible. The unique present, just as each point in the past, is unintelligible unless we understand the history of how it came to be. (Daniels, 1966, p. 5)

NCC, founded in 1959, held its first classes in the old Nassau County Courthouse on Long Island in Mineola, New York. Thirty faculty members taught 500 full-time and 900 part-time students. In 1963, the college relocated to its permanent home, the decommissioned Army Air Corps Base at Mitchell Field in Garden City, New York. The Army Air Corps Base was built around the parade grounds—a quadrangle rimmed with large chestnut trees (Nicholson, 2018).

Nicholson (2018) observed that the runways provided for ample parking and airplane hangars served as theater and gym. He noted that the "brick buildings, houses and trees contributed to a uniquely pleasant campus environment that was not typical of most community colleges" (pp. 4, 5). Breneman (1994) observed that the 1960s were marked by a "strong, non inflationary economy," and many characterized the early 1960s as the golden years of US higher education.

NCC's early years coincided with a period of change in colleges and universities. The civil rights movement and the Vietnam War precipitated a period of campus unrest as faculty and students began to examine their campus decision-making processes. Many of the issues of concern to the students, however, had little to do with academics or campus governance. Millett (1978) observed that "the student revolution was an excuse for, rather than the cause of, new forms of campus-wide governance" (p. xi). He noted that student disruptions provided faculty members with an opportunity to increase their influence in college and university affairs.

Some NCC students were participants in activities during that time of unrest. A current faculty leader in NCCFT, the full-time faculty union, was a veteran in 1970 when he enrolled in NCC. He became a student leader during that time, serving as Nassau's campus coordinator for Students for a Democratic Society and a member of the student Vietnam-era Veterans Against the War (Nicholson, 2018, p. 1).

The report of the Task Force on Faculty Representation and Academic Negotiation of the American Association for Higher Education identified the main source of faculty discontent as the "nonrecognition or non-accommodation of a faculty desire to participate in policies affecting the professional status and performance of facilities" (AAHE Report, 1967, quoted in Millett, 1978, p. 4). Some institutions founded senates during this period. Faculty in other institutions began to examine and strengthen their bylaws. Another mechanism for increasing faculty participation in decision making that developed during the 1960s and 1970s was collective bargaining. Millett (1978) described this era as a "period of innovation in campus governance" (p. xi).

Founded during this "period of innovation," NCC implemented many initiatives noted in the literature to "participate in policies affecting the professional status" of the faculty. Shortly after its founding, in 1962 NCC received the first AAUP chapter charter granted to a community college. Nicholson relates years of contention between administrators and faculty, describing situations at the college where "democratic decision making was virtually non-existent." The faculty senate served as the first bargaining unit in 1969. The centrality of the 1940 AAUP statement on academic freedom and tenure was acknowledged by the senate. Acknowledging the usefulness of an established union, the faculty affiliated with the New York State United Teachers (NYSUT) in 1971. An adjunct faculty union was formed for collective bargaining followed in 1975. Kemerer and Baldridge (1976), authors of the Stanford Project on Academic Governance, a major research study examining the ramifications of unionism on the future of governance, identified the causes of unionization based on responses to a national survey: "Wages, benefits, and job security are clearly rated as the most important causes of unionization by all respondents. All respondents also included fear of budget cuts, problems of teacher surplus, and the desire for increased faculty influence in governance" (p. 39).

Kemerer and Baldridge (1976) examined the consequences of unionization and concluded that its effect for the faculty depended on the campus, noting that unions could help on campuses where faculty never had a governance role. They commented that in addition to the economic advantages, unionization legitimizes authority by encouraging "the elaboration and codification of campus governance procedures" (p. 209). They noted that unionization can enfranchise a faculty that had no governance role in other institutions. The authors commented that this was more likely to occur by stimulating "new forms and styles of governance in order to increase faculty influence" (Kemerer & Baldridge, 1976, p. 210, as quoted in Collins, 1996, pp. 174–75).

Commenting on changes in governance at NCC, Nicholson (2018) notes that "when the 1971 contract placed the Academic Senate within the collective bargaining agreement, the era of benevolent administrative paternalism began to fade away. In contrast to the original Senate, which as a union only included faculty, the newly negotiated structure included student and administrative representatives" (p. 9).

A glimpse of NCC during this formative period of faculty governance and the establishment of the senate is useful. The legality of the senate bylaws becomes a major issue for the college in 2016 when the MSCHE found the college noncompliant with seven standards of accreditation, including governance.

These developments at NCC in the 1970s were preceded by the publication of the AAUP Statement on Government of Colleges and Universities. The "beauty of the statement" as noted by the AAUP, was the emphasis on the "shared functions of faculty, administration, and trustees and on the joint responsibility of all components for the success of an institution's mission" The statement was jointly formulated by the AAUP, the American Council on Education (ACE) and the Association of Governing Boards and Universities (AGB) (AAUP, 2001, p. 135). The Statement on Government of Colleges and Universities became the standard on this topic for academe. It stresses the interdependence between the various constituencies and delineates the responsibilities of the board of trustees, the president, and the faculty (Collins, 1996, pp. 166–67). As noted in the following section on the AAUP, this statement formed the basis of Article I of the NCC Academic Senate Bylaws.

During a relatively brief period of time, as described by Nicholson, a retired NCC union leader, the faculty took full advantage of opportunities to assume active participation in governance at the college. Although it is beyond the scope of this essay to present a full history of faculty governance issues at NCC, it is worth noting that the MSCHE also addressed issues at the college in 1975 during the first accreditation and again in 1989 (Nicholson, 2018, pp. 6–11). The 2004 self-study (NCC, 2004) did not generate a negative response on governance.

Mintzberg on Power in and Around Organizations

Mintzberg's framework defines power as the "capacity to effect (or affect) organizational outcomes" (1983, p. 4). Collins (1996) used Mintzberg's conceptualization of the power of internal and external influencers to effect change within an organization. According to Mintzberg, influencers are those "who seek to control the organization's decisions and actions." At NCC, 11 groups—6 internal and 5 external—vie for organizational power. Internal influencers are those full-time employees who are charged "with making the decision and taking the actions on a permanent, regular basis: it is they who determine the outcomes, which express the goals pursued by the organization" (Mintzberg, 1983, pp. 22–26). The internal influencers of interest to Collins (1996) were the faculty. External influencers are "non employees who use their bases of influence to try to affect the behavior of the employees" (pp. 22–26). Important influencers for academic organizations include the professional associations and the education departments of federal and state governments. The external influencers of interest to Collins (1996) were the MSCHE and the AAUP.

Academic organization internal influencers at NCC of interest to this study include the president, the board of trustees, administrators, and faculty leaders: the Academic Senate Executive Committee, NCCFT executive committee, and the chair of chairs. These faculty positions provide leadership for the faculty at the college.

The Role of Professional Associations in Guiding Governance

A goal of associations such as the MSCHE and AAUP is to assist the institution in adopting or maintaining the accepted standard in academe of some aspect of organizational policy (Collins, 1996). The influence of these associations on NCC at different points in time is explored and illustrated in the following sections.

The AAUP

AAUP committees developed standards on significant aspects of academic practice, for example, academic freedom and tenure (Committee A) and governance (Committee T). These policy statements provided specific content for faculty to use as they attempted to implement governance changes on their own campuses (Collins, 1996, p. 177).

The AAUP Policy Documents and Reports Tenth Edition (AAUP, 2006) includes two statements that influenced faculty governance in the founding years of the college. In 1971 as part of the process for the first contract negotiations, the NCC Faculty Senate determined that "academic freedom and faculty rights would conform to the *1940 Statement of Principles on Academic Freedom and Tenure*" (Nicholson, 2018, p. 7). This statement was widely implemented in a variety of institutions beginning in 1941 and into this century due in part to the number of prestigious organizations that endorsed it (AAUP, 2006, pp. 7–9).

The influence of another AAUP statement—the Statement on Government of Colleges and Universities—is evident in the NCC Academic Senate Bylaws Article I, Purpose (NCC, 2008; see Appendix A). Article I's five statements use the words *recommend*, *propose*, *formulate* and *provide a forum* in describing the purpose of the Academic Senate. These concepts are in keeping with the 1966 Statement on Government of Colleges and Universities calling for "appropriately shared responsibility and cooperative action among the components of the academic institution." These components include the board of trustees, administrators, students and faculty. The statement is "intended to foster constructive joint thought and action" (AAUP, 2006, p. 135).

This sense of shared responsibility is not evident in the NCC Academic Senate Article II Procedure, which states that actions shall "be communicated to the President of the College and unless vetoed in writing within 10 teaching days of receipt by the President, shall become the policy of the College." Article II goes on to note that "a Senate action vetoed by the President . . . could be followed by a motion to override the veto, and if passed the motion will be referred to the Board of Trustees" (NCC 2008, p. 2; see Appendix A).

In 2016, when the NCCFT contract was up for renewal, Article I of the Academic Senate Bylaws was retained in the newly negotiated contract. Like most faculty and other college professional organizations had done over time, NCC had adopted and retained this AAUP statement in their Academic Senate Bylaws (Article l, Purpose) as encompassing the essential faculty role in colleges and universities. However, not every article included in the NCC Academic Senate contract, when the senate was the bargaining unit in 1971, were included in the 2017 bargaining agreement. As discussed in the following sections, Article II of the Academic Senate Bylaws was of particular concern and was addressed in 2017 when the college and NCCFT engaged in binding arbitration to come into compliance with the MSCHE standard on governance.

NCC, 2016–2018:
The Years Leading up to the Golden Anniversary

The six years that preceded the submission of the 2016 self-study document to the MSCHE were characterized by "a period of instability relative to institutional administration and governance." The comments by the team included the observation that "the observed culture and reality of organization and lines of authority, on the ground at NCC, do not mirror the written documentation provided to the team." The team commented that "the Academic Senate, through its 27 committees, is the driving entity for a large array of policy decisions. Interviews with the President's Cabinet revealed a feeling of frustration by administrators to enact meaningful change—a feeling similarly expressed by the Board of Trustees." The team also noted that "the climate on campus is hostile and uncivil" (MSCHE, 2016a, pp. 12, 13).

Most important, the MSCHE team observed that "Article I is included in the Senate Bylaws and the NCCFT contract for 9/1/13 to 8/1/17." Their observations of NCC note "that the NCCFT contract and the Academic Senate Bylaws appear to be in conflict with Article II: Procedure of the Academic Senate Bylaws." The report references the statement in Article II that "the Board of Trustees under normal circumstances shall not formulate policies or modify existing policies in areas where the Academic Senate has responsibility and powers before the Senate has adequate opportunity to discuss policy and formulate recommendations."

The 2016 team report clearly identifies a concern with Article II of the NCC Bylaws. "These statements, along with the complex process for Presidential veto and Academic Senate veto have coalesced to form a difficult process for effective and efficient policy making decisions to occur on campus" (MSCHE, 2016a, p. 13).

Last, the team recommended that "the College must complete a formal review of the roles and responsibilities and authority of all constituencies and staff of the College, including but not limited to issues of policy creation/revision, policy final approvals, and policy implementation. The results of this review must be clearly communicated to all constituencies of the college" (MSCHE, 2016a, p. 14).

The roles of the president, faculty, and board were at issue at NCC. The April 2016 report recommendations noted above were addressed and did affect the roles of Mintzberg's influencers at the college. The new president arrived in August 2016 and immediately focused on communication with relevant constituencies, particularly the faculty. Phone conversations between the president and faculty leaders preceded his arrival and helped frame the first face-to-face meetings with the group. Faculty leaders and others were consulted in the appointment of an interim vice president of academic affairs. These conversations began a process that continued during the 2016–2017 academic year of numerous ongoing meetings between the president, two vice presidents, and identified faculty leaders. This is in keeping with the role responsibilities delineated in the AAUP *Statement on Government of Colleges and Universities*:

> The president, as chief executive officer of an institution of higher education, is measured largely by his or her capacity for institutional leadership. The president shares responsibility for the definition and attainment of goals, for administrative action, and for operating the communication system that links the components of the academic community. The president's leadership role is supported by delegated authority from the board and faculty. (AAUP, 2006, p. 138)

These conversations ultimately led to a binding arbitration agreement between the NCCFT and the college to revise the Academic Senate bylaws in September 2017. See Appendix A and Appendix B to view both articles as written in spring 2008 and following the September 2017 bylaws revision.

The September 2017 Academic Senate bylaws identify the appropriate faculty role in keeping with the AAUP *Statement on Government of Colleges and Universities* as follows:

> The faculty has primary responsibility for such fundamental areas as curriculum, subject matter and methods of instruction, research, faculty status, and those aspects of student life which relate to the educational process. On these matters the power of review or final decision lodged in the governing board or delegated by it to the president should be exercised adversely only in exceptional circumstances, and for reasons communicated to the faculty. (AAUP, 2006, p. 139).

This statement constituted a key element of the NCC board's 2017 resolution directing the Academic Senate bylaws revision. Also implemented after the 2016 MSCHE Team Report to NCC and the arrival of the new president was the board's decision to hire a consultant to review board processes and provide direction to commence passing college policies during the 2016–2017 academic year. This activity speaks to the role of the board of trustees as follows:

> The governing board of an institution of higher education in the United States operates, with few exceptions, as the final institutional authority. . . . The governing board of an institution, while maintaining a general overview, entrusts the conduct of administration to the administrative officers—the president and the deans—and the conduct of teaching and research to the faculty. The board should undertake appropriate self-limitation. One of the governing board's tasks is to ensure the publication of codified statements that define the overall policies and procedures of the institution under its jurisdiction. (AAUP, 2006, pp. 137–38)

Hiring a consultant to conduct workshops on the board's roles and responsibilities, among which was discussion of board self-evaluation and drafting policies, was a significant basis for the MSCHE team visitors to determine that NCC was now compliant with the accreditation standard of integrity (MSCHE, 2016b).

The Middle States Commission on Higher Education

> The existence of true faculty self-government is a necessity for continuing healthy faculty morale. (MSA Commission on Higher Education, 1953, p. 2)

The above statement, an early guideline in an publication on the faculty governance role, is from the Standards for Accreditation, an important document in the history of the Middle States Association (Collins, 1996, p. 93).

A purpose of the accrediting process is to assist an institution in improving educational effectiveness. NCC's March 2016 self-study was one of the last self-studies completed at the end of a 10-year cycle. Under the revised MSCHE process currently in place, self-studies will be completed every eight years. NCC's March 2016 self-study required an analysis of 14 standards, including governance. The April 2016 team report based on the March 2016 NCC self-study and subsequent campus visit, as noted already, found the Academic Senate bylaws to be a major concern. The April 2016 team found NCC noncompliant with seven of the MSCHE standards, including governance.

Historically, the relationship between the self-study process and changes in faculty governance was not well documented in the literature (Collins, 1996, pp. 8–10). Some have argued that accreditation has little long-term effect on the institution. For example, Bender (1983) stated that accreditation is not seen as a continuous process of self-evaluation and self-improvement but as a series of widely spaced visits by representatives of an external body for which hectic preparations must be made. After reaffirmation of accreditation, many institutions end self-evaluation activity until the 5- or 10-year period has passed and the institution must once again prepare for the visit (Bender, 1983, p. 83). Elliott (1983) notes that "in far too many instances, colleges and universities view accreditation as a troublesome outside force that they have to contend with periodically" (p. 9). On the other hand, one study found that the accreditation self-study process "tends to drive a variety of changes, including major examinations of institutional goals / mission and changes in faculty governance" (Finkelstein, 1984, p. 250).

Mintzberg (1983) noted that the actions of the professional associations are society's way of influencing the behavior of an organization. Collins (1996) found that Mintzberg's theories provided a mechanism to explain how the MSCHE influenced organizational behavior and the methods used by the internal influencers, the faculty and their presidents, to alter the power dynamics at the institution. The MSCHE used direct access to the decision makers and the authority to affect accreditation status to influence them. The success of this method was because of the contacts between the MSCHE professional staff, the visiting team chairpersons, and team visitors. The college addressed the MSCHE standards in the self-study report. When aspects of the report contradicted the standards, the college received recommendations from the MSCHE team. MSCHE monitored whether these recommendations were implemented through the use of the periodic report, and follow-up reports and special MSCHE visits as necessary (Collins, 1996, pp. 478–79).

Conclusion

Two organizations, the Middle States Commission on Higher Educations and the American Association of University Professors, exerted influence on the development of governance at Nassau Community College.

The MSCHE pattern of direct access to influence organizational behavior is apparent at NCC. After the March 2016 self-study and subsequent team visit, NCC was found noncompliant with 7 of the 14 MSCHE standards, including governance. NCC was required to submit two more monitoring reports and host two more MSCHE small team visits (August 2016 and Nov. 2016) until the college was found to be in compliance with the MSCHE standards. MSCHE team reports to the college and reports by the college to MSCHE addressed governance (NCC 2016, 2017a; MSCHE 2016a, 2016b, 2017).

At NCC between 2016 and 2018, the self-study accreditation process had a significant effect on changes in faculty governance. Historically, the MSCHE standards for accreditation have provided a standard of reference for an academic institution to emulate in virtually all aspects of institutional policy. "Accreditation is the means of self-regulation and peer review adopted by the educational community" (MSCHE, 2006, p. 14).

AAUP committee statements influenced NCC early in its history as the Academic Senate and collective bargaining agreement were put in place to allow faculty to "participate in policies affecting the professional status" of the faculty and 50 years later as it revised Academic Senate bylaws.

As noted above and in Appendix A and B, Article I of the 2017 Academic Senate bylaws was changed to remove the "Board of Trustees" from the first and third responsibilities and powers, thereby clarifying that the recommendation by the senate is to the president. The revised 2017 bylaws include an introduction that concludes with "the Academic Senate is the means by which the faculty provides a voice and representation of its respective constituencies, and through which recommendations are made to the President of the College" (NCC, 2017a, p. 4). These changes move Nassau's Senate in line with appropriate AAUP academic institutional roles.

As noted in Appendix A and B, following binding arbitration between the college and the NCCFT in summer 2017, changes were made to the NCC Academic Senate bylaws to bring them in line with usual senate procedures. These included (1) an introduction to the document, and (2) a rewriting of Article II, Procedures, noting that "All formal actions of the Academic Senate in areas where the Senate has powers and responsibilities shall be recommended to the President by the Academic Senate Executive Committee on behalf of the Academic Senate."

Afterward: Sustaining the Corrective Measures Put in Place at NCC in 2017

After removing NCC from probationary status and finding the institution in compliance with all MSCHE standards, the commission, in their wisdom, requested another monitoring report due September 2018 documenting how NCC would sustain the corrective measures put in place in 2017.

These corrective measures included continuation of the president's ongoing meetings with faculty leaders, NCCFT's and NCC administrators' agreement for binding arbitration, and subsequent changes to the Academic Senate bylaws. Another measure put in place in 2017 that was instrumental in addressing role confusion at NCC was the removal of the Planning Committee from the Academic Senate and the establishment of the Institutional Planning Committee with direct report to the president (NCC, 2017b, 2018).

The September 2018 NCC Monitoring Report to MSCHE provided evidence of how the college was sustaining these corrective measures. The section on governance included the following examples to document sustainability: narratives from faculty leaders and administrators attesting to the improved campus climate and good communication between faculty and administrators, including implementation of college-wide and Academic Senate surveys on governance; and college colloquia in 2017 on shared governance and 2018 on student recruitment and retention.

In November 2018 the president of MSCHE sent a letter to the NCC president. MSCHE accepted the 2018 NCC monitoring report as written. No additional information from the college (other than the usual reports) was required. This was the best possible response for the college and was well received by the NCC community.

Final Comment

The 2017 MSCHE visiting team that found NCC in compliance with all 14 standards of accreditation provided an insightful observation that both commended the college on its accomplishments and warned that change in campus culture has just begun:

> An operating system of governance that is in accord with the norms of Higher Education and the SUNY system, regulations

of the State of New York, the Standards of Accreditation of the Middle States Commission on Higher Education, and AAUP Policy now exists at NCC. Effective operationalization requires, as the former Team stated, that "each constituency group embrace their roles and responsibilities." We recognize that NCC's campus culture must evolve to enable this embracing of roles. Trust is a necessary component of this evolution. (MSCHE, 2017, p. 8)

It remains to be seen if the NCC campus culture, at odds for a long time with the usual higher education expectations regarding roles and responsibilities, can successfully meet this challenge. Sustaining respect and trust over time between faculty leaders, the president, administrators, and the board is a necessary component of this equation. Ongoing meetings with this group now called the College Leadership Council continue. The Institutional Planning Committee meets regularly to update the Strategic Plan and address issues of concern to maintain a positive momentum.

From the perspective at Nassau Community College in the fall 2018 Semester: so far, so good.

Note

In the years up through 2016, negative comments about challenges at NCC appeared in the local media. NCC was a topic of conversation in the area and at SUNY.

At the request of Nina Tamrowski, President of the SUNY Faculty Council of Community Colleges, the author presented "Surviving Middle States with Shared Governance" at the 2018 SUNY Voices Conference. At the suggestion of Middle States representatives, three members of the NCC community, including the author, presented at the 2018 Middle States Commission on Higher Education annual conference. The title of the presentation was "Responding to Accreditation Challenges through Governance Changes at Nassau Community College" (Keen, Lupino, & Collins, 2018).

The reason for these presentations was to demonstrate that, as the Middle States Representative noted, an institution can come back successfully after failure of half of the standards for accreditation. One of the faculty leaders noted the truth of this statement, and added "if everyone works together."

References

American Association of University Professors. (2001). *Policy documents and reports*. 9th ed. AAUP. Washington, DC.

American Association of University Professors. (2006). *Policy documents and reports*. 10th ed. AAUP. Washington, DC.
Bender, L. W. (1983). Accreditation: Misuses and misconceptions. In K. Young, C. Chambers, and H. Kelly's (Eds.), *Understanding accreditation* (pp. 71–86). San Francisco: Jossey-Bass.
Breneman, D. (1994). *Liberal arts colleges*. Washington, DC: Brookings Institution.
Collins, V. H. (1996). *The faculty role in governance: A historical analysis of the influence of the American Association of University Professors and the Middle States Association on academic decision making*. Doctoral dissertation, UMI Dissertation Services (9609387).
Collins, V. H. (1997). The faculty role in governance: A historical analysis of the influence of the American Association of University Professors and the Middle States Association on academic decision making. Paper presented at the 1996 Annual Meeting of the Association for the Study of Higher Education (Monograph 97-5). Institute For Higher Education Law & Governance, Houston, TX.
Collins, V. H. (2018). Surviving Middle States with shared governance. Presentation at SUNY Voices Conference.
Daniels, R. V. (1966). *Studying history*. Englewood Cliffs, NJ: Prentice Hall.
Elliot, L.H. (1983). How to make accreditation a constructive experience. In K. E. Young, C. M. Chambers, and H.R. Kells (Eds.), *Understanding accreditation*. San Francisco: Jossey-Bass.
Finkelstein, M. J. (1984). *The American academic profession*. Columbus: Ohio State University Press.
Keen, W. H., Lupino, P., & Collins, V. (2018). Responding to accreditation challenges through governance changes at Nassau Community College. Panel discussion at Middle States Commission on Higher Education Annual Conference.
Kemerer, F. R., & Baldridge, J. V. (1976). *Unions on campus*. San Francisco: Jossey-Bass.
Middle States Association Commission on Higher Education. (1953). *Standards for accreditation*. Philadelphia: MASCHE.
Middle States Association Commission on Higher Education. (1991). *Designs for excellence: Handbook for institutional self-study*. Philadelphia: MASCHE.
Middle States Commission on Higher Education. (2006). *Characteristics of excellence*. Philadelphia: MSCHE.
Middle States Commission on Higher Education. (2016a, April 16). *Report to the trustees, administration, faculty and students of Nassau Community College*. Philadelphia: MSCHE.
Middle States Commission on Higher Education. (2016b, Nov. 28–30). *Report to the trustees, administration, faculty and students of Nassau Community College*. Philadelphia: MSCHE.
Middle States Commission on Higher Education. (2017, Nov.). *Report to the trustees, administration, faculty and students of Nassau Community College*. Philadelphia: MSCHE.

Middle States Commission on Higher Education. (2018, Nov. 20). Letter to Dr. Hubert Keen, president, NCC from Elizabeth Sibolski, president, MSCHE.

Millett, J. D. (1978). *New structures of campus power*. San Francisco: Jossey-Bass.

Mintzberg, H. (1983). *Power in and around organizations*. New Jersey: Prentice Hall.

Nassau Community College. (2004). *Self-study report*. Garden City, NY: NCC.

Nassau Community College. (2008). Academic senate bylaws. Garden City, NY: NCC.

Nassau Community College. (2016, March). Monitoring report to Middle States Commission on Higher Education. Garden City, NY: NCC.

Nassau Community College. (2017a). Academic Senate bylaws. Garden City, NY: NCC.

Nassau Community College. (2017b). Monitoring report to Middle States Commission on Higher Education. Garden City, NY: NCC.

Nassau Community College. (2018). Monitoring report to Middle States Commission on Higher Education. Garden City, NY: NCC.

Nicholson, Philip Y. (2018). *Reflections on a golden anniversary: The NCCFT at NCC 1968–2018*. Unpublished manuscript, Nassau Community College, Garden City, NY.

Appendix A
2008 NCC Academic Senate Bylaws

Nassau Community College Academic Senate Bylaws

Revised Spring 2008

[No Introduction to the Bylaws]

Article I. Purpose

It is the Academic Senate of Nassau Community College that shall provide the College community with a voice in general educational goals and policies as well as other matters of concern to the College community. The Academic Senate shall have responsibilities and powers in the following areas unless otherwise restricted by law and the provisions of the Collective Bargaining Agreement.

    a) To examine, approve and recommend curriculum for examination by the President and the Board of Trustees.

b) To recommend requirements for admissions, degrees, and graduation.

c) To formulate and propose academic college policies including policies on class size, academic advisement, educational TV, and academic calendar for the consideration of the President and the Board of Trustees.

d) To provide a forum for the consideration of academic matters of interest to the College community

e) To formulate and propose policies in those aspects of student life which relate to the educational processes.

Article II. Procedure

All formal actions (actions which affect the policies and procedures of the College and /or the Academic Senate in areas where the Academic Senate has powers and responsibilities) shall be communicated to the President of the College and unless vetoed in writing within ten (10) teaching days of receipt by the President, shall become the policy of the College. Senate action vetoed by the President shall be presented at the next regularly scheduled Senate meeting for discussion. If appropriate, a motion to override the veto may be called for and if carried by a two-thirds vote of the members of the Senate present, the action will be referred to the Board of Trustees for discussion at its next regularly scheduled meeting. The Executive Committee of the Academic Senate must be provided with the opportunity for discussion of the issue with the Board of Trustees prior to Board action. The Board of Trustees under normal circumstances shall not formulate policies or modify existing policies in areas where the Academic Senate has responsibility and powers before the Senate has adequate opportunity to discuss policy and formulate recommendations. Under circumstances during which the Senate cannot be convened, the Board of Trustees shall receive input from the Chair of the Academic Senate or designee.

An action of the Academic Senate may be reversed by a two-thirds vote of those present and voting at a special meeting of faculty and administration called for the purpose of reviewing Senate actions.

Only faculty and administrators may vote at such a meeting. A quorum shall be considered present when a simple majority of faculty and administration are in attendance.

A proposal for reversing one or more actions of the Academic Senate is initiated by a petition signed by at least ten (10) percent of the eligible faculty and administration, in which case the Executive Committee of the Academic Senate must within ten (10) days request the President to call a special meeting. This petition must be filed with the Executive Committee of the Academic Senate working days after the specific Academic Senate and the College President within nine (9) working days after the specific Academic Senate action has been taken.

Appendix B
2017 Bylaws Revision

Nassau Community College

Academic Senate Bylaws

Revised September 2017

Introduction

These Bylaws constitute the Academic Senate of Nassau Community College (Senate) as the representative body of the full-time faculty (as defined by the Nassau Community College Federation of Teachers (NCCFT) Collective Bargaining Agreement) in fulfilling its role in the shared governance of the College. The Bylaws guide the Senate's operations and are in accord with New York State Educational Law, New York State Rules and Regulations governing public institutions of higher education, Rules of Procedure of the Nassau Community College Board of Trustees, Middle States Commission guidance on collegial governance, and Section 20 of the Collective Bargaining Agreement between Nassau Community College and the NCCFT. The Academic Senate is the means by which the faculty provides a voice and representation of its respective constituencies, and through which recommendations are made to the President of the College.

Article I. Purpose

The Purpose and statements remain as written in the Revised 2008 Academic Senate Bylaws with the following exceptions:

A. To examine, approve and recommend curriculum for examination by the President [and the 'Board of Trustees' was removed].

C. To formulate and propose academic College policies including policies on class size, academic advisement, educational technology, and academic calendar for the consideration of the President [and the Board of Trustees was removed].

Notes on Article II. Procedure

The 2017 Article II, Procedure differs significantly from the 2008 Article II, Procedure as noted above. Most importantly, the phrase 'recommend to the President' is included in the first sentence.

Also in the first paragraph, 'the President will review with the Senate reasons why a formal action of the Senate was not affirmed.' There is no statement on 'a motion to override the veto' as in the 2008 Article II Procedure as noted above.

In the 2017 Bylaws, Article II Procedure, the process 'for reversing an action of the Senate' is 'limited to membership in the Senate.' In the 2008 Bylaws, 'a proposal for reversing one or more actions of the Academic Senate is initiated by a petition signed by at least ten (10) percent of the eligible faculty and administration'

Article II. Procedure

All formal actions of the Academic Senate in areas where the Senate has powers and responsibilities shall be recommended to the President by the Executive Committee on behalf of the Academic Senate. The Academic Senate Executive Committee shall review matters that are under consideration by the Senate with the President. The President will respond to formal actions of the Academic Senate before he next meeting of the Senate. If the formal actions of the Senate are not affirmed by the President, then the President will review the reasons with the Academic Senate Executive Committee.

An action of the Academic Senate may be reversed by a two-thirds vote of those present and voting at a special meeting of the membership represented by the Senate called for the purpose of reviewing Academic Senate actions.

Only members represented by the Senate may vote at such a meeting. A quorum shall be considered present when a simple majority of the membership represented by the Academic Senate is in attendance.

A proposal for reversing one or more actions of the Academic Senate is initiated by a petition signed by at least ten (10) percent of the eligible membership represented by the Academic Senate, in which case the Executive Committee of the Academic Senate must within ten (10) regular teaching days call a special meeting. This petition must be filed with the Executive Committee of the Academic Senate within nine (9) regular teaching days after the specific Academic Senate action has been taken.

12

Accreditation Academy!

An Organic Approach to Preparing for an MSCHE Site Visit

Olin Stratton and Wendy Tarby

> *If you are part of an accredited college in New York State, you are familiar with the Middle States Commission on Higher Education. Middle States accredits all colleges in the middle of the Eastern Seaboard and relies on decennial reviews to determine the effectiveness of each school. Onondaga Community College (OCC) recently finished our review. Our self-study has been written, and our campus visit wrapped up in 2018, but the long journey to get to this point started three years earlier. Our campus president wanted to ensure that this process would be transparent and inclusive to all members of the OCC community. A top-down self-study would not be an option for our college. This chapter focuses on how faculty and administrators worked together to kick off the accreditation process and discusses how shared governance was infused into every step along the way.*

How does a college with roughly 10,000 students, 616 full-time and adjunct faculty, and 439 full-time employees inform everyone that the way their accreditor has assessed them in the past has dramatically changed? In 2008, Onondaga Community College (OCC) completed their self-study and reaccreditation visit from the Middle States Commission on Higher Education (MSCHE). At that time, MSCHE had 14 standards and 10 requirements for affiliation. By June 2014, MSCHE had approved a revised set of accreditation standards, with a focus on the student learning experience and emphasis on continuous improvement. Because OCC was in the midst of simultaneously developing a new strategic plan and preparing for the next reaccreditation visit, it became apparent that the college needed a creative way to fully inform and engage the campus community about the new expectations. Through OCC's shared governance system, the Accreditation Academy was established. This was a cross-institutional team of faculty, staff, and administrators whose job was to inform campus constituents about the new standards and the timeline for submission of our 2018 self-study and campus visit. More important, the academy engaged our campus in a thoughtful and collaborative discussion that both delivered and collected information from the community. The academy set the tone for the reaccreditation project. It wasn't going to be a top-down initiative, it was going to be a process that involved the collective knowledge and work of representatives from every academic and administrative department on campus. OCC's Accreditation Academy was developed by and delivered to faculty, staff, and administrators, which led to exceptional participation in the further planning and development of the college's self-study.

OCC Overview and Important Recent Milestones in Shared Governance

Established in 1961, OCC is an accredited, two-year, comprehensive community college in Onondaga County, New York. OCC attracts a diverse student body of approximately 10,000 students, which includes recent high school graduates, working adults and displaced workers, veterans, traditionally underrepresented minorities, English language learners, international students, parents, students with disabilities, low-income students, and first-generation college students, as well as those with a postsecondary credential preparing for new careers.

OCC offers 45 degree and certificate programs that prepare students for transfer to four-year colleges and entry into high-demand careers. The college maintains articulation and 2+2 agreements with many local and regional colleges and universities. OCC also offers certificate programs that can be completed in two to three semesters and short-term workforce training to meet the needs of local employers. Day, evening, online, and extension courses are available in fall and spring semesters, and eight academic programs are available fully online. Three summer sessions and an accelerated winter session are also offered.

The college's last reaccreditation visit ended with the following results:

> At its session on June 26, 2008, the Middle States Commission on Higher Education acted: To reaffirm accreditation and to request a

progress letter, due by April 1, 2010, documenting (1) the development and implementation of a comprehensive, organized, and sustained process for the assessment of institutional effectiveness with evidence that assessment results are used for improvement in all areas (Standard 7); (2) the development and implementation of a comprehensive student advising system (Standard 9); and (3) the development of a comprehensive, organized and sustained assessment process to evaluate and improve student learning (Standard 14). The Periodic Review Report is due June 1, 2013. (2008 MSCHE Accreditation Letter)

The president took immediate action toward an increased focus on assessment and continuous improvement by hiring an experienced professional with extensive background in planning, assessment, and governance systems in complex organizations. In collaboration with key stakeholders, a highly effective, comprehensive assessment plan engaging the college in continuous improvement in all areas of operation relative to its mission and strategic plan was developed. From the president to all campus constituents, goals, outcomes, and measures are tracked and monitored in a centralized online system, in support of the college's mission. OCC also developed a comprehensive system of assessing student learning focused on a set of common institutional learning outcomes. The campus community uses assessment results to identify strengths and opportunities for improvement to enhance student learning and success.

In 2011, the president initiated a Shared Governance Faculty-Trustee Ad Hoc Committee. The committee recommended replacing the president's cabinet with a College Leadership Council (CLC), an entity with broad representation to review and deliberate on cross-institutional issues and make recommendations to the president or forward to appropriate governance channels. This action blended the planning and assessment functions the cabinet facilitated in the past with a new role—as the central vehicle through which recommendations from the Faculty Senate, Staff Association, Administrators' Council, Student Association, and College Committees are collaboratively discussed and deliberated for consideration by the president. This concept was not a radical step for the college, but it held great promise as a bridge to dramatically improve the clarity and consistency of deliberations surrounding recommendations as they made their way through the governance system. The result was a much simpler structure to create a higher level of communications, consistency, and transparency in our decision-making processes, to ensure procedural justice, and to enable us to "tap the collective intelligence" of our college community more effectively. The CLC conducts annual self-assessments to ensure systems, structures, and processes are consistent with the college's goals for shared governance. Suggestions for possible refinements have included strategies for communication practices to promote greater awareness of the shared governance process and increased opportunities for constituent groups to make meaningful contributions in support of the college's mission and goals.

The CLC relies on three committees to investigate specific issues. The Programs and Academic Support Committee, the Student Experience Committee, and the Institutional Effectiveness and Resources Committee all play critical roles in informing the CLC. More important, these committees follow the model of shared governance that is important to the college. For example, each committee is co-chaired by one faculty member and one administrator. The membership of these committees represents a cross-section of the campus. Any faculty member serving on these committees is first vetted by the Faculty Senate and then formally asked to participate by the president of the college. In 2015, the Programs and Academic Support Committee worked in conjunction with the Student Experience Committee to lead the college's mission, vision, and values review, foundational to the development of Lazer Focus: 2016–2021 Strategic Plan. Likewise, the development and presentation of the Accreditation Academy by the Institutional Effectiveness and Resources Committee demonstrated and reinforced OCC's mission review through a deeper understanding of the revised MSCHE standards. The committees all work in tandem in support of the college's mission and goals.

New MSCHE Requirements

In 2015, MSCHE updated their Accreditation Standards and Requirements of Affiliation to comprise 7 standards and 15 requirements, which serve as OCC's roadmap for compliance. There is an emphasis on the importance of continuous improvement, and assessment is built into every standard. In 2015, OCC quickly acknowledged that prior to organizing for reaccreditation in 2018, everyone at the college needed to be fully informed about the new standards, including the emphasis on mission, students at the front, and the importance of planning and governance in support of students. In the spirit of collaboration, the Institutional Effectiveness and Resources Committee was charged with designing and implementing a learning opportunity for all faculty, administrators, and staff members to gain a deeper understanding of standards and an awareness of the "student-centered" principle that truly drives the college's work.

Institutional Effectiveness and Resources Committee

In fall 2014, the active members of the Institutional Effectiveness and Resources Committee (IE committee) were comprised of four faculty members and nine administrators. The president charged them with:

> the development, organization and presentation of an Accreditation Academy to ensure that the full OCC community is prepared to conduct a meaningful self-study, responding to these standards. The Academy should include a full explication of the new standards, an awareness of the College's documentation system, and the opportunity for participants to understand the relationship of their work to the accreditation process. The Committee should recommend a small group to represent OCC at the annual Middle States' Convention in December. The Committee should also develop a plan and recommend a timeline and steering committee for the purposes of developing the College's self-study for submission in a timely way. Those recommendations should be delivered to the CLC by the end of February 2015 so that the CLC can advise the President before the end of the 2014–15 academic year, thereby enabling the self-study steering committee to be formed prior to the 2015–16 academic year.

This charge started the ball rolling for OCC's self-study. The 13 committee members met monthly to develop the Accreditation Academy. The first step was to familiarize themselves with the new standards. In December of that year, a group of five administrators and two faculty members attended the MSCHE conference in Philadelphia. Five who attended were on the IE committee. This was the first annual conference where MSCHE rolled out the new standards. The keynote speakers focused on the development of the revised standards and expectations for institutions moving forward. After the conference, the IE committee met to talk about the new expectations. Now that the committee had a better understanding of what was expected in the reaccreditation process, it was time to develop an engaging program to inform the campus.

Because the IE committee represented different administrative departments and academic divisions, committee members were assigned specific standards linked to their role at the college. For example, the vice president of Human Resources was assigned to review Standard II, Ethics and Integrity, and faculty were assigned to Standard III, Design and Delivery of the Student Learning Experience, and Standard V, Educational Effectiveness Assessment. Tying committee members to standards that were close to their job function helped them develop interesting and appealing presentations for the Accreditation Academy curriculum. Each standard's group was encouraged to use a slide deck and multimedia platforms in a creative way. Members developed engaging, interactive activities for each standard to help facilitate the conversation, rather than delivering boring slides of information. The IE committee used meeting time to rehearse the show as if it were a play. Each standard became an act and performance, complete with a script. The committee members gave feedback to each other to help improve performances and determine what activities needed to be shortened, extended, or cut. They spent a tremendous amount of time crafting a show that was entertaining and engaging.

The Accreditation Academy Performance

The Accreditation Academy was going to be presented to groups of faculty, staff, and administrators. Most performances targeted one of those specific groups, but the IE committee also held open performances that anybody could attend. Vice presidents would set up specific academies for their staff, and multiple sessions were given at times when faculty could attend. The organizers of the Accreditation Academy worked with everybody on campus to set up performances that could reach the largest number of people possible. Since the presentations were in large lecture halls, and rooms packed with people, it was important that the performance grab everybody's attention quickly and hold it using interactive activities and discussion. The format for the Accreditation Academy started with a clever and amusing introduction, followed by an act for each standard and explanation of compliance requirements. The following outline of each act describes our approach and offers insights into the academy.

Prologue: An audience invited to a discussion on MSCHE standards does not have high expectations for an engaging meeting. This makes the introduction the most critical part of the show. A well-respected professor in the Business Department was given the task of getting people's attention. Instead of going with a slide that showed all 14 of the old standards and a cross-walked slide showing the 7 new standards, he took a very different approach. He showed a clip from the movie *Moneyball*. The premise of the clip is that continuing to operate in the same manner as you always have will not work in a competitive, regulated environment. The professor had participated in the last three MSCHE reviews and stressed that the college had to think and act differently this time because new expectations were on the horizon. The prologue served as an ice-breaker of sorts with the intent of engaging the audience and reducing accreditation anxiety.

Act 1, Standard I: Mission and Goals

The associate vice president of Institutional Planning, Assessment and Research presented this act. She described five learning outcomes for the discussion:

- Identify key components of Standard I that are most relevant to OCC's goals and activities.
- Describe the collaborative process used to develop and periodically review the college's mission and goals.
- Locate OCC's current mission statement and goals as presented to internal and external stakeholders.
- List examples of the college's strategy to ensure programs and services are consistent with its mission.
- Articulate individual roles/contributions in support of Standard I.

These outcomes were met primarily through interactive discussion. The presenter talked for two or three minutes and facilitated a small group activity. The audience was asked: "How do you personally contribute to the college's mission? What is your role in improving the effectiveness of your department/division, and what improvements have been made recently?" After participants had a chance to discuss in small groups, people were asked to share their responses with the entire group. Those responses were the key for the presenter to be able to meet the five outcomes for Standard I. The facilitator could have put all of her information on a slide, but she used the audience's responses to shape the conversation. This set the tone for many of the standards to come. Information about standards was not dictated to the audience. Instead, the audience's responses and participation were used to direct them to the correct answer during a conversation, not a lecture.

Act 2, Standard II: Ethics and Integrity

The vice president of Human Resources presented this act and had six learning outcomes for the discussion:

- List examples of evidence of ethical responsibility (academic freedom, commitment to diversity, etc.).
- Describe how the college meets Title IX expectations.
- Discuss policies and procedures governing student/faculty/staff complaints.
- Describe areas in which potential conflicts of interest could exist.
- Discuss ways the college provides and promotes financial literacy to students.
- Describe the college's compliance program.

The presenter relied on two different ethics case studies to discuss these learning outcomes. The first case involved a doctoral student who was working at a local community college. The student borrows supplies and student demographic and retention data from the community college to support her work in her graduate school class. The second case study centered on a large alcoholic beverage company that wants to donate a significant sum of money to the college. This contradicts the college's focus on recruiting Muslim students, who do not consume alcohol. Should the college accept or reject this sizable gift? The participating audience could clearly identify the main ethical concerns in these case studies, but the finer points that were not as clear-cut led to great discussion, and gave the presenter a chance to express OCC's stance on specific ethical concerns. In addition, there was a simple question that always sparked interesting conversations: "Who is OCC's Title IX coordinator?" Gauging the audience's understanding of Title IX legislation helped identify future training needs.

Act 3, Standard III: Design and Delivery of the Student Learning Experience

This act was co-presented by a professor from Human Services and Teacher Education and a professor from the Business Administration department. They had five learning outcomes for their discussion:

- Describe the collaborative process used to design, deliver, and assess student-learning activities regardless of the modality in academic programs.
- Locate resources where programs of study are clearly and accurately described.
- Identify the learning opportunities and resources used to support the college's academic programs and the student's progress.
- Describe how general education outcomes are integrated into the student's learning experience.
- Describe the periodic assessment of the effectiveness of academic programs.

These presenters copied and pasted the MSCHE wording for Standard III into a word cloud to give a visual summary of the most important components of this standard. They could summarize much of what Standard III said by reading the key words (see Figure 12.1 on page 226). "A student should have a rigorous learning experience regardless of the program's modality."

In addition, the presenters facilitated a conversation about how the college designs curriculum backward from the Institutional Learning Outcomes and delivers information forward from the Learning Outcomes of a particular lesson.

Figure 12.1. Word cloud summarizing key points of MSCHE Standard III.

The presenters led a discussion about the necessity of comprehensive course syllabi based on an educational malpractice case study. This was a very instructive conversation, emphasizing the critical need to communicate curricula to students via a detailed syllabus and helping students meet the expectations of the instructor in a standard and consistent manner.

Act 4, Standard IV: Support of the Student Experience

This act was co-presented by the director of the Collegiate Science and Technology Entry Program and associate vice president of Student Engagement. The presenters had three learning outcomes for their discussion:

- Identify key components of Standard IV that are most relevant to the college's goals and activities.
- Describe the college's initiatives, strategies and goals to support the student experience.

- List the resources available that document/illustrate the availability of student access to services that support their academic engagement and path to graduation.

This standard had the greatest impact on the participants and took longer than any other to discuss. The presenters used a film crew to record student responses when they were asked these four questions:

1. What is the college doing to support your success?
2. What could the college do better to support you?
3. What resources are you aware of on campus?
4. How could these resources become better?

The presenters edited out perfunctory statements about bad cafeteria food and not enough parking to reveal some significant truths about how our students viewed the college. Watching students voice fundamental concerns made many audience members feel uncomfortable. Depending on which group of participants were in the audience, the video sometimes led to finger pointing between faculty and staff. When participants saw actual student responses, it was very difficult for them to recognize how their role in the college could possibly affect the problem. After two or three presentations of the Accreditation Academy, the presenters of Standard IV became adept at taking comments from the audience, shaping potential solutions, and steering the conversation in a positive direction.

Act 5, Standard V: Education Effectiveness Assessment

This act was co-presented by two professors, one from the Health Information Technology department and one from the Mathematics department. They had three learning outcomes for their discussion:

- Identify key components and criteria of Standard V relating to assessment at the college.
- Describe the processes through which the college ensures each degree and certificate program supports institutional goals and student learning outcomes.

- Describe how the college uses assessments of student learning outcomes to affect program and curricular changes.

While assessment is now infused into all of the Middle States standards, Standard V really drives the point home. Lecturing an audience about assessment can cause them to shut down quickly, so the presenters took a different approach. They put up a slide that showed assessment results for a fictional program's learning outcomes. They asked the audience to analyze the results. Which results were surprising? What outcomes are students proficient in? Which outcomes need work? These are the fundamental questions that every department should be answering on a regular basis. Once again, the presenters used the participants' responses to deliver the information that they needed to know.

Act 6, Standard VI: Planning, Resources, and Institutional Improvement

This act was presented by the associate vice president of Administrative Services and included four learning outcomes:

- Identify institutional objectives and know where to locate these objectives, how they are linked to the mission and goals of the institution, and how they are used for planning and resource allocation.
- Describe the planning, improvement, and decision-making processes that are used on campus.
- Describe the financial planning and budgeting process at the college and how it is aligned with the institution's mission and goals.
- Articulate individual roles/contributions in support of Standard VI.

To deliver these outcomes, the presenter challenged the audience to break into small groups and develop a three-minute elevator pitch for a new program designed to enhance or support the student experience. This led to discussions on how programs and initiatives worked their way through the college for approval and funding.

Act 7, Standard VII: Governance, Leadership, and Administration

The vice president of Finance presented this act, and had two learning outcomes for the discussion:

- Articulate the college's governance structure that outlines roles, responsibilities, and accountability for decision making by each constituency, including governing body, administration, faculty, staff, and students.

- Describe how the college's senior leadership team demonstrates effectiveness, including how well it interacts with other governing entities, including faculty and students.

The presenter displayed OCC's interactive shared governance website and drilled into entities pertinent to the audience, emphasizing their role and contributions toward achieving the college's mission and goals.

Act 8, Verification of Compliance with Accreditation-Relevant Federal Regulations

The Communication and Project coordinator for the Institutional Planning, Assessment, and Research office, assistant to the Chief Information Officer, and associate vice president of Enrollment Development presented this act and had four learning outcomes for their discussion:

- Identify key components of MSCHE compliance with federal regulations that are relevant to the college.

- List examples of the college's strategies to ensure compliance with federal regulations.

- Locate documentation/evidence regarding applicable federal regulations on the public and/or employee websites.

- Articulate individuals' and/or departments' roles and contributions in support of the federal regulations.

This team had the difficult task of relaying to the audience the important details of OCC's compliance with federal regulations. Verification of identity of online students is a great example. How does the College know that the student who signed up for the course is the same student who finishes, and gets the grade for the course? To lighten the mood, this group found a video that depicted what can happen when the professor of a class does not know the names of his students. This team did not go into detail on every federal regulation but did a cursory overview of the important ones.

Finally, the presenters appealed to the audience on a light note, modifying Tom Hanks's famous movie line from *A League of Their Own* to "there's no crying in accreditation."

As a follow up, participants were asked to respond to an electronic quiz a few days after they participated in the Accreditation Academy. The quiz reinforced a handful of the important takeaways. The feedback validated that learning occurred and identified areas in need of further training opportunities.

How Did the Performances Go?

The IE committee did a dress rehearsal to tighten the performance. Presenters had a chance to cut extraneous information or activities that did not really help the audience meet the learning outcomes. The dress rehearsal also gave the group a chance to interact with a well-built slide deck that included embedded videos and graphics. The first performance was for a large group of senior administrators. Despite the fact the information and activities were well received, the session was deemed excessively long. The first performance took nearly three hours, which is a long time to keep an audience's attention. The feedback from the participants, however, informed the next show. The IE committee decided that each act needed both an in-depth and a short version of each standard. The committee had to tailor the presentation to the specific audience. When the Accreditation Academy was presented to a group of administrators, the presenters focused on the acts that dealt with ethics and integrity, planning, and verification of compliance. When the Accreditation Academy was presented to a group of faculty, the presenters emphasized the acts that dealt with curriculum and assessment of student learning. Each time an Accreditation Academy was performed, it became shorter and tighter until it eventually ran like a well-oiled machine. It was difficult for each presenter to free up their schedule for each performance, but as time went on, presenters no longer needed their notes and could come just in time for their performance and quickly return to their job when they were done.

Time limitations were an important concern. The IE committee spent significant time planning and prepping for each performance, as well as delivering repeat performances. Scheduling two hours in the middle of the day to present the Accreditation Academy was a challenge, to say the least. It worked much better when the presenters could show up just in time to give their performance, and then get back to work in the office or classroom.

The first Accreditation Academy was performed for a large group consisting of the president and her extended leadership team. They were impressed by how the presentation brought the entire scope of the college into focus, so they started asking for more performances for their employees. Entire departments would send their staff to the Accreditation Academy. The IE committee would host a presentation for Student Services employees one day, and then secretaries and other staff the next day. They hosted many presentations for faculty at different times of the day so everybody had a chance to participate. The Student Association was also encouraged to attend many of the open sessions. When all was said and done, about 500 administrators, faculty, adjuncts, staff, and students participated in the 15 Accreditation Academy presentations that were given.

Recommendations for a Successful Accreditation Academy

The buzz that the Accreditation Academy created was exactly what the IE committee was looking for. People wanted to know more about how their role in the college was going to affect the reaccreditation process. In previous rounds of reaccreditation, only a select group of people in the college participated. After the Accreditation Academy, the whole campus was talking about MSCHE expectations. The academy created this buzz because the IE committee took a couple of simple but important steps at the beginning of the process and learned from mistakes.

First and foremost, if you choose to kick off your accreditation process with an Accreditation Academy, it is critical to keep the discussion light. Do not drill the audience with facts written on a slide. Embed videos and activities, so it is not simply a parade of talking heads. It is much more effective for the audience members to determine for themselves how they fit into the big picture of a college. That level of active participation will drive points home much more effectively than simply giving employees information on the new standards.

Be smart about whom you pick to present. There is a wealth of hidden talent in your college. Find people to present who are charismatic and engaging to the audience. Although a vice president of a division might have the title and be a draw, if they are just going to read from a slide, they are not the person you want leading the charge. Instead, find someone lower in the division who can engage an audience and welcomes a professional development opportunity. Moreover, you will probably need to give this presentation many times, so you might not want to tie up a vice president's busy schedule.

Last, it is critical to have support for a project like this from the leaders of your campus community. The president of the college can make participation in this presentation mandatory or highly encouraged. The head of your Faculty Senate can get the word out that this presentation is important. The head of your Student Association can be a strong ally in getting students to participate. At OCC, our president backed the Accreditation Academy 100 percent. She spoke the praises of the academy to everyone on campus. Finding true leaders with the respect of the faculty and staff will significantly increase the participation of the campus community.

The IE committee is particularly proud of the number of participants who went up to the presenters after the show and said, "I had no idea that OCC did . . ." People become insulated in their job and forget to look at the college holistically. It is difficult to see the achievements and challenges that all members of the campus community share when one is focused solely on their daily work routine.

The Accreditation Academy is a spectacular example of how the shared governance process can create a program that affects the entire campus. The academy broke people out of their roles and introduced them to how the college and their colleagues worked. By using a wide range of creative and flexible teaching and learning techniques, the academy brought out the best in the participants. It helped people realize that they are part of the big picture on campus and that their contributions are truly important to student success. The academy opened the doors to all divisions and demonstrated to each member of the administration, faculty, and staff that what they do is vital to achieving the mission and goals of OCC overall. In the end, it set the stage for completing a successful MSCHE self-study and reaccreditation visit. Because of the buzz generated by the Accreditation Academy, the college was able to engage over 120 faculty, staff, students, and administrators to serve on steering committees and work groups for each standard. Those participants from every level of the college helped send the message to MSCHE that our campus was taking the reaccreditation process seriously and was willing to do the work necessary to earn reaccreditation.

13

A Comparative Analysis of Regional Accreditors

Role of Shared Governance in Accreditation

Peter L. K. Knuepfer

Seven regional accrediting organizations are authorized by the US Department of Education to oversee accreditation of colleges and universities. Each has a set of expectations and criteria providing the framework for evaluating whether academic institutions should be awarded or retain accreditation. Among other things, the criteria address the governance of an institution and the expected role of many constituencies, including the faculty. The description of faculty's role in establishing and overseeing the curriculum and governance structures varies among the accreditors. The accrediting agencies share the expectation that the institution has mechanisms to ensure that faculty are engaged in appropriate areas of governance, although the specific mechanisms may not be clearly defined. Some of the commissions recognize the role of shared governance among faculty and administration in institutional governance. Others do not address shared governance. Several commissions have weakened their language about how faculty should be engaged in the governance of the institution in their most recent revision of criteria. The Higher Learning Commission, on the other hand, has clarified the importance of shared governance in their latest revision of accreditation criteria. Overall, despite some explicit support, there has been an erosion of the expectations for shared governance in higher education accreditation.

Accreditation is designed to ensure the quality and stability of institutions of higher education in the United States. The process is overseen by accrediting organizations that are private, nonprofit groups. These groups need to be recognized by the US Department of Education to be eligible for federal funding. The Department of Education describes its role:

The Department provides oversight over the postsecondary accreditation system through its review of all federally-recognized accrediting agencies. The Department holds accrediting agencies accountable by ensuring that they enforce their accreditation standards effectively. Also, as a part of the Department's oversight roles, the Secretary of Education is required by law to publish a list of nationally recognized accrediting agencies that the Secretary determines to be reliable authorities as to the quality of education or training provided by the institutions of higher education and the higher education programs they accredit. (DAPIP, 2019)

It is thus important to note that although the Department of Education plays an important oversight role in ensuring the integrity of the accreditation process, the accrediting agencies are in fact independent of the government. Eaton (2015, p. 1) clarifies that "The federal government relies on accreditation to assure the quality of institutions and programs to which the government provides federal funds and for which the government provides federal aid to students."

Federally recognized accrediting groups can be institutional or programmatic. Institutional accreditors can be regional or national. Most public and private nonprofit colleges and universities are accredited by a regional commission, and these are the focus of the current discussion. Six regional accrediting associations exist in the United States, with one (the Western Association) subdivided into separate commissions for associate-granting institutions and baccalaureate-granting institutions. Their jurisdictions are listed in Table 13.1. These commissions are composed of institutional members (accredited colleges and universities that pay dues to the organization and are entitled to vote on commission policies and procedures), an elected group of commissioners representing the members, and a staff to oversee commission activities.

A primary duty of the commissions is to ensure that member institutions meet the criteria that the commission (and its members) has established for accreditation. These criteria typically include institutional structure and governance, financial health of the institution, support of the student experience, appropriate qualifications of instructors and curriculum, and assessment and continual improvement. The role of shared governance in an academic institution is part of the first set of criteria noted above, but the standards differ from region to region. In most cases, there has been a recent step back from more prescriptive criteria for the role of faculty governance. The remainder of this essay focuses on these regional criteria about shared governance in accreditation standards and the changes that the accrediting commissions have produced.

Table 13.1. Regional Accrediting Commissions

Commission	States and US Territories Covered
Higher Learning Commission (HLC)	Arizona, Arkansas, Colorado, Illinois, Indiana, Iowa, Kansas, Michigan, Minnesota, Missouri, Nebraska, New Mexico, North Dakota, Ohio, Oklahoma, South Dakota, West Virginia, Wisconsin, Wyoming
Middle States Commission on Higher Education (MSCHE)	Delaware, District of Columbia, Maryland, New Jersey, New York, Pennsylvania, Puerto Rico, the Virgin Islands
New England Commission of Higher Education (NECHE)	Connecticut, Maine, Massachusetts, New Hampshire, Rhode Island, Vermont
Northwest Commission on Colleges and Universities (NWCCU)	Alaska, Idaho, Montana, Nevada, Oregon, Utah, Washington
Southern Association of Colleges and Schools Commission on Colleges (SACSCOC)	Alabama, Florida, Georgia, Kentucky, Louisiana, Mississippi, North Carolina, South Carolina, Tennessee, Texas, Virginia
Accrediting Commission for Community and Junior Colleges, Western Association of Schools and Colleges (ACCJC)	Associate degree–granting institutions in California, Hawaii, and the Pacific Basin
Western Association of Schools and Colleges Senior College and University Commission (WSCUC)	Baccalaureate degree or higher institutions in California, Hawaii, and the Pacific Basin

Accreditation Criteria Related to Faculty Governance

Each accreditation commission has established a set of criteria or guidelines for accreditation providing the framework for evaluating whether academic institutions should be awarded or retain accreditation. As noted already, these criteria are approved by the member institutions. Most regional commissions have revised their criteria in recent years, especially increasing the focus on student learning and an institution's ability to provide that learning. Part of that ability centers on the financial resources a campus has available, and part of it centers on adequate staffing to deliver the curriculum. An important part of the criteria centers on the presence of established governance processes and procedures to provide oversight of the curriculum and the institution's progress in meeting its mission and goals while also meeting the expectations of the accrediting body. The description of the role of faculty in establishing and overseeing the curriculum and governance structures in support of those duties varies among the regional accreditors. The following sections provide an update to the article, "Regional Accreditation Standards Concerning Academic Freedom and the Faculty Role in Governance," by the American Association of University Professors (AAUP, undated, ca. 2007).

Middle States Commission on Higher Education (MSCHE)

The MSCHE revised its Standards for Accreditation and Requirements for Affiliation in 2014 (MSCHE, 2015) after considerable review and commentary from member institutions. MSCHE defines 15 requirements that institutions must satisfy for affiliation and 7 standards for accreditation and reaccreditation. One of the requirements addresses expectations about the faculty, and three of the standards address the role of faculty in the institution.

Requirements of Affiliation

> 15. The institution has a core of faculty (full-time or part-time) and/or other appropriate professionals with sufficient responsibility to the institution to assure the continuity and coherence of the institution's educational programs. (MSCHE, 2015, p. 3)

Standard I: Mission and Goals

In the broad description of expectations about what an institution should include in its mission statement and outline of institutional goals, the commission focuses on the general roles of the various constituents.

The mission must be clearly defined and "guide faculty, administration, staff, and governing structures in making decisions related to planning, resource allocation, program and curricular development, and the definition of institutional and educational outcomes" (MSCHE, 2015, p. 4).

Standard III: Design and Delivery of the Student Learning Experience

Middle States defines this standard:

> An institution provides students with learning experiences that are characterized by rigor and coherence at all program, certificate, and degree levels, regardless of instructional modality. All learning experiences, regardless of modality, program pace/schedule, level, and setting are consistent with higher education expectations. (MSCHE, 2015, p. 7)

Eight criteria are specified, describing what an institution is expected to do in meeting this standard. Criterion 2 describes the role of faculty in supporting the design and delivery of the curriculum, requiring an institution to provide "student learning experiences that are designed, delivered, and assessed by faculty (full-time or part-time) and/or other appropriate professionals" (MSCHE, 2015, p. 7). Note that this criterion does not allocate exclusive design and delivery of the curriculum to faculty, nor does it offer any guidance as to how faculty "or other appropriate professionals" should implement this oversight of the curriculum. The remainder of the criterion describes expectations of the qualifications of those who exercise this design, delivery, and assessment role, again without explicitly identifying process. Criterion 7 provides additional guidance to the institution on how to accomplish the standard, requiring it to provide "adequate and appropriate institutional review and approval on any student learning opportunities designed, delivered, or assessed by third-party provider" (MSCHE, 2015, p. 8).

Standard V: Educational Effectiveness Assessment

This standard addresses the expectations for institutional assessment:

> Assessment of student learning and achievement demonstrates that the institution's students have accomplished educational goals consistent with their program of study, degree level, the

institution's mission, and appropriate expectations for institutions of higher education. (MSCHE, 2015, p. 10)

Criterion 2 addresses faculty's role in the assessment process by indicating that institutions are expected to undertake "organized and systematic assessments, conducted by faculty and/or appropriate professionals, evaluating the extent of student achievement of institutional and degree/program goals" (MSCHE, 2015, p. 10). Again, the mechanism for involvement of faculty is left open.

Standard VII: Governance, Leadership, and Administration

The final standard directly addresses the role of governance for the institution.

> The institution is governed and administered in a manner that allows it to realize its stated mission and goals in a way that effectively benefits the institution, its students, and the other constituencies it serves. Even when supported by or affiliated with governmental, corporate, religious, educational system, or other unaccredited organizations, the institution has education as its primary purpose, and it operates as an academic institution with appropriate autonomy. (MSCHE, 2015, p. 13)

The criteria mainly address the role of the governing authority (e.g., board of trustees), campus president/chief executive, and administration. However, the first criterion broadly addresses the role of faculty governance, instructing the institution to demonstrate that it has "a clearly articulated and transparent governance structure that outlines roles, responsibilities, and accountability for decision making by each constituency, including governing body, administration, faculty, staff and students" (MSCHE, 2015, p. 14).

In summary, the current standards defined by MSCHE emphasize the broad role of the faculty in campus governance, particularly in curriculum development and delivery. However, the standards do not articulate a specific role for faculty *governance*, leaving it to the institutions to demonstrate the mechanism(s) by which they meet the standards and criteria.

New England Commission of Higher Education (NECHE)

NECHE revised its standards for accreditation in 2016, with nine standards that are expected to be met by institutions (NECHE, 2016). The principal description of the expectations of the faculty role is contained in Standard 3.

Standard 3: Organization and Governance

Several sections of Standard 3 address the role of faculty and their position within an institution's governance structure. The overall general statement about governance is contained in the introduction to this section of their standards document.

> The institution has a system of governance that facilitates the accomplishment of its mission and purposes and supports institutional effectiveness and integrity. Through its organizational design and governance structure, the institution creates and sustains an environment that encourages teaching, learning, service, scholarship, and where appropriate, research and creative activity. It demonstrates administrative capacity by assuring provision of support adequate for the appropriate functioning of each organizational component. The institution has sufficient independence from any other entity to be held accountable for meeting the Commission's Standards for Accreditation. (NECHE, 2016, p. 5)

The first subsection of Standard 3 provides a general description of the commission's expectations.

> 3.1 The authority, responsibilities, and relationships among the governing board, administration, faculty, staff, and sponsoring entity (if any) are clearly described in the institution's bylaws, or an equivalent document, and in a table of organization that displays the working order of the institution. The board, administration, staff, and faculty understand and fulfill their respective roles as set forth in the institution's official documents and are provided with the appropriate information to undertake their respective roles. (NECHE, 2016, p. 5)

NECHE goes on to describe first the expected responsibilities of the governing board and then, in some detail, the expectations for internal governance. Here the commission gets more specific about the roles that administrators and faculty (among others) are expected to play in institutional governance.

> 3.13 In accordance with established institutional mechanisms and procedures, the chief executive officer and senior administrators consult with faculty, students, other administrators, and staff, and are appropriately responsive to their concerns, needs, and initiatives. The institution's internal governance provides for the appropriate participation of its constituencies, promotes communications, and effectively advances the quality of the institution.
>
> 3.14 The institution's chief academic officer is directly responsible to the chief executive officer, and in concert with the faculty and other academic administrators, is responsible for the quality of the academic program. The institution's organization and governance structure assure the integrity and quality of academic programming however and wherever offered. Off-campus, continuing education, distance education, correspondence education, international, evening, and weekend programs are clearly integrated and incorporated into the policy formation, academic oversight, and evaluation system of the institution.
>
> 3.15 The institution places primary responsibility for the content, quality, and effectiveness of the curriculum with its faculty. Faculty have a substantive voice in matters of educational programs, faculty personnel, and other aspects of institutional policy that relate to their areas of responsibility and expertise. (NECHE, 2016, p. 6)

Thus, the roles of the faculty of the institution are defined, albeit in somewhat general terms (e.g., relating to their areas of responsibility), and NECHE emphasizes the importance of consultation and substantive voice through mechanisms and procedures established by the institution. Even though a faculty governance structure is not explicitly mentioned, it is clear that the commission requires institutions to make decisions through consultative procedures involving established structures; a faculty senate or its equivalent certainly is one such structure at most universities and colleges.

Standard 4: The Academic Program

NECHE describes its general expectation for the structure and quality of undergraduate academic programs through a general statement of expectations and specific requirements. The general expectations are provided in the opening statement of the standard and in the first few subsections.

> The institution's academic programs are consistent with and serve to fulfill its mission and purposes. The institution works systematically and effectively to plan, provide, oversee, evaluate, improve, and assure the academic quality and integrity of its academic programs and the credits and degrees awarded. The institution sets a standard of student achievement appropriate to the degree or certificate awarded and develops the systematic means to understand how and what students are learning and to use the evidence obtained to improve the academic program. (NECHE, 2016, p. 8)

The commission provides a further clarification of the faculty role in institutional governance in Standard 4. Specifically, the important role of faculty participation in overseeing and reviewing academic programs is explicitly defined.

> 4.5 Through its system of academic administration and faculty participation, the institution demonstrates an effective system of academic oversight, assuring the quality of the academic program wherever and however it is offered.
>
> 4.6 The institution develops, approves, administers, and on a regular cycle reviews its academic programs under institutional policies that are implemented by designated bodies with established channels of communication and control. Review of academic programs includes evidence of student success and program effectiveness and incorporates an external perspective. Faculty have a substantive voice in these matters. (NECHE, 2016, p. 8)

Clearly, then, NECHE has many expectations about the areas in which faculty are involved in institutional and academic governance. They defer to an institution's decisions on appropriate structures, as is typically the case among accrediting bodies, but they also make it clear that institutional structures and processes need to exist to enable the faculty (and students) to provide substantive input and oversight into academic matters.

The Higher Learning Commission (HLC)

The HLC oversees accreditation of colleges and universities across a wide swath of the central part of the United States. HLC revised its criteria for accreditation in 2019 for implementation in September 2020 (HLC, 2019). This review summarizes the criteria as amended, in the context of guiding values and assumed practices last updated in the 2018 resource guide (HLC, 2018).

Guiding Values

The HLC provides a set of 10 guiding values that give a high-level outline of the framework that leads to specific expectations for accreditation. Guiding Value 7 describes the general expectations for the governance structure of an institution.

> Governance for the Well-Being of the Institution. Governance of a quality institution of higher education will include a significant role for faculty, in particular with regard to currency and sufficiency of the curriculum, expectations for student performance, qualifications of the instructional staff, and adequacy of resources for instructional support. (HLC, 2018, p. 6)

Criteria for Accreditation

The HLC criteria for accreditation were most recently revised in 2019. HLC lists five criteria, each of which has core components that must be addressed by institutions.

Criterion 2: Integrity: Ethical and Responsible Conduct

HLC expects that an institution will conduct itself in an ethical and responsible fashion. Core Component 2.C describes expectations for the behavior of the institution's governing board. Point 2.C.5 remarks on the relationship between the governing board and other campus constituencies: "The governing board delegates day-to-day management of the institution to the institution's administration and expects the faculty to oversee academic matters" (HLC, 2019, p. 3).

Criterion 3: Teaching and Learning: Quality, Resources, and Support

The HLC describes five core components of expectations an institution must follow in providing high-quality educational opportunities. One aspect of these expectations that describes the faculty role is contained in Core Component 3.C, which addresses the requirement that sufficient and appropriate faculty and staff are needed to provide a high-quality academic and student services program. Point 3.C.1 notes that the number and quality of faculty must be sufficient to provide "oversight of the curriculum and expectations for student performance" (HLC, 2019, p. 4).

Criterion 4: Teaching and Learning: Evaluation and Improvement

This criterion covers the expectations for assessment of the teaching and learning experience. Core Component 4.B addresses the commitment of the institution to this assessment process. Point 4.B.3 requires that "the institution's processes and methodologies to assess student learning reflect good practice, including the substantial participation of faculty, instructional and other relevant staff members" (HLC, 2019, p. 5). Although the criterion does not specify the structure, HLC clearly expects well-defined processes that involve faculty directly in the assessment of student learning.

Criterion 5: Resources, Planning, and Institutional Effectiveness

This criterion addresses HLC's expectations regarding the sufficiency of the institution's resources to carry out its mission, including the need for a planning process. Core Component 5.A emphasizes the nature of shared governance: "Through its administrative structures and collaborative processes, the institution's leadership demonstrates that it is effective and enables the institution to fulfill its mission" (HLC, 2019, p. 5). Specifically, point 5.A.1 states: "Shared governance at the institution engages its internal constituencies—including its governing board, administration, faculty, staff and students—through planning, policies and procedures" (HLC, 2019, p. 5). Point 5.B.3 addresses the need for appropriate institutional structures for overseeing the academic program by faculty and other key institutional constituents: "The institution's administration ensures that faculty and, when appropriate, staff and students are involved in setting academic requirements, policy and processes through effective collaborative structures" (HLC, 2019, p. 5). This emphasis on shared governance, formal structures, and a collaborative effort is particularly noteworthy.

Assumed Practices

HLC also provides a set of four Assumed Practices that are foundational to the values and criteria previously discussed. Assumed Practice B addresses expectations across the range of teaching and learning quality, resources, and support. Practice B.2 describes the faculty roles and qualifications. It is worth noting that HLC is quite specific about its expectations regarding faculty qualifications, particularly in terms of degree or postgraduate course qualifications for teaching in general education and graduate areas. Point B.2.d addresses faculty responsibilities with language similar to that used in the criteria:

d. Faculty participate substantially in:

   a. oversight of the curriculum—its development and implementation, academic substance, currency, and relevance for internal and external constituencies;

   b. assurance of consistency in the level and quality of instruction and in the expectations of student performance;

   c. establishment of the academic qualifications for instructional personnel;

   d. analysis of data and appropriate action on assessment of student learning and program completion. (HLC, 2018, p. 15)

In summary, the HLC retains a more prescriptive set of criteria for the role of faculty in the governance of the institution than is typical of the other accreditation commissions.

Northwest Commission on Colleges and Universities (NWCCU)

NWCCU oversees accreditation in seven states and most recently revised their Accreditation Handbook in 2017. The commission has established five standards for accreditation, of which two address some aspects of the faculty roles and responsibilities.

Standard 2: Resources and Capacity

NWCCU covers a wide range of aspects of the operation of accredited institutions in its second standard. Several of these sections are especially relevant for defining the faculty role in the governance of the institution and oversight of the curriculum. The expectations for institutional governance speak in a general way to the role of faculty while not describing the mechanism by which the views of the faculty should be incorporated.

Section 2.A. Governance, Subsections on Governance

> 2.A.1 The institution demonstrates an effective and widely understood system of governance with clearly defined authority, roles, and responsibilities. Its decision-making structures and processes make provision for the consideration of the views of faculty, staff, administrators, and students on matters in which they have a direct and reasonable interest. (NWCCU, 2017, p. 23)

On the other hand, the subsection that describes the requirements for human resources is more explicit about the faculty role in oversight of the curriculum. Similarly, the subsection on education resources is clear about the requirement that faculty input to curricular decisions is achieved through well-defined structures and processes.

Section 2.B. Human Resources

> 2.B.4 Consistent with its mission, core themes, programs, services, and characteristics, the institution employs appropriately qualified faculty sufficient in number to achieve its educational objectives, establish and oversee academic policies, and assure the integrity and continuity of its academic programs, wherever offered and however delivered. (NWCCU, 2017, pp. 26–27)

Section 2.C. Education Resources

> 2.C.5 Faculty, through well-defined structures and processes with clearly defined authority and responsibilities, exercise a major role

in the design, approval, implementation, and revision of the curriculum, and have an active role in the selection of new faculty. (NWCCU, 2017, p. 27)

The role of faculty oversight in developing and administering undergraduate programs is not further explicitly described in the subsection on undergraduate programs. However, the subsection on graduate programs notes a particular role for faculty-developed policies.

Section 2.C. Subsection on Graduate Programs

2.C.13 Graduate admission and retention policies ensure that student qualifications and expectations are compatible with the institution's mission and the program's requirements. Transfer of credit is evaluated according to clearly defined policies by faculty with a major commitment to graduate education or by a representative body of faculty responsible for the degree program at the receiving institution. (NWCCU, 2017, p. 29)

The role of the faculty in continuing education and noncredit programs is also spelled out.

Section 2.C. Subsection on Continuing Education and Non-Credit Programs

2.C.17 . . . Faculty representing the disciplines and fields of work are appropriately involved in the planning and evaluation of the institution's continuing education and special learning activities. (NWCCU, 2017, p. 29)

NWCCU further requires that the faculty and other campus constituencies have clearly defined participation in institutional financial planning, although again the mechanism is not specified.

Section 2.F. Financial Resources

2.F.3 The institution clearly defines and follows its policies, guidelines, and processes for financial planning and budget development that include appropriate opportunities for participation by its constituencies. (NWCCU, 2017, p. 32)

Standard 4 addresses the institution's responsibilities to assess its progress and to have mechanisms to support continuous improvement. The faculty role is defined in terms of both program and course assessment.

Section 4.A. Assessment

> 4.A.2 The institution engages in an effective system of evaluation of its programs and services, wherever offered and however delivered, to evaluate achievement of clearly identified program goals or intended outcomes. Faculty have a primary role in the evaluation of educational programs and services.
>
> 4.A.3 The institution documents, through an effective, regular, and comprehensive system of assessment of student achievement, that students who complete its educational courses, programs, and degrees, wherever offered and however delivered, achieve identified course, program, and degree learning outcomes. Faculty with teaching responsibilities are responsible for evaluating student achievement of clearly identified learning outcomes. (NWCCU, 2017, p. 35)

In summary, the NWCCU highlights a number of central roles for the faculty in both the governance of the institution and the development, oversight, and assessment of the curriculum.

Southern Association of Colleges and Schools Commission on Colleges (SACSCOC)

SACSOC oversees accreditation for institutions across the southeastern part of the United States. The association recently (2018) updated its principles of accreditation. Fourteen principles are provided and explained as sections of the guidelines (SACSCOC, 2018). Several sections describe aspects of the faculty's roles and responsibilities in institutional governance.

Section 4. Governing Board

Although this section deals with the role of an institution's governing board, it also addresses the relationships among the governing board and the institution's faculty and administration.

2.b [The Governing Board] ensures a clear and appropriate distinction between the policy-making function of the board and the responsibility of the administration and faculty to administer and implement policy. (SACSCOC, 2018, p. 4)

Section 6. Faculty

Section 6 describes SACSCOC's expectations regarding the faculty of the institution. This includes the expected qualifications of the faculty and the role of shared governance. The preamble to this section summarizes the criteria.

> Qualified, effective faculty members are essential to carry out the mission of the institution and to ensure the quality and integrity of its academic program. The tradition of shared governance within American higher education recognizes the importance of both faculty and administrative involvement in the approval of educational programs. Because student learning is central to the institution's mission and educational degrees, the faculty has responsibility for directing the learning enterprise including overseeing and coordinating educational programs to ensure that each contains essential curricular components, has appropriate content and pedagogy, and maintains discipline currency.
> Achievement of the institution's mission with respect to teaching, research, and service requires a critical mass of full-time qualified faculty to provide direction and oversight of the academic programs. Due to this significant role, it is imperative that an effective system of evaluation be in place for all faculty members that takes into account the institution's obligations to foster intellectual freedom of faculty to teach, serve, research, and publish. (SACSCOC, 2018, p. 6)

The remainder of the section clarifies expectations about what the institution must do to meet these general goals, but it does not specify a particular structure to ensure faculty oversight of the education programs and curriculum.

Section 10. Educational Policies, Procedures, and Practices

SACSCOC provides more detailed expectations regarding the kinds of policies that institutions enact to achieve desired academic outcomes. The preamble provides a broad description of the goals of such policies, with nine points providing more detail.

> Sub-point 4. The institution (a) publishes and implements policies on the authority of faculty in academic and governance matters, (b) demonstrates that educational programs for which academic credit is awarded are approved consistent with institutional policy, and (c) places primary responsibility for the content, quality, and effectiveness of the curriculum with its faculty. (SACSCOC, 2018, p. 10)

In summary, SACSCOC provides both broad guidance to institutions about expectations of the role and specific requirements about the responsibility of the faculty in overseeing the curriculum. The language explicitly addresses the importance of shared governance between the faculty and the administration, in keeping with the long tradition of higher education in the United States.

Western Association of Schools and Colleges (WASC)

WASC oversees accreditation in California, Hawaii, and Pacific territories of the United States and other areas in the Pacific and East Asia regions. The association accredits baccalaureate institutions separately from those that offer associate's degrees. Accreditation criteria from the WASC Senior College and University Commission are discussed first, followed by discussion of the criteria from the WASC Accrediting Commission for Community and Junior Colleges.

WASC Senior College and University Commission (WSCUC)

The *Handbook of Accreditation* for senior colleges and universities that are overseen by WASC was most recently developed in 2013 with revisions in 2015 and editorial updates in 2018 (WSCUC, 2018). WSCUC defines four standards for accreditation. Three of the standards provide guidance regarding the role and responsibilities of faculty in the governance of the academic enterprise.

Standard 2: Achieving Educational Objectives through Core Functions

WSCUC reviews core functions of the institution in three areas: teaching and learning, scholarship and creative activity, and student learning and success. There is little explicit indication of the role of faculty governance in overseeing the teaching and learning activities, although section 2.4 indicates the faculty's responsibility for determining the standards for student achievement.

> 2.4 The institution's student learning outcomes and standards of performance are developed by faculty. . . . The institution's faculty take collective responsibility for establishing appropriate standards of performance and demonstrating through assessment the achievement of these standards. (WSCUC, 2018)

Although WSCUC does not specify what is meant by "collective responsibility," the association provides further guidance in Standard 3.

Standard 3: Developing and Applying Resources and Organizational Structures to Ensure Quality and Sustainability

Standard 3 focuses the institution on "an appropriate and effective set of organizational and decision-making structures" (WSCUC, 2018), with 10 sections. The first three directly address review criteria regarding the institution's responsibilities with respect to faculty and staff; the first of these notes the role of the faculty in academic policies.

> 3.1 . . . The faculty and staff are sufficient in number, professional qualification, and diversity to achieve the institution's educational objectives, establish and oversee academic policies, and ensure the integrity and continuity of its academic and co-curricular programs wherever and however delivered. (WSCUC, 2018)

The last five sections address the governance structure of the institution. The requirement for clear decision-making authority is addressed in section 3.7, but the role of the faculty is more directly outlined in section 3.10.

> 3.7 The institution's organizational structures and decision-making processes are clear and consistent with its purposes, support effective decision making, and place priority on sustaining institutional capacity and educational effectiveness.
> *Guideline:* The institution establishes clear roles, responsibilities, and lines of authority.

3.10 The institution's faculty exercises effective academic leadership and acts consistently to ensure that both academic quality and the institution's educational purposes and character are sustained. (WSCUC, 2018)

Thus, WSCUC establishes the role of the faculty as one of leadership over the educational aspects of the institution, within an overall framework that defines how this role fits with other lines of authority (particularly administrative).

Standard 4. Creating an Organization Committed to Quality Assurance, Institutional Learning, and Improvement

Standard 4 addresses institutional planning, assessment, and continuous improvement. Seven sections provide criteria for review in the areas of quality assurance processes (4.1 and 4.2) and institutional learning and improvement (4.3–4.7). Section 4.4 refers to faculty involvement in assessment of learning and teaching; section 4.6 discusses expectations that all institutional constituencies be engaged in evidence-based reflection and planning at the institutional level.

4.4 The institution, with significant faculty involvement, engages in ongoing inquiry into the processes of teaching and learning, and the conditions and practices that ensure that the standards of performance established by the institution are being achieved. The faculty and other educators take responsibility for evaluating the effectiveness of teaching and learning processes and uses the results for improvement of student learning and success. The findings from such inquiries are applied to the design and improvement of curricula, pedagogy, and assessment methodology.

4.6 The institution periodically engages its multiple constituencies, including the governing board, faculty, staff, and others, in institutional reflection and planning processes that are based on the examination of data and evidence.

In total, WSCUC directs institutions to involve faculty through appropriate structures in the governance of the institution, particularly on aspects related directly to academic aspects and student learning.

WASC Accrediting Commission for Community and Junior Colleges (ACCJC)

The state of California and the ACCJC have had a difficult relationship in recent years (e.g., California State Auditor, 2014). Nonetheless, ACCJC continues to accredit community colleges throughout its regional area of California, Hawaii, and the Pacific Islands. The current accreditation standards were most recently adopted and published in 2014 (ACCJC, 2014). They comprise four standards, of which two address the roles and responsibilities of faculty in institutional governance.

Standard II. Student Learning Programs and Support Services

Standard II describes expectations on instructional programs (II.A), library and learning support services (II.B), and student support services (II.C). The faculty role in overseeing academic programs is outlined in the first section. Section II.A.2 underwent changes effective in 2020; both the current and changed sections are included here.

> 2 *(Applicable to institutions with comprehensive reviews scheduled through Fall 2019.)* Faculty, including full time, part time, and adjunct faculty, ensure that the content and methods of instruction meet generally accepted academic and professional standards and expectations. Faculty and others responsible act to continuously improve instructional courses, programs and directly related services through systematic evaluation to assure currency, improve teaching and learning strategies, and promote student success.

> *(Applicable to institutions with comprehensive reviews scheduled after Fall 2019)* Faculty, including full time, part time, and adjunct faculty, regularly engage in ensuring that the content and methods of instruction meet generally accepted academic and professional standards and expectations. In exercising collective ownership over the design and improvement of the learning experience, faculty conduct systematic and inclusive program review, using student achievement data, in order to continuously improve instructional courses and programs, thereby ensuring program currency, improving teaching and learning strategies, and promoting student success. (ACCJC, 2014, p. 5)

The new language differs from the existing criteria in a few key ways. First, the role of faculty in ensuring the quality of instruction shifts from "ensure" to "regularly engage in ensuring"—a change that can be regarded as weakening the faculty role, on one hand, or a clearer requirement for regular review, on the other. The changes to the second sentence emphasize the role of the faculty in program design and review, with a clearer requirement that this be a collective faculty ownership.

Section 12 outlines the role of faculty in developing and implementing the general education curriculum at the institution.

> A12 . . . The institution, relying on faculty expertise, determines the appropriateness of each course for inclusion in the general education curriculum, based upon student learning outcomes and competencies appropriate to the degree level. (ACCJC, 2014, p. 6)

Standard IV. Leadership and Governance

The expectations for institutional governance include the requirement that the institution has established governance structures: "Through established governance structures, processes, and practices, the governing board, administrators, faculty, staff, and students work together for the good of the institution. In multi-college districts or systems, the roles within the district/system are clearly delineated." Section A describes the decision-making roles and processes in more detail, with the first four (of seven) subsections specifically including faculty responsibilities.

1. Institutional leaders create and encourage innovation leading to institutional excellence. They support administrators, faculty, staff, and students, no matter what their official titles, in taking initiative for improving the practices, programs, and services in which they are involved. When ideas for improvement have policy or significant institution-wide implications, systematic participative processes are used to assure effective planning and implementation.

2. The institution establishes and implements policy and procedures authorizing administrator, faculty, and staff participation in decision-making processes. The policy makes provisions for student participation and consideration of student views in those matters in which students have a direct and reasonable

interest. Policy specifies the manner in which individuals bring forward ideas and work together on appropriate policy, planning, and special-purpose committees.

3. Administrators and faculty, through policy and procedures, have a substantive and clearly defined role in institutional governance and exercise a substantial voice in institutional policies, planning, and budget that relate to their areas of responsibility and expertise.

4. Faculty and academic administrators, through policy and procedures, and through well-defined structures, have responsibility for recommendations about curriculum and student learning programs and services. (ACCJC, 2014, p. 14)

The emphasis, then, is on the use of participatory processes, but with clearly defined structures and responsibilities. The following sections of Standard IV address the institution's chief executive and governing body, along with appropriate considerations for community college districts and systems (as opposed to individual institutions). The responsibility of the faculty is not defined in further detail, but there are several reiterations of the importance of participatory processes. For example, in section B (regarding the chief executive), subsection 3 instructs "Through established policies and procedures, the CEO guides institutional improvement of the teaching and learning environment by establishing a collegial process that sets values, goals, and priorities" (ACCJC, 2014, p. 15), among other enumerated duties. Subsection 4 notes that "Faculty . . . also have responsibility for assuring compliance with accreditation requirements" (ACCJC, 2014, p. 15).

Changing Emphasis in Accreditation Standards

As should be clear, few of the accrediting commissions explicitly address the faculty role as *shared governance* of an institution. Instead, they typically use phrase like "established structures" in lieu of terms like "faculty governance" or "shared governance." There are exceptions, of course. Notably, the HLC clearly defines shared governance without calling it by that name and, more important, is considering revisions to its criteria that explicitly cite the role of shared governance. Likewise, SACSCOC explicitly identifies the importance of shared governance in an institution, particularly in the context of curriculum oversight. The other commissions are far less prescriptive about what they mean when requiring that institutions have established structures or processes through which faculty engage in the governance of the institution (or through which chief executives interact with faculty and other constituencies in the decision-making process).

It is instructive to see how the language around faculty governance, shared governance, and so on has changed as commissions have updated and revised their criteria for accreditation. Around 2007 the American Association of University Professors (AAUP) summarized existing criteria as they related to faculty governance and academic freedom. Their summary, coupled with a direct review of the previous version of each commission's criteria for accreditation, informs the following discussion.

MSCHE Changes in Criteria for Accreditation

The 2015 MSCHE Standards for Accreditation updated the previous criteria that had been published in 2009. This was a significant overhauling of the standards, reducing them from fourteen to seven, and changing language in many instances. One of the more significant changes in terms of the role of shared governance occurred in the standard dealing with leadership and governance. This was part of Standard 4 in the 2009 MSCHE criteria, whereas the equivalent standard is now part of a broader Standard VII.

Standard 4 (Leadership and Governance) from the revision to the 12th edition of MSCHE's criteria for accreditation (MSCHE, 2009) sought assurance that institutional governance was shared and collegial.

> [The commission] expects a climate of shared collegial governance in which all constituencies (such as faculty, administration, staff, students and governing board members, as determined by each institution) involved in carrying out the institution's mission and goals participate in the governance function in a manner appropriate to that institution. Institutions should seek to create a governance environment in which issues concerning mission, vision, program planning, resource allocation and others, as appropriate, can be discussed openly by those who are responsible for each activity. Within any system of shared governance, each major constituency must carry out its separate but complementary roles and responsibilities. Each must contribute to an appropriate degree so

that decision-makers and goal-setters consider information from all relevant constituencies. While reflecting institutional mission, perspective, and culture, collegial governance structures should acknowledge also the need for timely decision-making. (MSCHE, 2009, p. 12)

Specific requirements under Standard 4 are largely preserved in Standard VII of the 2015 document, but this broader commitment to shared governance is no longer part of the governing document. This is not to imply that MSCHE no longer values the role of shared governance; nonetheless, it is far less visible in the standards.

The 2009 document also had a standard specifically related to the qualifications and roles of the faculty (Standard 10, Faculty; MSCHE, 2009, pp. 37–39). The key elements of this standard are now incorporated across several standards in the 2015 version. But the specific focus on the faculty qualifications and role has been lost, as the commission refocused its standards on the student learning experience.

NECHE Changes in Criteria

Previous language in NECHE requirements, summarized by AAUP, is equivalent to section 3.15 as provided above. Thus, their current update has not significantly enhanced or diminished the role of faculty—nor does the present or past language explicitly address shared governance.

HLC Changes in Criteria

The previous (HLC, 2003) *Handbook of Accreditation* addressed the role of shared governance in the first of its criteria for accreditation: mission and integrity. Core Component 1d indicates that "The organization's governance and administrative structures promote effective leadership and support collaborative processes that enable the organization to fulfill its mission" (HLC, 2003, p. 3.1.3). They elaborated on this expectation by requiring that "the organization must have structures through which decisions are made, responsibilities assigned, and accountability for end results established. Shared governance has been a long-standing attribute of most colleges and universities in the United States" (HLC, 2003, p. 3.2.4). Examples included: "Faculty and other academic leaders share responsibility for the coherence of the curriculum and the integrity of academic processes" (HLC, 2003, p. 3.2.4) and "Effective communication facilitates governance processes and activities" (HLC, 2003, p. 3.2.4).

The essential message had not changed in the criteria that were revised in 2014 (HSC, 2018), although the structure of the guidance was modified. The revised criteria adopted in 2019 for implementation in 2020 puts a much greater emphasis on shared governance within the institution. The changes to Criterion 5 not only explicitly address the nature of shared governance that is expected, but makes it the first point in explaining the first core component of institutional effectiveness. This represents a significant increase in the commission's expectations for the role of shared governance.

NWCCU Changes in Criteria

The 2003 NWCCU Handbook on Accreditation included Standard 2 on the educational program and its effectiveness. Point 2.A.7 spoke to the faculty role in oversight of the curriculum:

> Responsibility for design, approval, and implementation of the curriculum is vested in designated institutional bodies with clearly established channels of communication and control. The faculty has a major role and responsibility in the design, integrity, and implementation of the curriculum. (NWCCU, 2003, p. 28)

The revised standards still identify the major role of the faculty, although changed wording (and its location in the document) is less clear about the nature of how this role is to be implemented. This does not appear to be a significant rollback in expectation; nonetheless the lack of a statement about "designated institutional bodies" may well reduce the role of shared governance.

Likewise, the requirements for faculty's role in academic and institutional planning and curriculum oversight have been diluted. Standard 4 addressed the faculty. Section 4.A.2 stated "Faculty participate in academic planning, curriculum development and review, academic advising, and institutional governance" (NWCCU, 2003, p. 63). Furthermore, Standard 6.D, Faculty Role in Governance, provided clear expectations for the faculty involvement in institutional governance: "The role of faculty in institutional governance, planning, budgeting and policy development is made clear and public; faculty are supported in that role" (NWSCC 2003, p. 74). The current criteria are far less explicit about the role that the faculty are to play in the governance of the institution.

SACSCOC Changes in Criteria

The SACSCOC 1997 Criteria for Accreditation (SACSCOC, 1997) addressed the role of the faculty in a number of subsections of Section IV, Educational Programs. The role of faculty governance was addressed in section 4.8.8, The Role of the Faculty and Its Committees:

> Primary responsibility for the quality of the educational program **must** reside with the faculty. The extent of the participation and jurisdiction of the faculty in academic affairs **must** be clearly set forth and published. Much of their business will normally be conducted through such structures as committees, councils, and senates, operating within the broad policies determined by the administration and governing board. (SACSCOC, 1997, p. 49; emphasis in original)

In subsequent years this explicit set of requirements for faculty governance changed. The 2006 interim edition of Principles of Accreditation had 14 standards of accreditation (SACSCOC, 2007). The faculty role was covered in different parts of the standards. Standard 3.4 addressed all educational programs, and Standard 3.4.10 clearly documents the role of faculty in curriculum: "The institution places primary responsibility for the content, quality, and effectiveness of the curriculum with its faculty. (**Responsibility for curriculum**)" (SACSCOC, 2007, p. 12). Standard 3.7, Faculty, spoke to the faculty role in governance: "3.7.5 The institution publishes policies on the responsibility and authority of faculty in academic and governance matters. (**Faculty role in governance**)" (SACSCOC, 2007, p. 13). Subsequent revisions retain this language. As noted previously, however, the current version of the SACS requirements emphasizes the importance of shared governance as a hallmark of American higher education.

WSCUC Changes in Criteria

The 2001 WASC *Handbook of Accreditation* (WSCUC, 2001) provided detailed guidance regarding standards and the evidence that institutions were expected to include in their self-study reports. Standard 3, Developing and Applying Resources and Organizational Structures to Ensure Sustainability, provided a standard on faculty involvement in institutional governance and a question for institutions to address regarding the nature of that involvement. "3.11. The institution's faculty exercises effective academic leadership and acts consistently to ensure both academic quality and the appropriate maintenance of the institution's educational purposes and character" (WSCUC, 2001, p. 27). Question 5 for institutional engagement under this standard asks institutions, "How does the institution interpret and put into practice shared governance through appropriate faculty participation in planning and decision-making in pursuit of the institution's purpose and character?" (WSCUC, 2001, p. 28). It is noteworthy that although the current WSCUC handbook maintains the language regarding the faculty role (though now as Standard 3.10; WSCUC, 2018), the guiding language regarding shared governance has not been retained in the handbook. This doesn't imply a reduction in the commission's expectations regarding faculty involvement in the academic mission of the institution, it erodes the guidance on how this involvement should be institutionalized.

ACCJC Changes in Criteria

The Accreditation Standards that ACCJC had in place for institutions prior to its 2014 revisions (ACCJC, 2012) addressed the role of faculty in two standards.

Standard II, then as now, dealt with student learning programs and services. Point II.A.2.a stated that "The institution uses established procedures to design, identify learning outcomes for, approve, administer, deliver, and evaluate courses and programs. The institution recognizes the central role of its faculty for establishing quality and improving instructional courses and programs" (ACCJC, 2012, p. 4). The following section, II.A.2.b, obliquely refers to shared governance by saying "The institution relies on faculty expertise and the assistance of advisory committees when appropriate" (ACCJC, 2012, p. 4).

Standard IV, Leadership and Governance, spoke to the structural role of the faculty. Section A addressed the institution's decision-making roles and responsibilities. Standard IV.A.2.a stated that "Faculty and administrators have a substantive and clearly defined role in institutional governance and exercise a substantial voice in institutional policies, planning, and budget" (ACCJC, 2012, p. 16). The following section specifies the importance of faculty structures in providing guidance for the student learning program: "The institution relies on faculty, its academic senate or other appropriate faculty structures, the curriculum committee, and academic administrators for recommendations about student learning programs and services." (ACCJC, 2012, p. 16). Finally, an effective definition of shared governance was provided in IV.A.3: "Through established governance structures, processes, and practices, the governing board, administrators, faculty, staff, and students work together for the good of the institution. These processes facilitate discussion of ideas and effective communication among the institution's constituencies" (ACCJC, 2012, p. 16).

The degree of specificity of the kinds of roles and structures that ACCJC expects institutions to use has thus shifted through time. The 2012 standards specify a formal faculty structure (senate or other), whereas the current standards are much more vague about how faculty should be engaged in institutional governance, simply calling for "well-defined structures."

Concluding Remarks

Regional accrediting commissions generally assign a substantial role to faculty in the development and oversight of curriculum and establishing and implementing criteria for evaluating and assessing student learning. The degree to which institutions are expected to facilitate faculty involvement through their (faculty) governance structures varies in language and emphasis. Importance is placed on recognizing respective roles of governing boards, administrative leadership, faculty, staff, and (sometimes) students. Many of the commissions also note the important role of the faculty in institutional planning, including consideration of institutional budgets, but this is not consistent in the standards and guidance.

Recognition of the formal role of shared governance has increasingly disappeared from accreditation criteria. Most accrediting bodies have moved away from prescriptive language about faculty or shared authority, whether over the curriculum or other academic matters. Rather than explicitly or implicitly addressing the importance of shared governance, terminology such as "established structures" has become common. There are important exceptions. HLC is considering reintroducing an explicit statement on the importance of shared governance, and SACSCOC notes the centrality of shared governance in higher education. All in all, though, what we see evolving is a de facto erosion of the emphasis on shared governance and, in most cases, a less well-defined role for faculty in institutional governance.

I experienced this rather directly at a public meeting that MSCHE held in 2014 in Albany, New York, to obtain comments on their proposed changes to the accreditation standards. I inquired of the commission why there was a lack of a clear responsibility for faculty in general, and faculty governance structures in particular, in the proposed criteria. The audience was informed that MSCHE was attempting to accommodate the nature of different roles for instructors in member institutions—some of which don't even have faculty in the traditionally defined way. Thus, MSCHE sought to establish the most general and universal criteria for implementation of their standards. Granted, this reflects the changing nature of the professoriate and (some) academic institutions. Certainly the rise of contingent faculty, whether full-time or (especially) part-time, has eroded the faculty role in institutional governance. There are fewer full-time tenure-track and tenured faculty with the freedom and expectation to engage in shared governance. But the step-back by so many of the accrediting commissions in the specificity of their expectations around faculty involvement in institutional governance, or shared governance more generally, is concerning.

Despite all of this, the institutional structures of shared governance still play an important role in the accreditation process. Two recent examples illustrate how the role of faculty governance on a campus can be a serious consideration when an institution's accreditation is at risk. Valerie Collins (chapter 11 in this volume) reports on the challenges that Nassau Community College faced when they failed 7 of the then-14 standards for accreditation during the MSCHE team's accreditation review in 2016. Although there were a number of issues around institutional governance that Nassau had to address, the ability of the faculty governance body to veto administrative action (or override an administrative veto of the faculty body's action) was one of the central issues. In this case, the MSCHE team found the faculty governance organization to be exerting too much authority, rather than shared authority, over the institution.

A different governance issue emerged at the University of Virginia in 2012 when the Board of Visitors in essence forced the president to resign and then reinstated her. The SACSCOC Board of Trustees issued a formal warning to the University of Virginia in December 2012 that the institution had failed to demonstrate compliance with Core Requirement 2.2 (governing board) and Comprehensive Standard 3.7.5 (faculty role in governance), with a required review by December 2013 (SACSCOC, 2012). *Virginia Magazine* explained the situation to the university community in their spring 2013 issue. The main issue was the action of a minority of the Board of Visitors, but the commission also faulted the university for failure to involve the faculty governance structure in this critical governance decision. The essential issue was the failure of the institution to follow established governance processes.

Shared governance remains a distinctive component of most higher education institutions in the United States. Regional accreditation commissions vary in their expectations about how governance is shared at an institution, and most have reduced how explicit they are about the kinds of shared governance structures that are expected of an accredited institution. Nonetheless, commissions clearly continue to have a high-priority expectation that institutions clearly demarcate authority for the academic program and that faculty (through some kind of mechanism) have a central role in this.

References

Accrediting Commission for Community and Junior Colleges, Western Association of Colleges (ACCJC). (2012). *Accreditation standards.* ACCJC, Novato, CA.

Accrediting Commission for Community and Junior Colleges, Western Association of Colleges (ACCJC). (2014). *Accreditation standards, annotated* (adopted June, 2014). ACCJC, Novato, CA.

American Association of University Professors. (n.d., ca. 2007). *Regional accreditation standards concerning academic freedom and the faculty role in governance.* AAUP. Retrieved March 8, 2019, from https://www.aaup.org/report/regional-accreditation-standards-concerning-academic-freedom-and-faculty-role-governance.

California State Auditor. (2014). *California community college accreditation; colleges are treated inconsistently and opportunities exist for improvement in the accreditation process.* California State Auditor Report 2013-123.

Database of Accredited Postsecondary Institutions and Programs (DAPIP). (2019). US Department of Education Office of Postsecondary Education. Retrieved March 8, 2019, from https://ope.ed.gov/dapip/#/home.

Eaton, J. S. (2015). *An overview of U.S. accreditation* Washington, DC: Council for Higher Education Accreditation.

Higher Learning Commission (HLC). (2003). *Handbook of accreditation*, 3rd ed. Chicago: HLC.

Higher Learning Commission (HLC). (2018). *Resource guide 2018.* Chicago: HLC.

Higher Learning Commission (HLC). (2019). *Criteria for Accreditation. Adopted Revisions Effective September 2020.* Chicago: HLC.

Middle States Commission on Higher Education (MSCHE). (2009). *Characteristics of excellence in higher education; requirements of affiliation and standards for accreditation.* Philadelphia: MSCHE.

Middle States Commission on Higher Education (MSCHE). (2015). *Standards for accreditation and requirements of affiliation*, 13th ed. Philadelphia: MSCHE.

New England Commission of Higher Education (NECHE). (2016). *Standards for accreditation.* Burlington, MA: NECHE.

Northwest Commission on Colleges and Universities (NWCCU). (2003). *Accreditation handbook*, 2003 ed. Redmond, WA: NWCCU.
Northwest Commission on Colleges and Universities (NWCCU). (2017). *Accreditation handbook*, January 2017 ed. Redmond, WA: NWCCU.
Southern Association of Colleges and Schools Commission on Colleges (SACSCOC). (1997). *Criteria for accreditation*, 11th ed. Decatur, GA: SACSCOC.
Southern Association of Colleges and Schools Commission on Colleges (SACSCOC). (2007). *Principles of accreditation: Foundations for quality enhancement*, interim ed. Decatur, GA: SACSCOC.
Southern Association of Colleges and Schools Commission on Colleges (SACSCOC). (2012). *Disclosure statement regarding the status of University of Virginia, Charlottesville, Virginia*. Letter to University of Virginia, December 20, 2012. Retrieved February 20, 2018, from www.virginia.edu/sacs/2013/sanctiondisclosure.pdf.
Southern Association of Colleges and Schools Commission on Colleges (SACSCOC). (2018). *Principles of accreditation: Foundations for quality enhancement*, 2018 ed. Decatur, GA: SACSCOC.
Virginia Magazine. (2013). Understanding the SACSCOC warning. *Virginia Magazine*, spring. Retrieved March 20, 2019, from http://uvamagazine.org/articles/understanding_the_sacscoc_warning.
Western Association of Schools and Colleges Senior College and University Commission (WSCUC). (2001). *Handbook of accreditation 2001*. Alameda, CA: WSCUC.
Western Association of Schools and Colleges Senior College and University Commission (WSCUC). (2018). *Handbook of accreditation 2013 revised*. Alameda, CA: WSCUC. Retrieved March 15, 2019, https://www.wscuc.org/book/export/html/924.

Contributors

Gordon Bigelow is a member of the English Department at Rhodes College, where he teaches nineteenth-century British and Irish literature and literary theory. His research interests center on the history of economic thought, with particular focus in the economics of the Irish famine and the Atlantic slave trade. Currently he is completing a book manuscript on the Irish novels of Anthony Trollope. Bigelow is the author of *Fiction, Famine, and the Rise of Economics in Victorian Britain and Ireland* (2003), and his essays have appeared in *English Literary History*, *Novel: A Forum on Fiction*, and *Harper's* magazine. He holds degrees from Brown University (BA in comparative literature), the University of New Hampshire (MA in English), and the University of California, Santa Cruz (PhD in literature). In 2010 he received the Clarence Day Award for Excellence in Teaching at Rhodes College. From 2015 to 2018 he served as the Presiding Officer of the Rhodes faculty, facilitating monthly meetings of the full faculty and participating in the work of the Rhodes Faculty Governance Committee.

Diane Bliss is professor emerita of English at Orange County Community College, where she taught from 1992 through 2019. She previously held teaching positions at Jamestown Community College and Alfred State College. She earned an AA in forest technology from SUNY College of Environmental Science and Forestry, a BA in creative writing, environmental concerns, and philosophy from Hartwick College, and an MA in English with a specialization in two-year college teaching from Binghamton University. She served in varying capacities in shared governance at Orange for 25 years, with 12 years as a voting member of executive committee, including 3.5 years as Governance vice president, and 5.5 years as Governance president. She completed two terms as Orange's delegate to the Faculty Council of Community Colleges, after previously serving as alternate delegate. While serving as delegate, Bliss chaired the Governance

Committee of the FCCC. Under her leadership, the committee crafted a number of resolutions related to shared governance, academic freedom, faculty purview over curriculum, and state funding for community colleges, and she was instrumental in the creation of a Campus Governance Leaders' Toolkit for community colleges. The committee's latest contribution to shared governance was the production and release of a rubric for assessing campus governance systems, which was primarily coauthored by Bliss and past FCCC President Tina Good. She has participated in several SUNY Voices events as a panelist or presenter. She received the SUNY Orange President's Award for Excellence in Faculty Service and the SUNY Chancellor's Award for Excellence in Faculty Service in 2018.

Noelle Chaddock currently serves as the vice president of Equity and Inclusion at Bates College in Lewiston, Maine. Their administrative duties include institutional, faculty, student, and administrative matters pertaining to diversity, equity, inclusion, access, and social justice. Chaddock has and continues to work closely with the faculty governance structures along with faculty committees tasked with the work of equity, inclusion, diversity, access, antiracism, and social justice work. Chaddock has demonstrated success in addressing issues of attracting, recruiting, hiring, orienting, mentoring, retaining, and otherwise supporting underrepresented and marginalized faculty, staff, and students. Chaddock previously served as the chief diversity officer at SUNY Cortland and was heavily engaged in shared governance at the college and across the SUNY system. Chaddock served as the state-wide faculty senate representative for SUNY Cortland and the second chair of the state-wide Faculty Senate committee on equity, inclusion, and diversity. Chaddock does a considerable amount of consulting with higher education institutions around cultivating inclusive leadership and diversifying faculty. Chaddock has facilitated diversity training for the Binghamton Police Department and facilitates inclusion dialogues with the Memphis Cultural Coalition, the Orpheum Theatre Group, Playback Memphis, and the Memphis College of Art. Chaddock earned their doctorate from Binghamton University in philosophy. Their areas of research and teaching include critical race theory, antagonizing white feminism, diversity and shared governance, Africana theater, and diversifying faculty. Chaddock is the coeditor of the forthcoming book *Antagonizing White Feminism: Women's Studies, Feminism, Gender Identity, and the Academy* (Lexington Books) and the creator and principal writer of the blog "Baby Girl: Examinations of Genealogical Inheritance and Disruption."

Valerie H. Collins has been the interim vice president of Academic Affairs and accreditation liaison officer for the Middle States Commission on Higher Education at Nassau Community College since 2016. She holds a bachelor's of science degree in nursing from Molloy College. She received a National Institute of Mental Health Graduate Education Traineeship to pursue a master's degree at NYU, where she also earned her doctoral degree in higher education administration. For several years Collins held the position of vice president of Academic Affairs and dean of Faculty at Molloy College. Early in her career, she was active in the Molloy Faculty Council, serving a term as faculty president. During this time she developed an interest in shared governance, having recognized the importance of this concept on the dynamics of working relationships in a college. This focus on shared governance later led to her doctoral dissertation exploring this topic from a historical case study perspective. Collins found her background and belief in shared governance especially useful at Nassau, where this concept is an important one.

Sharon F. Cramer is a SUNY Distinguished Service professor emerita and was a faculty member at SUNY Buffalo State from 1985 to 2011. During her career, she served as an academic leader in roles that included department chair (1995–1999), executive director of a Student Information System implementation team (SABRE) (1999–2004), chair of the College Senate (2007–2010), and chair of the Governance Committee of the SUNY University Faculty Senate (2007–2010). She was an officer, on the board of directors, of four professional and governance organizations, and received the highest award from each of them. She served as parliamentarian for the SUNY University Faculty Senate 2011–2019 and was recognized for her contributions to the UFS with the Chugh Award in 2011, and the Senator Emerita award in 2015. She completed her doctoral studies at New York University, earned an MAT degree from Harvard University and a bachelor's from Tufts University. Her publication record includes 3 scholarly books, editing 2 volumes and coediting a 3rd, on shared governance (published by SUNY Press), 26 scholarly articles, 34 reflective essays published in the *Buffalo News*, and 10 chapters in academic publications. Her sustained academic scholarship led to her receiving of the Albert Nelson Marquis Lifetime Achievement Award in 2017 for career longevity and unwavering excellence in chosen field, from the Marquis Who's Who Publication Board. She is listed in *Who's Who in America* (2006–present), *Who's Who in American Education* (2006–present), and *Who's Who in American Women* (2008–present).

Michael DeCesare is a professor of sociology at Merrimack College. Prior to joining Merrimack in 2007, he spent three years as an assistant professor of sociology at California State University, Northridge. An active member of the American Association of University Professors (AAUP), DeCesare guest-edited the May–June 2017 special issue of *Academe* magazine on academic governance. He was elected to a four-year term on the AAUP's national council in 2016 and has chaired the Committee on College and University Governance since 2015. In addition, he has served as vice president of the Massachusetts AAUP Conference since 2015 and as president of Merrimack's AAUP chapter from 2012 to 2019. His governance experience at Merrimack includes chairing the Sociology Department since 2011, serving twice on the Faculty Senate executive committee, and chairing the Appointment, Rank and Tenure Committee and the Faculty Development Committee. DeCesare has published several dozen scholarly articles, chapters, essays, and reviews. His books include *Death on Demand: Jack Kevorkian and the Right-to-Die Movement*, *New Directions in Sociology: Essays on Theory and Methodology in the 21st Century* (coedited with Ieva Zake), and *A Discipline Divided: Sociology in American High Schools*.

Philip L. Glick is a tenured professor of surgery at the Jacobs School of Medicine and Biomedical Sciences, University at Buffalo, and professor of management in the School of Management. In July 2015, Glick began a two-year term as the president of the University at Buffalo Faculty Senate and the chairperson of the University at Buffalo Faculty Senate Executive Committee. He was reelected for a second two-year term in 2017. He will continue as SUNY University Faculty Senate (UFS) health science sector senator through 2021. As sector head of the SUNY Healthcare Campuses, 2018–2020, he served as a member of the SUNY UFS executive committee. He has also been a member of the SUNY UFS Governance Committee. Since 2015, he has been a state-wide champion of shared governance throughout the 34 four-year college and four-year comprehensive research universities and the 30 two-year colleges. In 2019, Glick, Domenic Licata, their colleagues in the UB Faculty Senate and the UB Professional Staff Senate, UB student leaders, and UB administrators were co-recipients of 2018–2019 SUNY Shared Governance Award. In June 2019, Glick was elected president of UUP Buffalo HSC chapter.

Lisa M. Glidden is associate professor of political science at SUNY Oswego, where she also directs the Global and International Studies program and the sustainability studies minor. She was a representative to the

Faculty Assembly 2010–2017 and became its chair in 2017. In 2019, she was elected to serve as the convener of the Campus Governance Leaders of the SUNY University Faculty Senate, thereby serving as a member of the SUNY University Faculty Senate. She earned her doctorate from the University of Washington, Seattle, in 2007; MA in international relations from the City College of the City University of New York in 1999; and BA from St. Francis College in 1995. She teaches courses on global studies, Latin America, the Middle East, Africa, sustainability, and energy and the environment. Her publications include *Understanding Energy and Energy Policy* (2014, Zed Books), *Mobilizing Ethnic Identity in the Andes* (2011, Lexington Books), and articles on Cuba's energy policy, women's activism in Ecuador, and on Cuban society and US misperceptions of it.

Margaret Ann Hoose is associate professor and coordinator of the Early Childhood program at Morrisville State College, Norwich Campus. She earned an AAS at SUNY Cobleskill, BS at SUNY Oneonta, and MS at the College of Saint Rose. At Morrisville, Hoose has been involved in campus governance as a member of Faculty Congress, College Senate, and the Norwich Campus Liaison Committee. Hoose completed two two-year terms as College Senate president ending May 2019 and has been teaching at Morrisville since August 2006. She is a member of the Associate Degree Early Childhood Teacher Educators and the National Association for the Education of Young Children at the national, state, and local levels. Hoose currently serves as the secretary of the Morrisville UUP chapter and the recorder for College Senate.

Gwen Kay is professor of history and director of the honors program at SUNY Oswego, president of the Faculty Senate and vice president of the National Council of Faculty Senates. She joined the SUNY Board of Trustees on July 1, 2017. Kay earned her BA degree in biology and history from Bowdoin College and a PhD in history of medicine and science from Yale University. A member of Oswego's faculty since 2000, she specializes in the intersection of medicine, science and gender in the 20th-century United States. She has taught undergraduate and graduate courses in history, gender and women's studies and the honors program. She has been principal advisor to 20 honors theses and 5 master's theses. Kay has served Oswego, SUNY, and the community in myriad ways. She has fostered student engagement and involvement in research through her work in the honors program, supporting conference presentations. She has written two books, coauthored one, and coedited another, in addition to articles. Her current research investigates scientific education for women in college-level courses, using human ecology as a lens for inquiry. In particular, she is examining how a profession might shift or change its gendered identity, and what lessons this field might hold for other fields. Kay served as faculty senator, vice chair of the Faculty Assembly, and chair of the Personnel Policies Council at Oswego. Prior to assuming the presidency, she was vice president and secretary of the Faculty Senate. In this capacity, she serves on numerous SUNY-wide committees.

After 20 years as an art teacher and a designer in Istanbul, **Aslı Kinsizer** completed a second master's degree, in graphic design and digital media in May 2019 from SUNY Oswego. While a graduate student, Kinsizer twice received the prestigious Aulus W. Saunders Service Award. Kinsizer's work has been shown and presented at the TAG 55th Annual Juried Exhibition and the Best of SUNY student show. She views her role as an artist, "as being 'one of the exposers of the situation,' providing a voice for the oppressed, and offering an alternative that inspires change." Her goal with her ongoing project, "Strong Women," is to "remind people of women who realized the power within themselves to create change, amplifying their voices through the utilization of visual art, striving to be a universal language." Kinsizer's "Strong Women" projects have been shown in Washington, DC, and Rochester, New York, and in 2019 won first place in the three-minute faculty research competition at SUNY Oswego. She is currently an adjunct professor at SUNY Oswego.

Peter L. K. Knuepfer is associate professor of geological sciences and environmental studies at Binghamton University. He served as president of the SUNY University Faculty Senate from 2013 to 2017. In that role he represented the faculty of the 34 state-operated and statutory campuses of SUNY, and he served as a member of the SUNY Board of Trustees. His work with the UFS included contributions to policies on diversity and student sexual assault and implementation of a SUNY-wide seamless transfer initiative. He has coauthored articles on the SUNY Voices initiative and the governance approach that led to the SUNY policy on student sexual assault. Knuepfer earned his BS and MS degrees in geology from Stanford University and his PhD in geosciences from the University of Arizona. A member of Binghamton University's faculty since 1986, he has taught undergraduate courses in environmental studies and undergraduate and graduate courses in geology, as well as courses in the Binghamton University scholars program and freshmen seminars. He has been principal advisor to 11 master's and 4 PhD students, as well as serving on numerous master's and doctoral committees. Knuepfer's research has ranged from the study of earthquake hazards (including part of a team that assessed earthquake potential for the proposed Yucca Mountain Nuclear Waste Repository), to analysis of mountain growth in Taiwan and New Zealand to the glacial history of New York, to the assessment of past and potential future flooding in the Susquehanna River basin, to historical changes in river channel patterns in the Catskill Mountains of New York. He has authored or coauthored more than 40 scientific papers and 100 professional presentations and coedited three books.

Renee Lathrop is professor of physics at Dutchess Community College, where she has taught since 2003. She earned a BS in physics from Susquehanna University and an MS in physics from the University of Nebraska, Lincoln. She later earned an MA in educational psychology from Marist College. She is the author of the book *A Little Bit of Physics*, a workbook for students in their first year of studying physics. In 2013 she was recognized as a recipient of the SUNY Chancellors Award for Excellence in Teaching. From 2015 to 2017 she was the shared governance leader of Dutchess Community College after previously serving as Faculty Community College delegate for many years. Besides taking an interest in governance, she is an active member of the American Association of Physics Teachers, attending many national conferences and working closely with the two-year college committee to promote physics education.

Domenic J. Licata is an instructional support technician in the Department of Art at the University at Buffalo. He maintains a collaborative art- and design lab and has developed several courses in the areas of digital art, web design, and animation. He served as chair of the UB Professional Staff Senate from 2015 to 2019 and as 2018–2019 convener of the SUNY University Faculty Senate's Campus Governance Leaders group. He has presented at several SUNY Voices conferences on shared governance. Community-based governance experience includes six years as president of the board of directors of the Lexington Real Foods Community Cooperative. Licata has led and served on numerous committees and task forces across UB, including Stewardship within UB Sustainability, UBIT's Collaborative and Learning Space initiative, Teaching and Learning with Technology, the College of Arts and Sciences Educational Technology Advisory Group, FACT2 Mobile Technology in Teaching and Learning, and the UB Libraries Digital Challenges initiative.

Joe Marren is a professor and was the chair of the Communication Department at SUNY Buffalo State from January 2011 to July 2018. He was the Campus Governance leader at Buffalo State in 2018–2019 and 2019–2020. During that time, he was also chair of the University Faculty Senate's ad hoc Communication Committee (2016–2018) and the first chair of the committee when it became a fully constituted UFS committee in 2018. He won a Chancellor's Award for Excellence in Faculty Service in 2014. His outstanding, long-standing service to the UFS was recognized when he received the Chugh Award in 2019. He has taught journalism and communication classes for the past 20 years and recently started teaching a religious studies class. Marren is a summa cum laude graduate of Buffalo State with majors in journalism and history and a minor in anthropology. He also has a master's degree in history from St. Bonaventure University and certificates in communication from the Columbia University Graduate School of Journalism, the Newsplex at the University of South Caroline, the Poynter Institute, the American Press Institute, and the National Center for Business Journalism. He has certificates in theology from Christ the King Seminary in East Aurora, New York, and Yale Divinity School, and is working toward a certificate in theology and ministry from Princeton Theological Seminary. Marren has given or written more than 50 presentations, journal articles, and book chapters on topics from sports to journalism to pedagogy to history to religion. Prior to his academic career, he was a newspaper reporter for 7 years and an editor for another 11 years at various community newspapers in western New York, winning several state and national awards. His beats were cops and courts, sports, and business. Marren also was a stringer for the Associated Press and periodically wrote commentaries presented on WBFO, the National Public Radio station in Buffalo.

Belinda S. Miles has served as president of SUNY Westchester Community College since 2015, serving more than 25,000 students in one of the nation's largest metropolitan areas. Prior roles include system-wide Provost/EVP and president of the Eastern Campus at Cuyahoga Community College in Ohio. Miles serves on national and regional boards at organizations focused on expanding economic mobility, workforce development, and the impact of technology on the future of work including the American Association of Community Colleges, American Association of Colleges and Universities Presidents' Trust, Block Center for Technology and Society at Carnegie Mellon University, Hudson Valley Patterns for Progress, Westchester-Putnam Workforce Investment Board, and the

Business Council of Westchester. The recipient of numerous service and leadership awards, Miles is a highly regarded speaker on community college advocacy, student success, and leadership development. She earned master's and doctoral degrees from Columbia University Teachers College and a bachelor of arts degree from York College CUNY.

Deborah L. Moeckel has been assistant provost for Assessment and Community College Education at SUNY System Administration since June 2010. Since the beginning of her tenure, she has served as the liaison from SUNY System to the Middle States Commission on Higher Education. She has conducted a study of system-wide accreditation results and incorporated these into the SUNY Council on Assessment Institutional Effectiveness Rubric. She is also a staff liaison to the SUNY Council on Assessment and an ex officio member of the Assessment Network of New York Board of Directors. She serves as liaison to the Faculty Council of Community Colleges Academic and Student Affairs Committee and the University Faculty Senate Undergraduate Committee. Moeckel has served as a consultant on learning strategies, assessment, accreditation, and general education for such institutions as Hahnemann University Hospital, New York University, Mercy College, the Culinary Institute of America, and Al Kafaat University in Lebanon. She also served as a member of the executive committee of the SUNY Chief Academic Officers and was an active participant in accreditation activities at the campus and evaluation team levels. Particular professional interests include strategic and academic planning, curriculum development, applied or experiential learning, developmental education, assessment, accreditation, and shared governance. Moeckel earned her BS in French from North Park College, MS in Bilingual Education from Southern Connecticut State University and PhD in Reading/Writing/Literacy from the University of Pennsylvania.

Kenneth P. O'Brien currently holds the rank of professor emeritus, the College at Brockport. He came to SUNY in 1970 and served as history department chair, director of the College Honors Program, and director of Transfer Articulation among a number of other faculty-staff positions, as well as two terms as president of the College Senate. O'Brien earned his BA from Rutgers College in 1965 and his PhD in American history from Northwestern University in 1974. In 1965, he became a tutor in American political history for ABC News's Peter Jennings, his first professional teaching position, to prepare the young Canadian newscaster for the 1966 congressional elections. In 1974–75, he joined a year-long, interdisciplinary NEH-funded seminar for college teachers in residence at Columbia University, and from 1985 to 1987, he was a member of the Motion Picture Association of America's Ratings Board, viewing and rating 842 feature films over two years. He has also served on the New York State Historical Records Advisory Board for more than two decades. From 1990 to 1995, he was Monroe County Historian. In 1993, the office received the Edmund J. Wilson Award for leading a team of local historians to create "The War Comes Home," a major exhibit for the Strong Museum that explored the Rochester region during World War II. The recipient of both the SUNY Chancellor's Award for Excellence in Teaching (1981) and Excellence in Faculty Service (2005), O'Brien is the former president of the University Faculty Senate (2009–2013) and member of the SUNY Board of Trustees. O'Brien has given more than three dozen invited lectures, including a dozen panel presentations and papers at national scholarly conferences on scholarly topics and university shared governance. His major publications include *The Home-Front War* (coedited with Lynn Hudson Parsons); *SUNY at 60* (coedited with John Clark and W. Bruce Leslie); "The United States and War in the Twentieth Century," a chapter in *The Cambridge Companion to Modern American Culture* (2006); and "Education Markets in English and American Universities," with coauthor John Halsey, in Sarah Pickard (ed.), *Higher Education in the UK and the US* (2014). His chapter in this volume is his second in the SUNY Press Shared Governance series. O'Brien is currently under contract with Cambridge University Press for a chapter that examines US popular culture during World Wars I and II for an upcoming volume in their History of American Culture series.

Barry L. Spriggs presently serves as the provost at Morrisville State College. He previously served as dean of Academic Services at Lehigh Carbon Community College for six years. He earned his BS in criminal justice and MS in administration of justice/psychology at Shippensburg University and PhD in Sociology at South Dakota State University. He was an associate professor of criminal justice at County College of Morris and dean of Students at Keystone College, where he also served as chair of the Criminal Justice Programs. Spriggs established the first four-year program at Keystone as they were transitioning from a junior college to a four-year institution. During his tenure as dean of Students, he developed a department of Multicultural Affairs, First Year Experience, and a service learning center; spearheaded efforts in athletics to reach Division III status; and established learning communities in the residence halls. He has served as the assistant director of Alternative Rehabilitation Communities and assistant residential center supervisor at KidsPeace National Center for Kids in Crisis, where he developed and implemented various programs for adolescents with a variety of mental health issues. Spriggs has provided consultation to a number of organizations in the area of cultural competency, diversity, and social and emotional development, including Pennsylvania State Police, Keystone University Research Corporation, Pennsylvania Department of Public Welfare, and KidsPeace National Center for Kids in Crisis. He has presented on a variety of topics to constituents locally, regionally, and nationally, including topics such as inter gender relations, bullying, violence in the family, dealing with challenging and difficult behaviors, and dramaturgical analysis in a total institution. Spriggs presently serves on advisory boards for Preventive Measures, LLC, and Lincoln Leadership Academy. He has served on the board of directors for the Workforce Investment Board of Lehigh Valley as well as Vice President of PA National Association of Multicultural Education. He is a past president of the Brookings Humans Rights Committee and a past member of the American Sociological Association, Midwest Sociological Association, National Association for Staff and Organizational Development, National Association for Community Colleges Entrepreneurship, and Association for Student Judicial Affairs.

Deborah F. Stanley is the 10th president of SUNY Oswego. Her inclusive leadership and broad vision has driven increased academic excellence, campus renewal, successful fundraising, and the creation of a learner-centered environment. Stanley led the creation of the School of Communication, Media, and the Arts and established Oswego's Syracuse campus. Under her leadership, new programs such as electrical and computer engineering, human–computer interaction, biomedical and health informatics, and the online MBA programs were established. She pioneered the Oswego Guarantee for graduation and the $300 Graduation Return on Investment. Her ambitious campus-wide renewal plan encompasses hundreds of millions of dollars in renovations and construction, including the environmentally designated LEED Gold Shineman Center; the modernization of the college's arts building, Tyler Hall; and the recently renovated Wilber Hall to accommodate the departments of the School of Education. Stanley currently serves on the American Council on Education Board of Directors, is past chair of the American Association of State Colleges and Universities board of directors, and is a board member of the American Academic Leadership Institute. She served three years as board chair of CenterState

CEO. Stanley also served as a member of the CNY Regional Economic Development Council since its inception and was appointed its co-chair in 2019. Stanley was a director and chairman of the former community bank OCNB and a director of the former Alliance Bank. She earned a baccalaureate degree with honors and a JD from Syracuse University. Stanley was named a New York State Woman of Distinction and received the *Post-Standard*'s Person of Achievement Award.

Jeffrey Steele is associate professor of history and social science at Herkimer County Community College. He earned an AA in social science from Herkimer and a BA and MA in history from SUNY Albany. After Herkimer created a system of shared governance for the first time in its institution's history, in 2009, Steele was the initial president of its Academic Senate until term limited in 2013. He was elected to that position again in 2015. In addition to his shared governance service on his campus, since 2014, he has served as a delegate to the Faculty Council of Community Colleges, served as the secretary of the Faculty Council from 2015 to 2018, and is currently chair of their governance committee. Beyond academic service, he has served many terms as board member and president of the Herkimer County Historical Society. He received the Chancellor's Award for Excellence in Faculty Service in 2017.

Olin Stratton is an experienced educator in mathematics. He is currently an associate professor of mathematics at Onondaga Community College in Syracuse, New York. In addition to his teaching duties, Stratton has been a champion of promoting continuous improvement methods for his department and the college as a whole. He has delivered multiple presentations at the local, state, and national levels regarding the systematic use of assessment results to improve a department's performance. In particular, his talks focus on creating assessments that are simple and applicable to the professors in the classroom. Stratton holds a master's degree in applied and computational mathematics with a focus in operations research from the Rochester Institute of Technology. He is the chair of the Learning Outcomes and Assessment Committee at Onondaga Community College. In that role, he makes sure every academic department on campus systematically uses assessment to produce better results.

Nina Tamrowski was the president of the Faculty Council of Community Colleges and a member of the SUNY Board of Trustees between July 2015 and June 2019. During that time, she served on several shared governance advisory bodies at SUNY, including the Student Mobility Steering Committee, the General Education Working Group, the Applied Learning Steering Committee, and the MicroCredentialing Task Force. She received the Chancellor's Award for Excellence in Faculty Service in spring 2015, in recognition of her service in many arenas including her campus and the Faculty Council of Community Colleges (FCCC). Tamrowski served as a member of the Search Committee for the SUNY Chancellor in 2017 and served on the Search Committee for the SUNY Provost in 2014 and again in 2018. She has been heavily involved in planning many meetings and events for the SUNY Voices initiative. Tamrowski served as delegate to the FCCC from Onondaga Community College since 2009 and was a member of its governance committee. She served as secretary of the FCCC from 2011 to 2013, and as vice president from 2013 to 2015. She was the Faculty Council liaison to the University Faculty Senate's Governance Committee for five years. Tamrowski has been a professor of political science at Onondaga Community College since 1993 and was elected Faculty Senate president in 2019. At Onondaga, she has regularly taught American national politics, state and local politics, comparative politics, and women and politics. She served for four years as the chair of the Social Sciences and Philosophy Department. She has been a member of Onondaga's Faculty Executive Committee since 2009. She earned an MA in political science from Syracuse University and completed her PhD coursework in political science as well. Tamrowski's BA degree in Spanish and political science is from SUNY College at Brockport.

Wendy Tarby is a seasoned manager/leader in institutional educational services and health care, with visionary view, systems background, and customer-first philosophy. Her 30-year professional background includes building teams that carry out mission of support—gaining a quick understanding of where an organization wants to be, assembling teams, getting projects moving, and standardizing processes. Tarby has demonstrated her extensive background in technology, human resources, financial, quality, and grants and budget management with in-depth understanding of regulatory requirements and expectations. She enjoys project management and leading teams to focus on knowledge management, relevant technologies, and enterprise-wide success. Tarby holds a master's degree in information studies from Syracuse University, a BA in English and communication studies from SUNY Oswego, and a certificate in medical informatics from Stanford University. She has worked in academic institutions and private industry. Examples of her work include successful college and hospital reaccreditations, a Y2K system migration and conversion, and as adjunct faculty, participation in Syracuse University's Leadership Institutes. She has made numerous national and regional presentations and served on many professional boards throughout her career.

Cliff L. Wood is president emeritus of Rockland Community College, after retiring in June 2017. His career spanned five decades of service in six community colleges in five states. Wood also served as president of the New York Community College Association of Presidents. In 2010 he was appointed by Governor Andrew Cuomo to the Mid-Hudson Regional Economic Development Council and served until his retirement. For his work in economic development, Wood was honored by the NY Council of Industry, Patterns for Progress, the Rockland Business Association, and the Rockland Economic Development Council. He was also active in a number of community activities and served on several nonprofit boards.

Over the first four years of her tenure as president at SUNY Orange, **Kristine Young** significantly reshaped the student experience while expanding access to the college and cementing public–private partnerships that place SUNY Orange in the midst of academic and workforce training innovation. She successfully navigated the college through budgetary challenges and managed to halt enrollment declines that had continued for nearly a decade. Under Young's watchful eye, SUNY Orange opened the Sarfatti Education Center in Port Jervis, embarked on a SUNY Orange Experience initiative that will overhaul how the college ushers students through their academic career, and supported the implementation of grant-funded TRIO Student Support Services and Educational Opportunity Program. The college has enjoyed substantial growth in online enrollment, while overall enrollment has leveled out.

Index

Page numbers in *italics* indicate illustrations.

AAUP. *See* American Association of University Professors
academic freedom, 155–56, 158, 202–3, 257
academic governance, 179; Bahls on, 153; cultural shifts in, 151–55; future of, 147–59; shared governance versus, 148, 152–53; Stanford project on, 200; structural threats to, 150–51; traditional, 147–50
accessibility. *See* diversity
accountability: decision making and, 28; transparency and, *184*, 194
accreditation, xv, 4–5, 26, 94–95, 100; affiliation requirements and, 220–21; criteria for, 237–38, 244–46; by regional commissions, 235–64, *237*; standards for, 138–45, 206–10, 217–33, 257–62
Accreditation Academy, 220–23; establishment of, 218; participant feedback on, 230–31; recommendations for, 231–33
Accrediting Commission for Community and Junior Colleges (ACCJC), *237*, 254–57, 261–62
administrators, 110–11; collaboration with, 191–92; diversity programs and, 23; turnover among, 32–34

AGB. *See* Association of Governing Boards
alcohol policies, 224–25
American Association for Higher Education, 200
American Association of University Professors (AAUP), xiv; on academic freedom, 155–56, 158, 202–3, 257; on academic governance, 179; on decision making, 30; on effective planning, 75; on shared governance, 3–5, 29, 77, 99; *Statement on Government of Colleges and Universities* of, 3–4, 77, 147–50, 153–59, 205; on students in shared governance, 35
American Council on Education (ACE), 32–33, 148, 201
Anderson, Bill, 93, *95*
Arab Spring (2010–13), 158–59
assessment rubric for shared governance, 91–100, 112–13, *114–33*, 134–38
Association of Governing Boards (AGB), 17–18, 35, 201; on shared governance, 4–6, 153–54
Assumed Practices, 246–47
authority, 35; delegated, 28–29; Johnstone on, 51, 57

Bahls, Steven, 153–54
Baldridge, J. V., 200–201
Bender, L. W., 207
Bevin, Matt, 159
Bigelow, Gordon, xiii, 15–23
Bliss, Diane, xiii, 3–13, 93, 97
Board of Trustees, 102–5; faculty representatives on, 5; president and, 106; UFS and, 167–68, 180
Borowitz, Drucy, 188
Boyer, Richard K., 32
Breathe Free policy, 187, 189, 193
Breneman, D., 199
Brown, Owen, 65
bullying incidents, 20
bylaws, 7, 12, 42, 138, 203; Board of Trustees and, 104; changes to, 44, 186, 200; legality of, 201, 207; of NCC Academic Senate, 201, 203–9, 212–16

Camp, Sue, *89*
Campus Concept Committee, 75–88; challenges of, 84–87; goal of, 81; history of, 77–81; members of, *89*; successes of, 81–84
career development centers, 151–52
Chaddock, Noelle, xiii, 15–23
Chomsky, Noam, 63–64
City University of New York (CUNY), 172
Civil Service Employees Association, 188
Clark, John, 166
Click, Melissa, 151, 155
Coalition of Advocacy and Leadership (COAL), 186
collaboration, 195, 245–46; with administrators, 191–92; competencies of, *184*
collective bargaining, 30, 60, 106; at Nassau Community College, 200–201, 208, 212–14; PHEEIA and, 172–74, 178; protection of, 149

college councils, 30, 31, 96, 105, 111, 135
College Leadership Council (CLC), 210, 219–20
College of Saint Rose (N.Y.), 155–56
College Senate, 54; of Norwich campus, 41–42, 47–49
Collegiate Science and Technology Entry Program, 226
Collins, Valerie H., xv, 197–216, 263–64
committee(s), 8, 51, 53; ad hoc, 9, 56, 219; on credit transfer, 177; on diversity, 21–22, 50–51, 56; planning, 75, 198, 223–24, 229–30; on professional development, 57–58; subcommittees of, 86
communication, 7–9, 102; challenges of, 63–72; consistency in, 35; Olson on, 87; planning and, 148; press releases for, 69–72; Spriggs on, 44–45
community colleges, 11–12; accreditation of, *237, 254–57,* 261–62; college council model for, 30; governance of, vii
constitutions, 7, 138, 190
continuing education, 248–49
Continuing Education Series for Shared Governance, 187–88, 191–92
Cowen, Scott S., 29, 150
Cramer, Sharon F., xvii–xviii, 188
credit transfer policies, 175–78, 218, 248
Cross, Raymond, 50
Cuffee, Sallie, 65
cultural competency training, 188
cultural shifts, 151–55
culture, institutional, 27
Cuomo, Andrew, 174
curriculum, 8; credit transfer and, 175–77, 218, 248; responsibility for, 28, 246

Daniels, R. V., 199

INDEX 283

Database of Accredited Postsecondary Institutions and Programs (DAPIP), 236
DeCesare, Michael, xiv–xv, 147–59
decision making, 28–29; accountability and, 28; bylaws for, 7; consensus on, 76; deadlines for, 31; feedback on, 30; Hoose on, 50, 52–54; Spriggs on, 57–58, 61
DeSantis, Jerry, 89
Dickens, Charles, 165
diversity, 11, 46, 190, 194; accessibility issues with, 20, 23, 26, 34–35, 178; faculty role in, 15–23; planning for, 171; Daryl Smith on, 18; task forces on, 21–22, 50–51, 56; transparency of, 184. See also race
Donaghy, Kelley, 65
Dong, June, 89
Drucker, Peter, 27

Educational Effectiveness Assessment, 222, 227–28
Educational Opportunity Center (EOC), 41, 189
Educational Support Professionals, 46
effectiveness, 220–22, 230–31; assessment of, 112–13, *114–17*, 143–44, 239
Emerson, Ralph Waldo, 64, 66
emotional intelligence, 36
Engagement in Learning plan, 81, 89
Environmental Science and Forestry (ESF) College, 65, 105
environmentalism, 187, 189, 191, 193, 196
ethics, 140–41, 222, 224–25

faculty, 46, 107–10, 149–50; accreditation criteria and, 237–38, 250–51; assessments by, 240; diversity of, 15–23; hiring of, 21; presidential searches and, 157
Faculty Congress, 54

Faculty Council of Community Colleges (FCCC), 5; Board of Trustees and, 167; on credit transfer policies, 177; on shared governance, viii–xi, 6, 93–100, 109
Faculty Senate, University at Buffalo, 183, 185–88; activities of, 188–89; funding of, 191–92
FCCC. *See* Faculty Council of Community Colleges
Feck, Donald, 89
Ferrer-Muniz, Karen, 95
Finkelstein, M. J., 207
first-generation access, 23, 26
Flaherty, Michael, 89
focus groups, 154
Freedom of Information Act, 36
Frost, Robert, 64

gender equality, 20, 189
General Education Program, 79, 168, 176
Gerber, L. G., 147
Glick, Philip L., xv, 183–95
Glidden, Lisa M., xiv, 75–88
Good, Tina, 43–44
Goodman, Norman, 66, 167
Graci, Craig, 89
graduate programs, 248
Graduate Student Employee Association, 188
Grant, Joe, 89
Great Recession (2008), 170, 172
Gublo, Kristen, 89

Hebblethwaite, Chris, 89
Higher Education Commission, 176
Higher Learning Commission (HLC), 235, 237, 244–47, 257, 259
Hill, David, 81, 89
Hispanic-serving institutions, 34–35
Hoose, Margaret Ann, xiv, 41–44, 50–56, 61–62
Horvath, Virginia, 186, 193

inclusion. *See* diversity
Institutional Effectiveness and Resources Committee, 220–22, 230–31
institutional governance, 152–53
Institutional Planning, Assessment and Research (Onondaga), 223–24, 229–30
Institutional Planning Committee (Nassau), 198
interdependence, 77, 85, 101–2, 148, 150, 201

Jacobs School of Medicine and Biomedical Sciences, 190
Jagord, Steve, 188
job training, 151
Johnson, Allan, 156
Johnson, Kristina, viii, 25–26, 186
Johnstone, Bruce, 41, 50–61, 170
Jones, T., 27

Kallio, Ken, 99
Kant, Immanuel, 66
Kay, Gwen, xiii–xv
Kemerer, F. R., 200–201
Kennesaw State University (Ga.), 157
Kentucky State University, 156–57
Keystone College (Pa.), 45
King, David, 89
King, Martin Luther, Jr., 36
King, Robert L., 170
Knuepfer, Peter L. K., xv, 235–64

Lackey, Al, 89
Landel, Ann Marie, 188
Lathrop, Renee, xiii, 3–13
Laursen, Tod, 186
Lavallee, David, 177
leadership, 33–34, 255–57; assessment of, 123, 205; communications by, 80; diversity of, 15–17, 20–23; stability of, 170; standards of, 4–5, 26, 138–39, 198, 229; student, 35, 186; transformative, 150
Leadership Institute (SUNY Voices), 43–44, 185
learning outcomes, 249, 262; for Accreditation Academy, 223–30; institutional, 48, 49, 219; student, 112, 113, 252, 255
Leslie, W. Bruce, 166
LGBTQ+ community, 20, 23
Licata, Dominic J., xv, 183–95
Lojacono, Caroline, 188
Longfellow, Henry Wadsworth, 91

Maggio, Evelyn, 65
management styles, 48
Marano Campus Center (SUNY Oswego), 82
Marren, Joe, xiv, 63–72
McCall, H. Carl, 183
Merrimack College (Mass.), 151–52
Middle States Commission of Higher Education (MSCHE), xiv–xv, 237; accreditation standards of, 238–40, 257–58; affiliation requirements of, 220–21, 238; Nassau Community College and, xiv–xv, 197–98, 206–7, 263–64; shared governance standards of, 4–5, 26, 94–95, 100, 138–45; site visits by, 217–33
Miles, Belinda S., xiv, 25–37
Millett, J. D., 199, 200
minority-serving institutions, 34–35
Mintzberg, Henry, 197, 198, 201–2, 207
mission, 139–40, 238–39; institutional culture and, 27–28
Moeckel, Deborah L., xiv, 91–100
Monnier, N., 159n2
Morrisville State College, 46–56
MSCHE. *See* Middle States Commission of Higher Education
Muslim students, 224–25

Nassau Community College (NCC), 197–210, 263–64; Academic Senate Bylaws of, 201, 203–9, 212–16; Federation of Teachers of, 214
Nepkie, Janet, 93, 95–97
New England Commission of Higher Education (NECHE), 237, 241–44, 258–59
New President Programs, 33
New York State United Teachers (NYSUT), 173, 200
Newton, Eric, 67
Nicholson, Philip Y., 199–201
Nielsen, Jakob, 69–70
"no surprises" rule, 193–94
Northwest Commission on Colleges and Universities (NWCCU), 237, 247–50, 259–60
NYSUNY2020, 174–75
NYSUT. *See* New York State United Teachers

O'Brien, Kenneth P., xv, 165–80
O'Brien Center for Career Development, 151–52
Office of University Shared Government, 188, 191, 193
Olson, G. A., 27, 28, 86–87
Onondaga Community College (OCC), 217–22
Oswego Guarantee, 79, 88n4, 277

parliamentary procedure, 7, 188
Pataki, George, 169
Paterson, David, 172
PHEEIA. *See* Public Higher Education Empowerment and Innovation Act
PISCO plan, 61
planning, 144, 170–72, 217–20; AAUP on, 75; by college presidents, 35; committees for, 75, 198, 223–24, 229–30; communications and, 148; for diversity, 171

Poucher Hall (Oswego), 83, 84
presidents, college: as chief planning officer, 35; development programs for, 33; skill sets of, 36; turnover among, 32–33
press releases, 69–72
professional development, 151–52; committee on, 57–58; of nonteaching staff, 190
Professional Staff Senate, University at Buffalo, 183, 185–88; activities of, 189–91; funding of, 191–92; responsibilities of, 190
Programs and Academic Support Committee, 220
provost, 32, 53–54, 91–93, 158; role of, 43, 45, 47, 48; search committee for, 51
Public Higher Education Empowerment and Innovation Act (PHEEIA), 172–74, 178

quality of work life, 190

race, 16, 20, 23. *See also* diversity
rape, 23, 188
recycling efforts, 187, 191, 196. *See also* environmentalism
responsibility, 238; ethical, 224; shared, 148, 194
Rockefeller, Nelson, 169
Rogers, David E., 42–43, 50
Rush, Carolyn, 89

Safe Zones, 188
Salaita, Steven, 155
Sargent, David, 89
Scalzo, Kim, 95
Scharfenberger, Jim, 89
scheduling issues, 53, 58
SCoA. *See* SUNY Council on Assessment
self-studies, 206–7, 217, 221, 249

September 11th attacks, 170
sexual violence, 23, 188
shared governance, xiii–xv, 9–13, 101–12, 257; AAUP on, 3–5, 29, 77, 99; academic governance versus, 148, 152–53; accreditation standards for, 4–5, 235–64; AGB on, 4–6, 153–54; assessment rubric for, 91–100, 112–13, *114–33*, 134–38; Bahls on, 153, 154; Campus Concept Committee for, 75–88; components of, x–xi; conferences on, 178; Continuing Education Series for, 191–92; culture of, 10; definitions of, ix, 3–6, 77, 245; doctrine of, 194–96; elements of, 6–9; General Education Requirement and, 168; inclusivity of, 170–71, 178; litmus test of, 185–86; managing turnover in, 32–34; principles of, 76–77; self-assessment of, 120, *121–33*; transparency and, 183–95, *184*
Shared Governance Award, 26, 33, 178
Shared Governance Day, 186–88, 194–96
shared services model, 42–43
Smith, Daryl, 18
smoke-free campus policies, 187, 189, 193
social media, 69–72, 159, 189, 191
sociological theory, 45, 61
Southern Association of Colleges and Schools Commission on Colleges (SACSCOC), *237*, 250–51, 257, 260–61, 264
Southern Association of Colleges and Schools (SACS), 259
Spalding University (Ky.), 156
Spriggs, Barry, xiv, 41, 44–49, 54–62
stakeholders, 186; engagement of, 29; maintaining balance among, 31–32; readiness for change of, 28
Stanford Project on Academic Governance, 200

Stanley, Deborah F., xiv, 75–90
State Teachers Colleges, 175
Staub, Robert E., II, 36
Steele, Jeffrey, xiii, 3–13, 93, 95, 97
strategic planning. *See* planning
Stratton, Olin, xv, 217–33
StriveTogether program, 166
structural forces, 150–51
students, 11–12, 34–35; credit transfers for, 175–78, 218, 248; Oswego Guarantee of costs to, 79, 88n4, 277; position of, 35; shared governance responsibilities of, 35, 186
student affairs representative, 45–46
Student Assembly (SA), 5, 111–12; Board of Trustees and, 168; Joint Statement on Shared Governance of, viii–xi; Zimpher and, 167, 168
Student Association (Onondaga), 231, 232
student-centered principles, 221
Student Engagement, 226–27
Student Experience Committee, 220
student learning experiences, 81, 89, 141–43; academic program for, 242–43; standards for, 220, 222, 225–27, *226*, 238–39
Student Mobility Advisory Committee, 177
student trustees, 111
Student-Wide Judiciary, 186
Styrofoam elimination, 187. *See also* environmentalism
Sullivan, Robin, 188
SUNY Council on Assessment (SCoA), 91–100
SUNY Morrisville, Norwich Campus, 41–42, 47–49
SUNY Orange, 33
SUNY Oswego, 75–88
SUNY Polytechnic Institute (Utica), 42–43
SUNY system: budgetary crises of, 169–70; components of, vii; as engine

for economic growth, 172, 174–75; governance of, vii, 5; history of, 166–67; NYSUNY2020 and, 174–75; PHEEIA and, 172–74, 178
SUNY Voices, x, 96–99, 178; Kay on, xiii; Leadership Institute of, 43–44, 185; Tamrowski on, viii

Tamrowski, Nina, vii–ix
Tarby, Wendy, xv, 217–33
task forces, 9; for diversity, 21–22, 50–51, 56. *See also* committee(s)
tenure-track positions, 151, 202–3
terrorism, 170
Thomas theorem, 158
Title IX, 20, 87, 225
town hall meetings, 29
transparency, 9, 183–95; accountability and, *184,* 194; of governance structure, 101; "no surprises" rule and, 193–94
Tripathi, Satish, 185, 186, 190, 192–94
Trump, Donald, 152
tuition increases, 172–74
"tyranny of the urgent," 31–32

UFS. *See* University Faculty Senate
Union County College (N.J.), 150–51
unions. *See* collective bargaining
United States Department of Education, 235–36
United University Professions (UUP), 173, 188
University at Buffalo (UB), 183–95
University Faculty Senate (UFS), 5, 110; Board of Trustees and, 167–68; Joint Statement on Shared Governance of, viii–xi; PHEEIA and, 173–74, 178; plenaries of, 68; Zimpher and, 167
University of Illinois Urbana-Champaign, 155
University of Iowa, 150, 157
University of Louisville, 159
University of Missouri, 151, 155
University of Virginia, 264
Urbanek, David, 188
UUP. *See* United University Professions

Varhus, Sarah, *89*
Vietnam War protests, 199–200

Walpole, Casey, *89*
WASC. *See* Western Association of Schools and Colleges
Weisbuch, R., 31, 32
wellness programs, 190
Westchester Community College, 29
Western Association of Schools and Colleges (WASC), *237,* 252–57, 261–62
Wharton, Clifton, 169
White, Brian, 188
Wilson, Tom, 36
Wittgenstein, Ludwig, 63
Wood, Cliff L., xiv, 25–37

Young, Kristine, xiv, 25–37

Zimpher, Nancy L., 165–80, 186; Kay on, xiii; O'Brien on, xv, 165–80; Tamrowski on, vii
Zubrow, Ezra, 188
Zukoski, Charles F., 185, 192

www.ingramcontent.com/pod-product-compliance
Ingram Content Group UK Ltd.
Pitfield, Milton Keynes, MK11 3LW, UK
UKHW040643271224
453054UK00014B/85